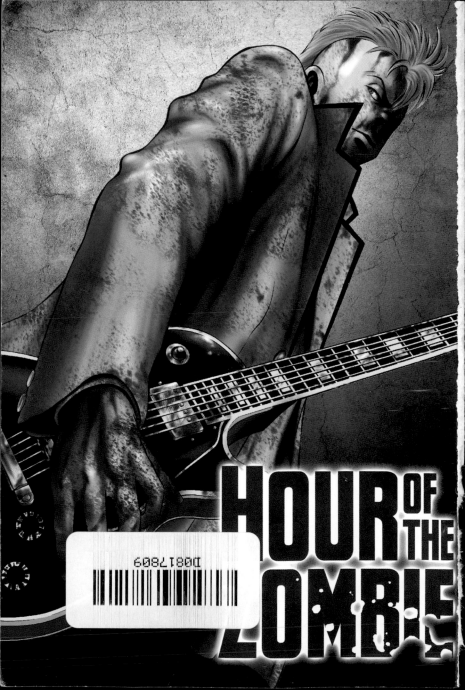

HOUR OF THE ZOMBIE

BOXING TEAM

Umezawa Reiji
ZOMBIE
- Boxing Team member, second-year.
- Placed fourth in the Interhigh championship. Trusts Akira.

BEST FRIENDS

Nikaidou Akira
- Boxing Team member, second-year.
- Wants to stop the war between zombies and humans. Believes they can reach a mutual understanding.

CRUSH

Akutsu Kurumi
ZOMBIE
- Second-year.
- Childhood friends with Akira.

CRUSH

Usa Sadaharu
ZOMBIE
- Band, third-year.
- A hardliner.

Furuchi Madoka
ZOMBIE **DEAD**
- Film Club president, second-year.
- Found himself zombified and committed suicide.

Igarashi Kaoru
ZOMBIE
- Rugby Team captain, third-year.
- Defies fate and is driven by his mission.

RESPECTS

BAD BLOOD

Houjou Shunichi
ZOMBIE
- Shogi Team co-captain, Student Council President, third-year.
- Is neither optimistic nor pessimistic. Only thinks of the future.

DATING

BEST FRIENDS

Togawa Yukiya
ZOMBIE
- Band, third-year.
- Plays drums. Devoted to Usa.

Kisaragi Takeru
- Craft Club member, first-year.
- Stuck in his own world.

Kubo Ryuuhei
ZOMBIE
- Craft Club member, first-year.
- Was betrayed by his best friend, Kisaragi.

CRAFT CLUB

Himehana Sara
ZOMBIE
- Tennis Team member, Student Council Vice President, second-year.

Ezaki

Kishi

Makimura Tadanobu
- Basketball Team captain, third-year.

BASKETBALL TEAM

Takeda Goushi
DEAD
- Kyudo Team captain, third-year.
- Died while defending Sagawa.

Sagawa Seiichirou
- Kyudo Team member, second-year.
- Admires Takeda.

KYUDO TEAM

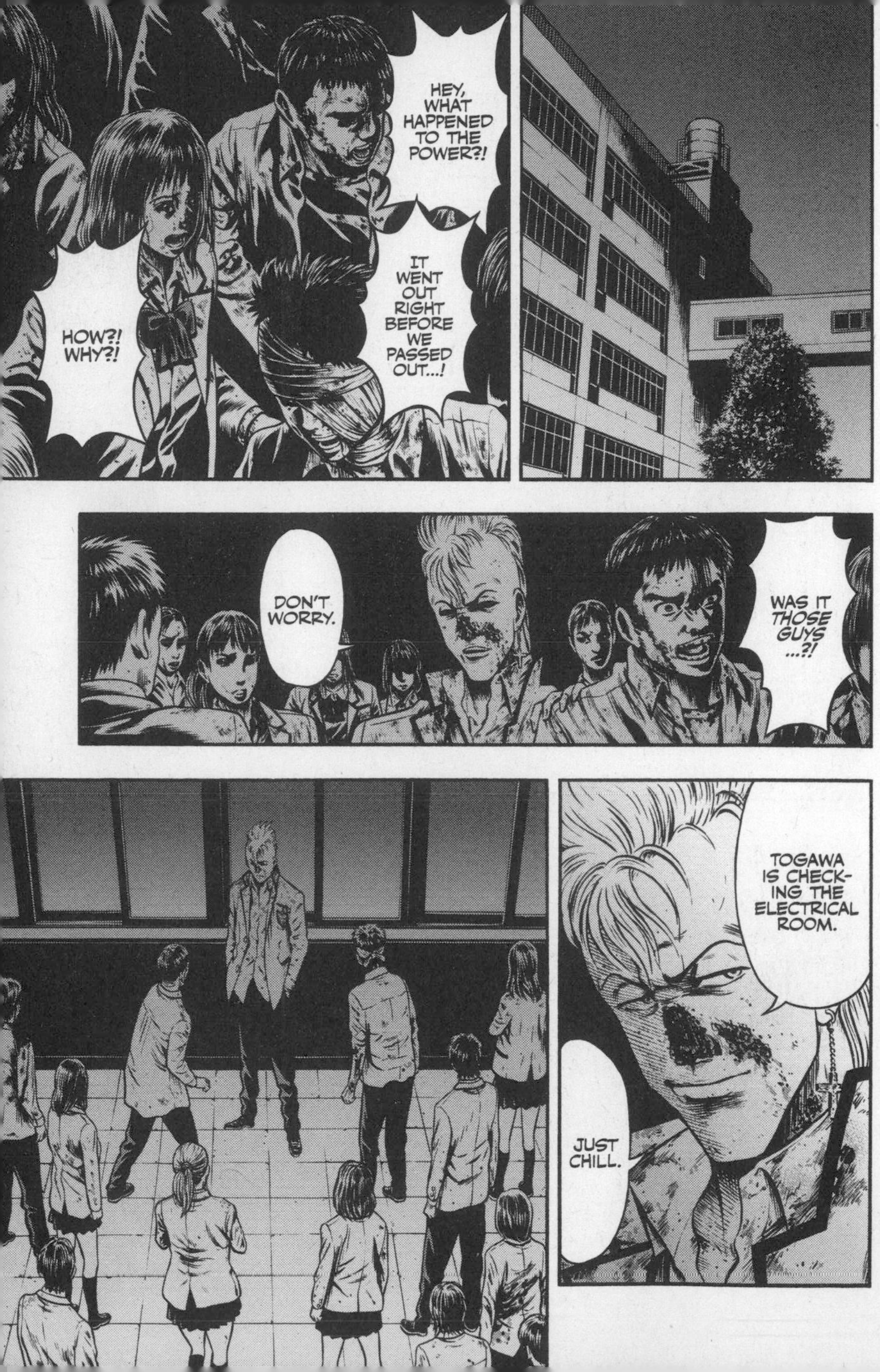
HEY, WHAT HAPPENED TO THE POWER?!
IT WENT OUT RIGHT BEFORE WE PASSED OUT...!
HOW?! WHY?!
WAS IT *THOSE GUYS* ...?!
DON'T WORRY.
TOGAWA IS CHECK-ING THE ELECTRICAL ROOM.
JUST CHILL.

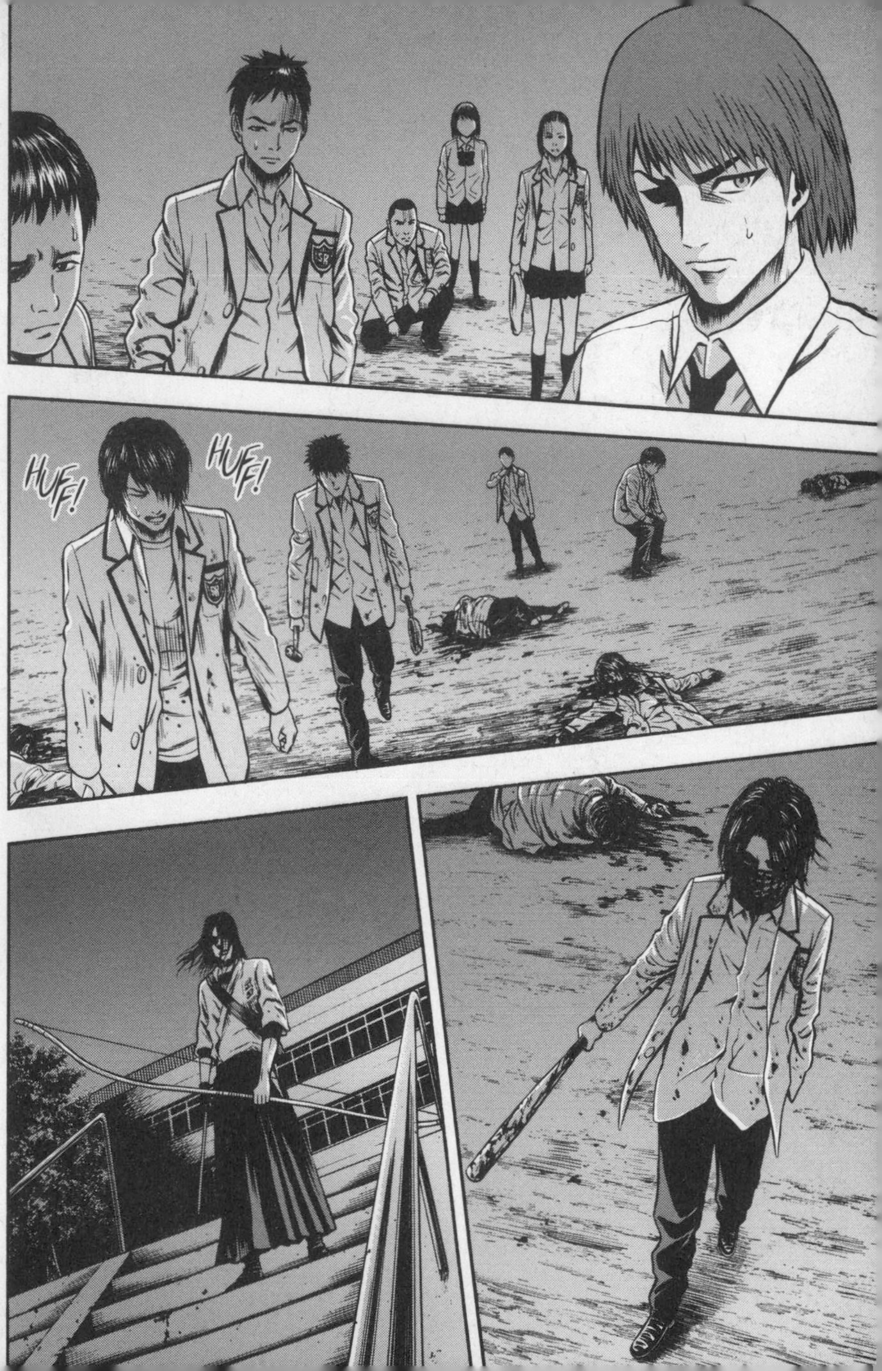
HUFF!
HUFF!

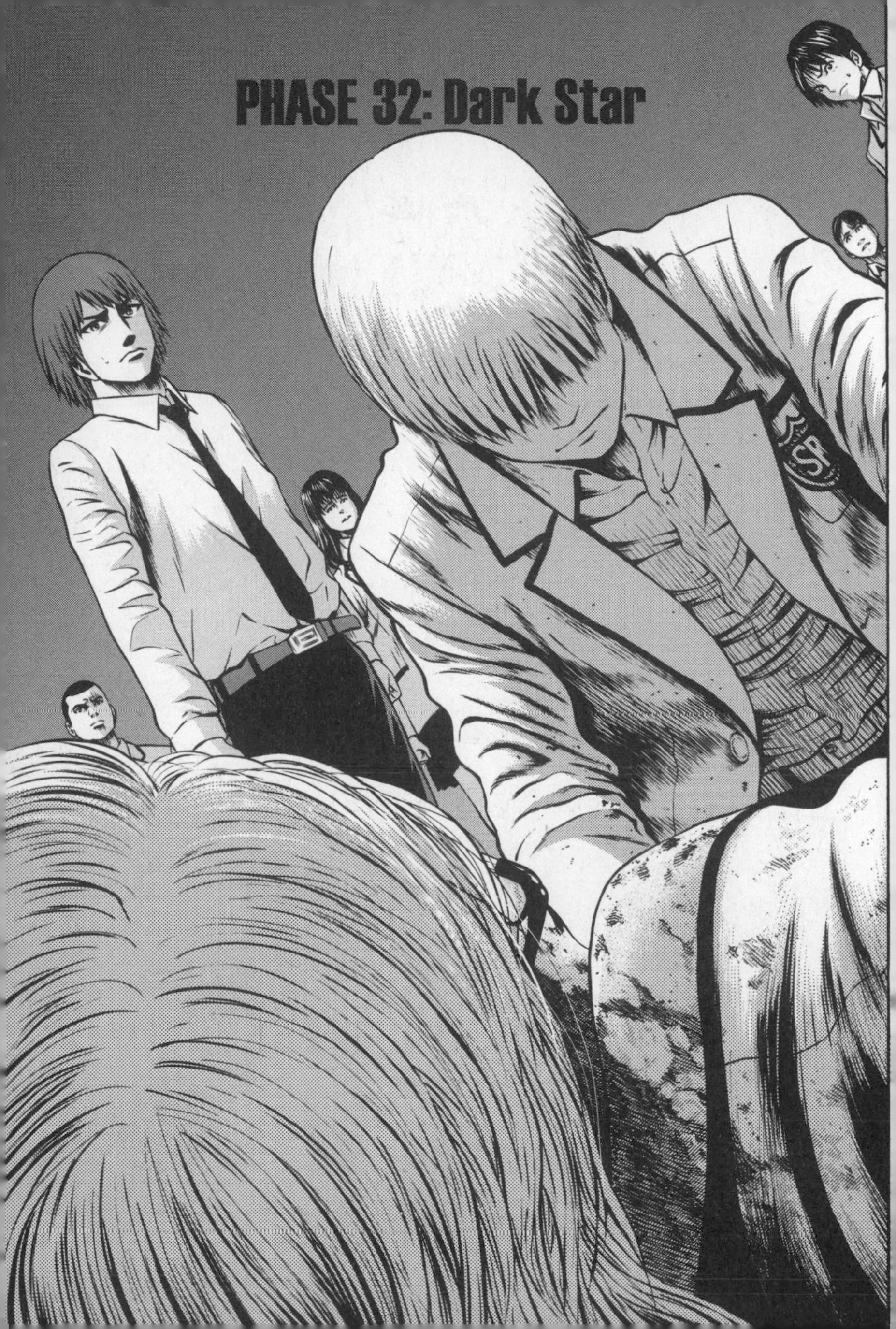
PHASE 32: Dark Star

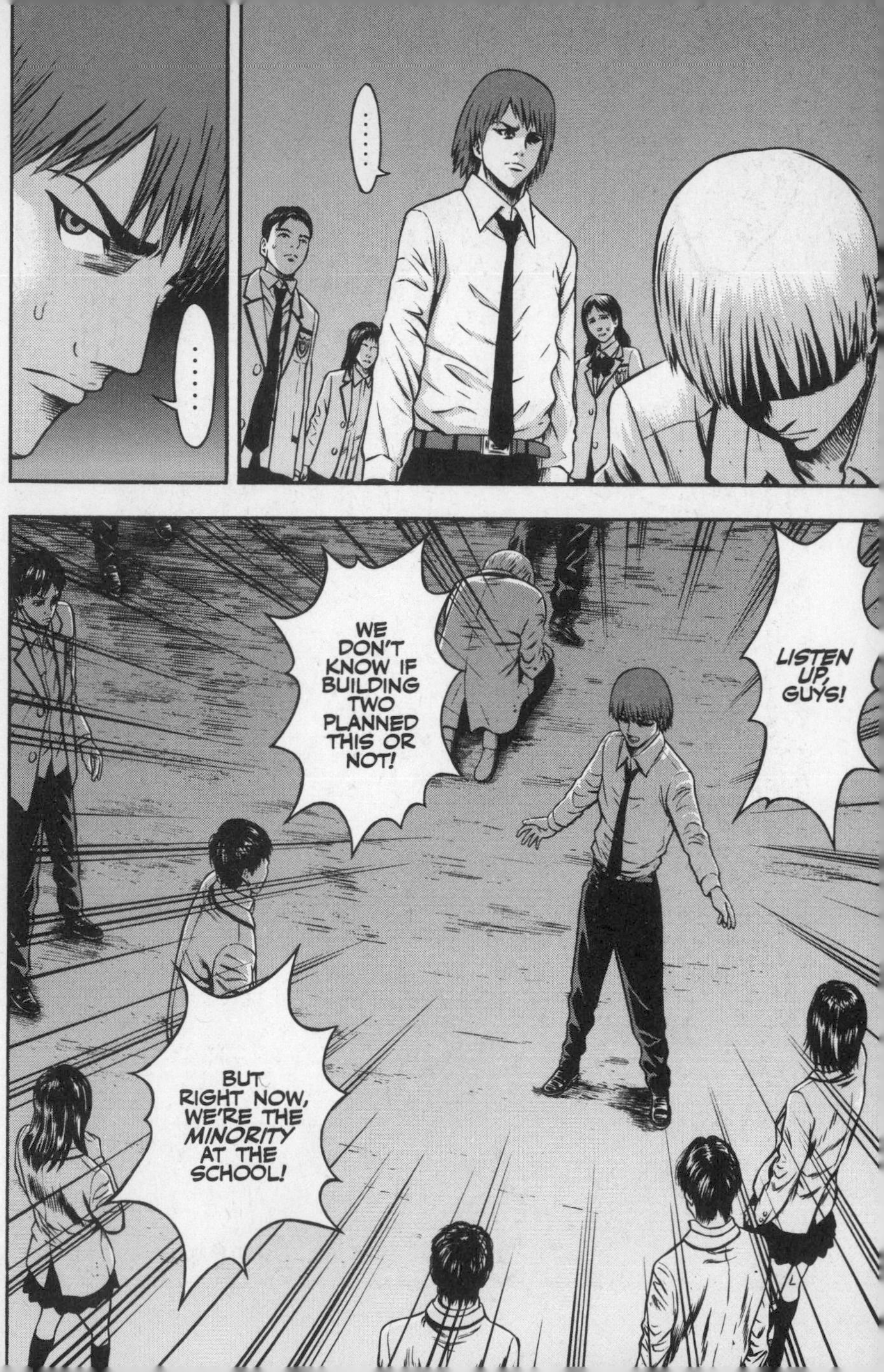
......
......
LISTEN UP, GUYS!
WE DON'T KNOW IF BUILDING TWO PLANNED THIS OR NOT!
BUT RIGHT NOW, WE'RE THE *MINORITY* AT THE SCHOOL!

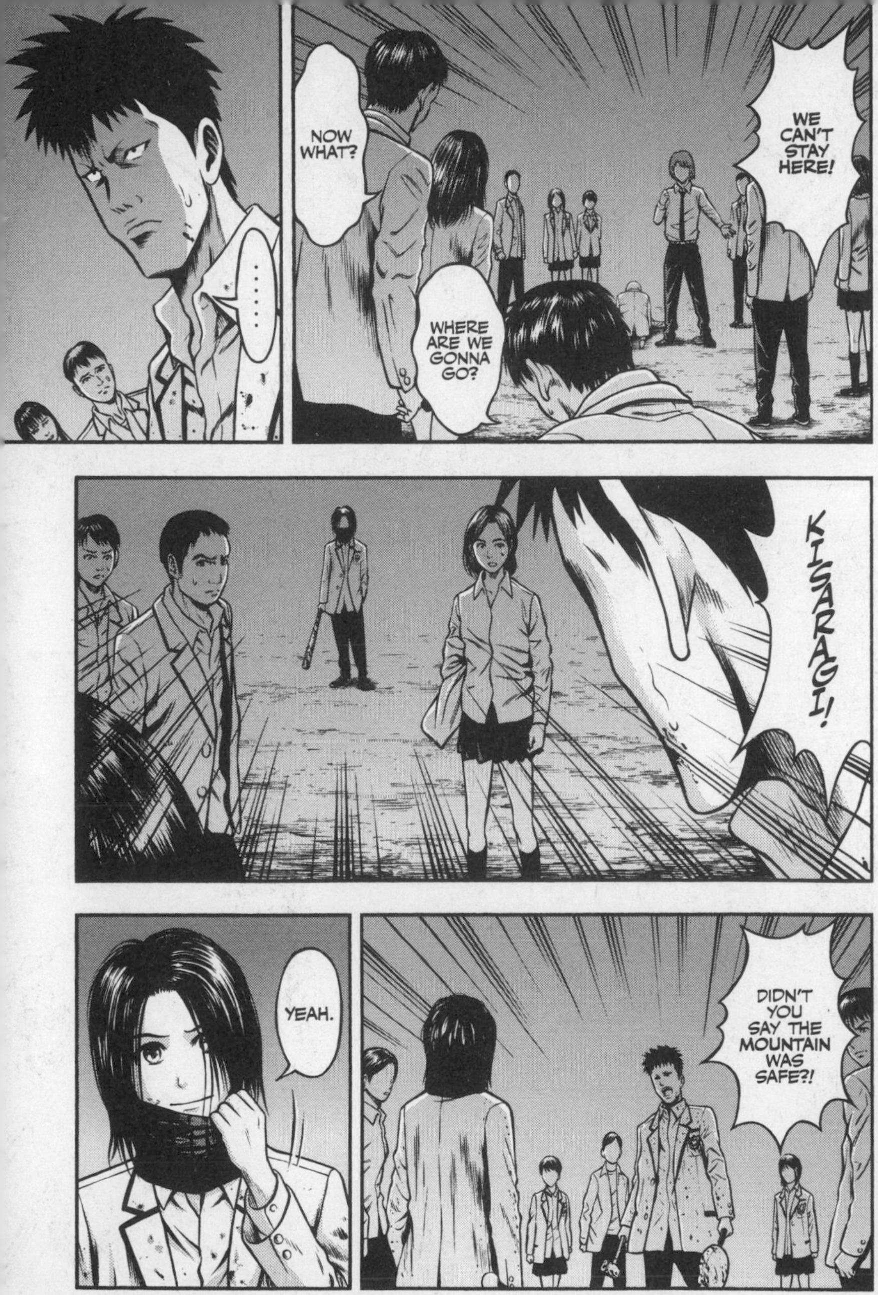
WE CAN'T STAY HERE!
NOW WHAT?
WHERE ARE WE GONNA GO?
......
KISARAGI!
DIDN'T YOU SAY THE MOUNTAIN WAS SAFE?!
YEAH.

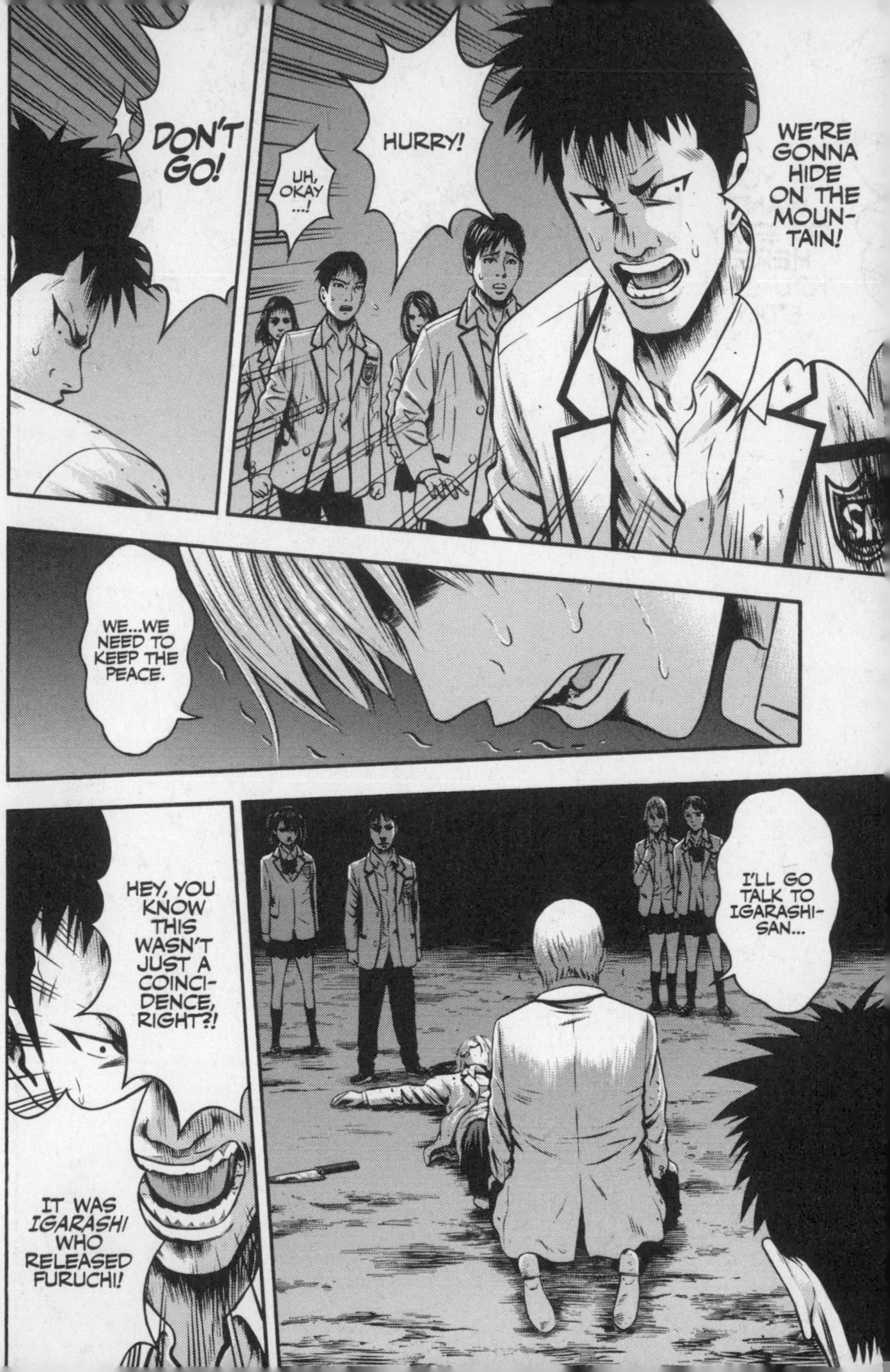
WE'RE GONNA HIDE ON THE MOUNTAIN!
HURRY!
UH, OKAY ...!
DON'T GO!
WE...WE NEED TO KEEP THE PEACE.
I'LL GO TALK TO IGARASHI-SAN...
HEY, YOU KNOW THIS WASN'T JUST A COINCIDENCE, RIGHT?!
IT WAS *IGARASHI* WHO RELEASED FURUCHI!

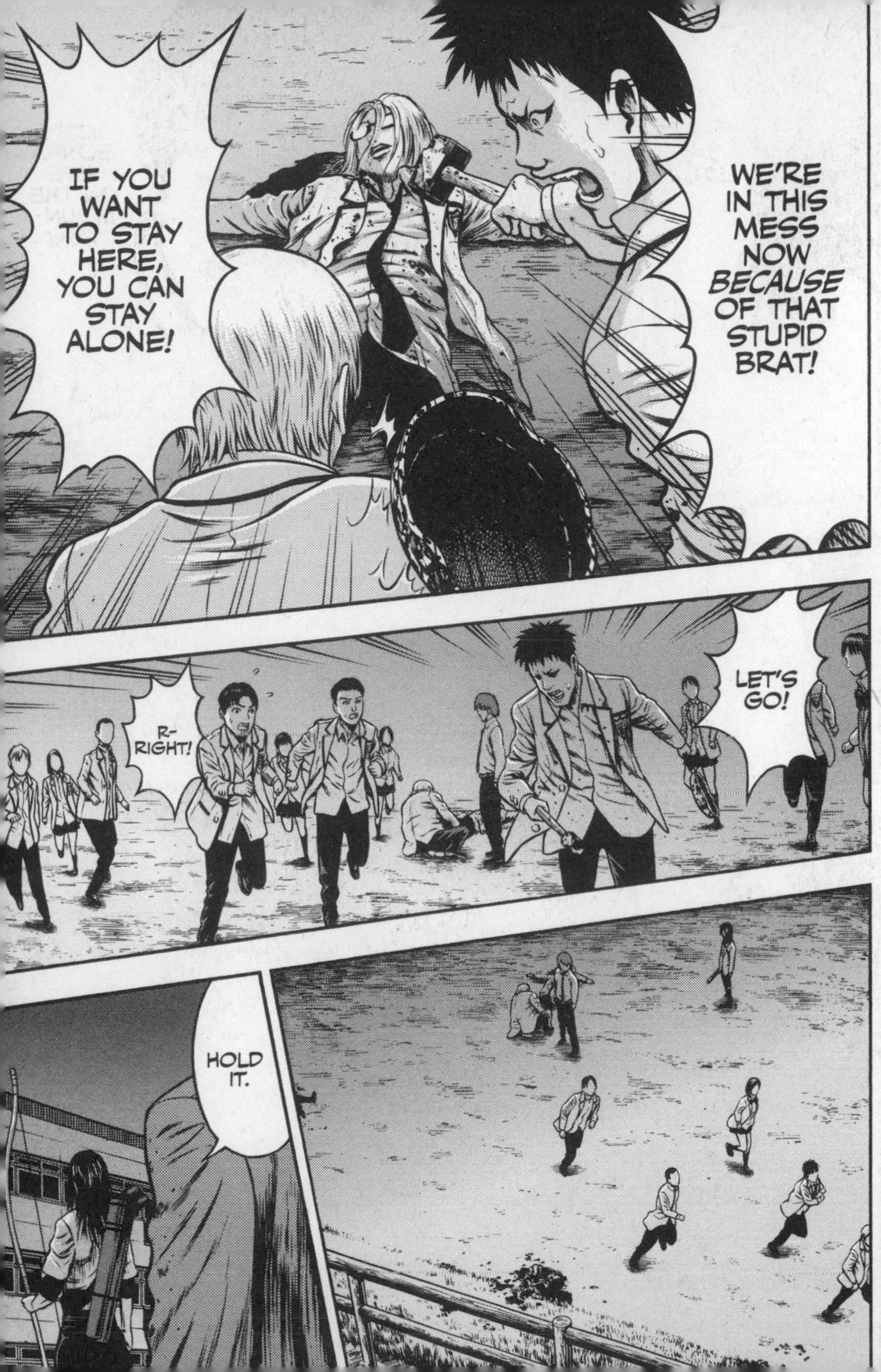
WE'RE IN THIS MESS NOW BECAUSE OF THAT STUPID BRAT!
IF YOU WANT TO STAY HERE, YOU CAN STAY ALONE!
LET'S GO!
R-RIGHT!
HOLD IT.

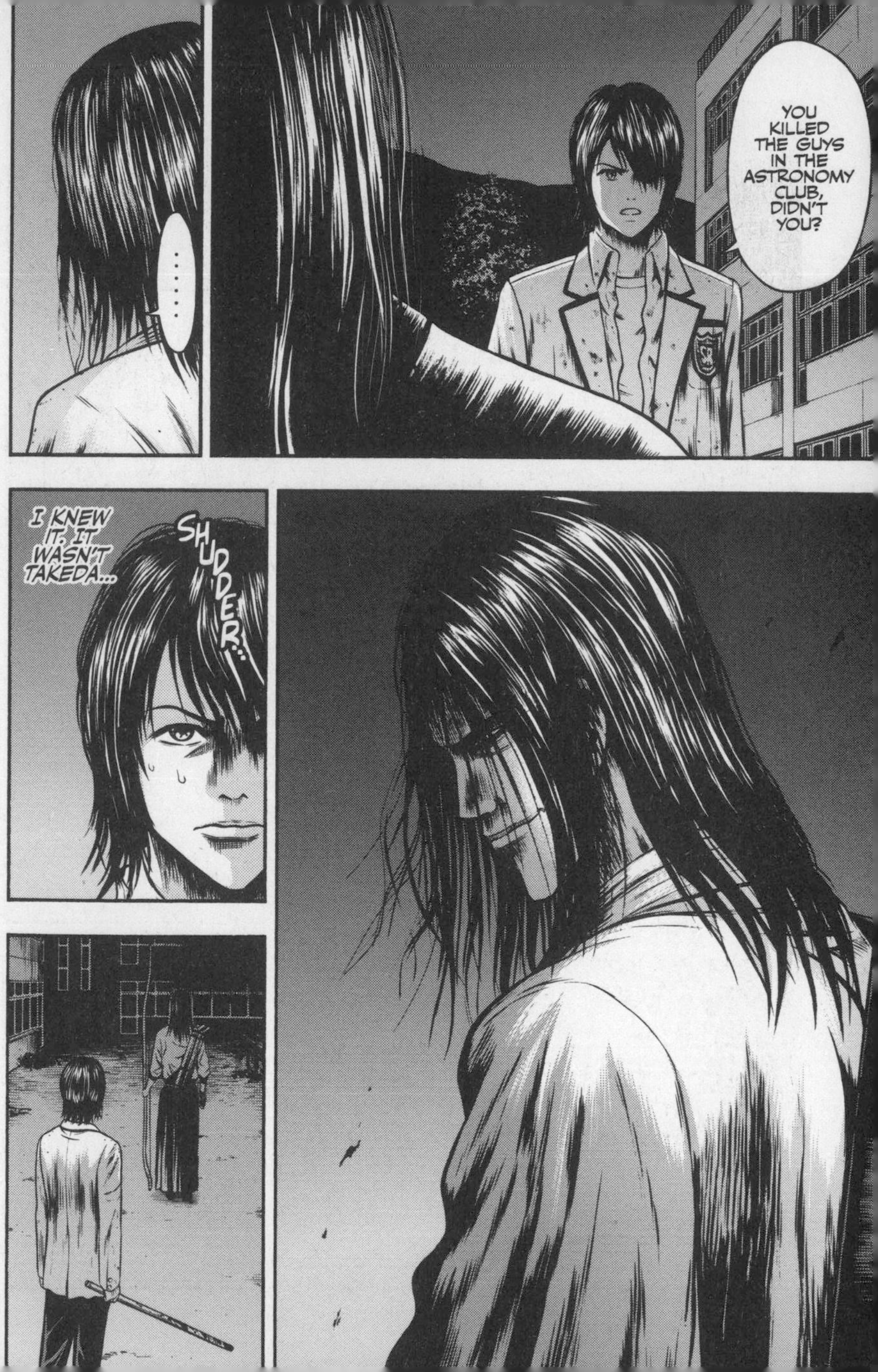
YOU KILLED THE GUYS IN THE ASTRONOMY CLUB, DIDN'T YOU?
......
SHUDDER...
I KNEW IT. IT WASN'T TAKEDA...

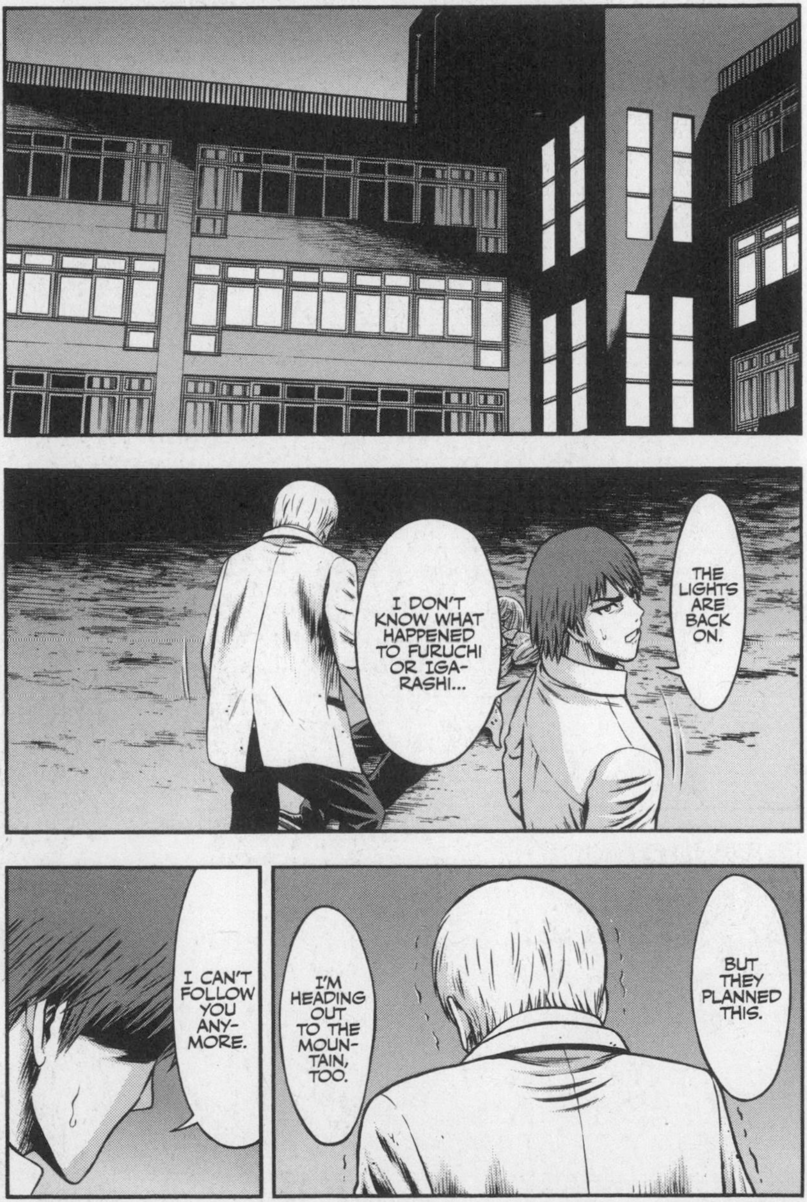
THE LIGHTS ARE BACK ON.
I DON'T KNOW WHAT HAPPENED TO FURUCHI OR IGA-RASHI...
BUT THEY PLANNED THIS.
I'M HEADING OUT TO THE MOUN-TAIN, TOO.
I CAN'T FOLLOW YOU ANY-MORE.

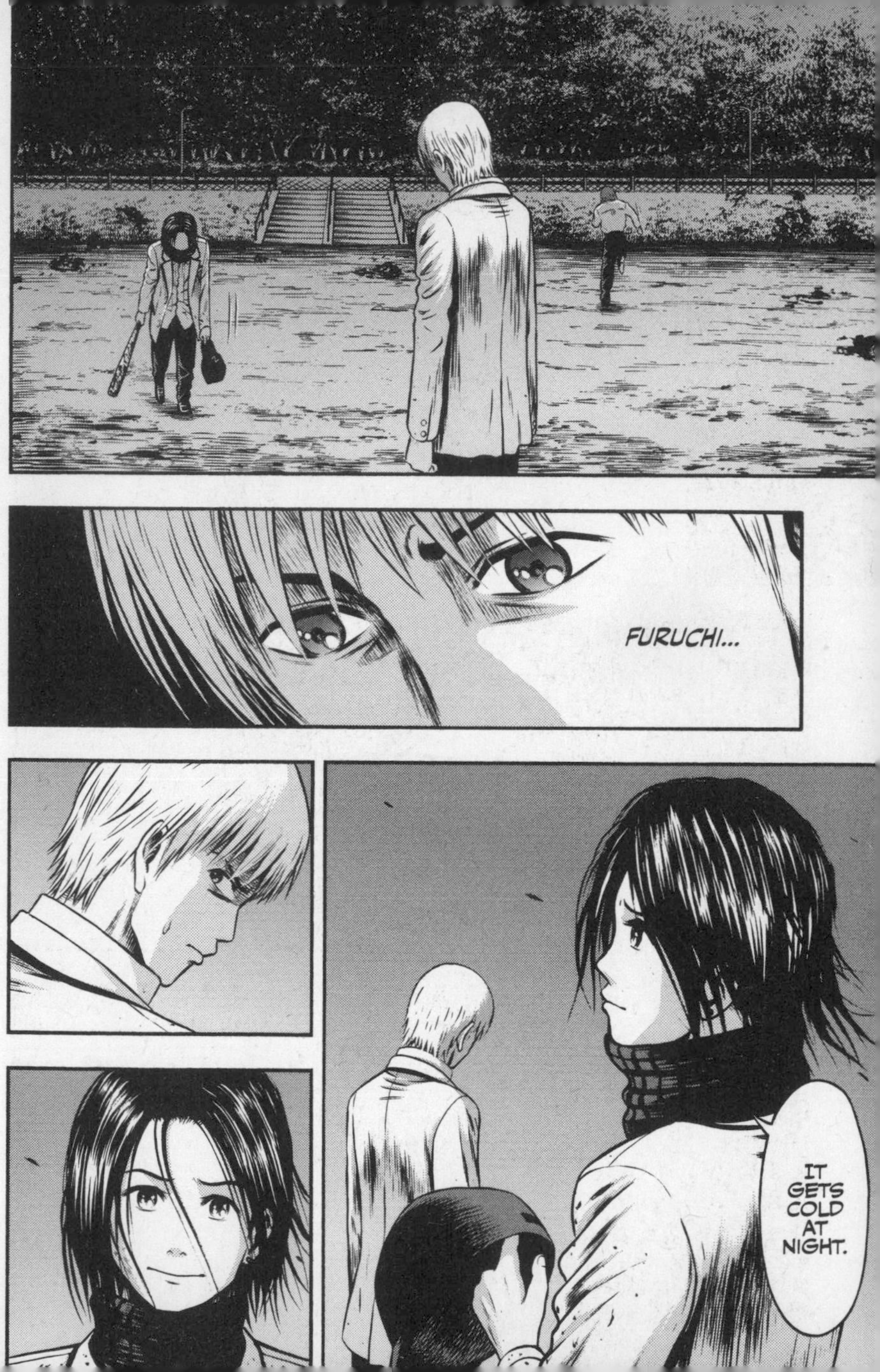
FURUCHI...
IT GETS COLD AT NIGHT.

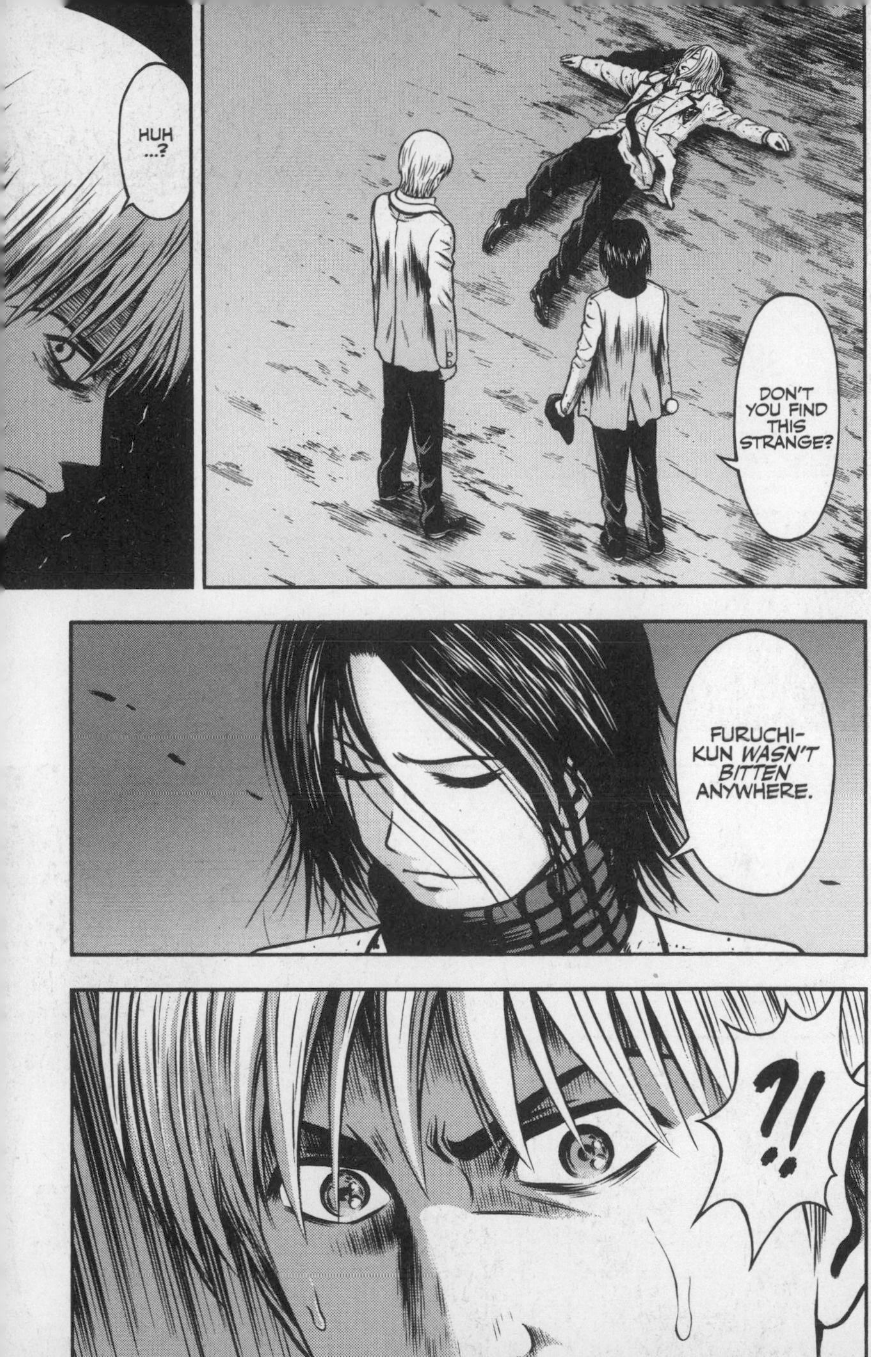
DON'T YOU FIND THIS STRANGE?
HUH ...?
FURUCHI-KUN WASN'T BITTEN ANYWHERE.
?!

HE DIDN'T GET BITTEN...!

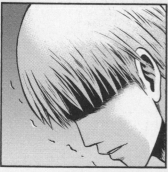

FURUCHI HAD NO IDEA...

THAT HE WAS ZOMBIFIED.

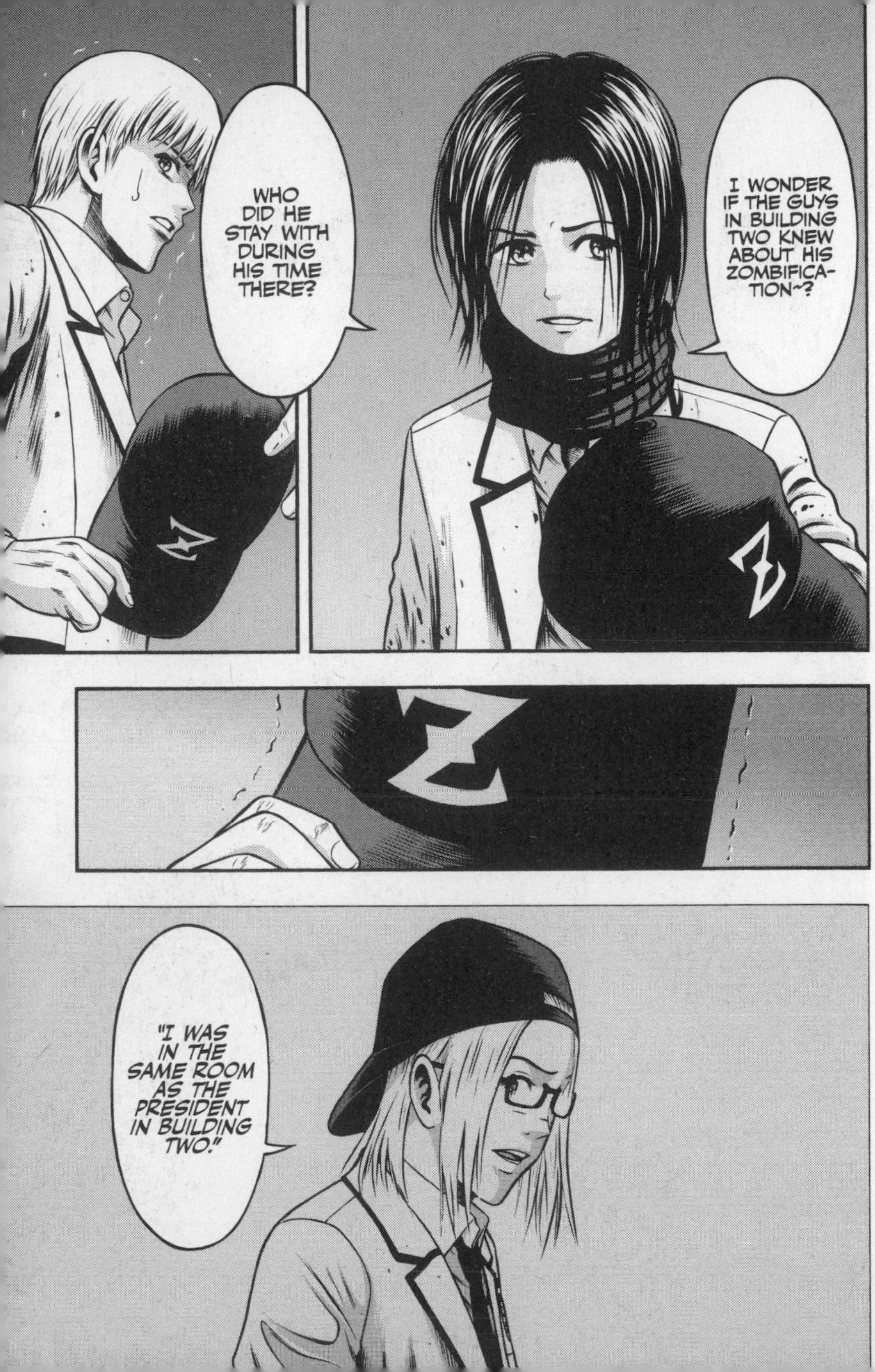
I WONDER IF THE GUYS IN BUILDING TWO KNEW ABOUT HIS ZOMBIFICA-TION~?
WHO DID HE STAY WITH DURING HIS TIME THERE?
"I WAS IN THE SAME ROOM AS THE PRESIDENT IN BUILDING TWO."

HOUJOU!

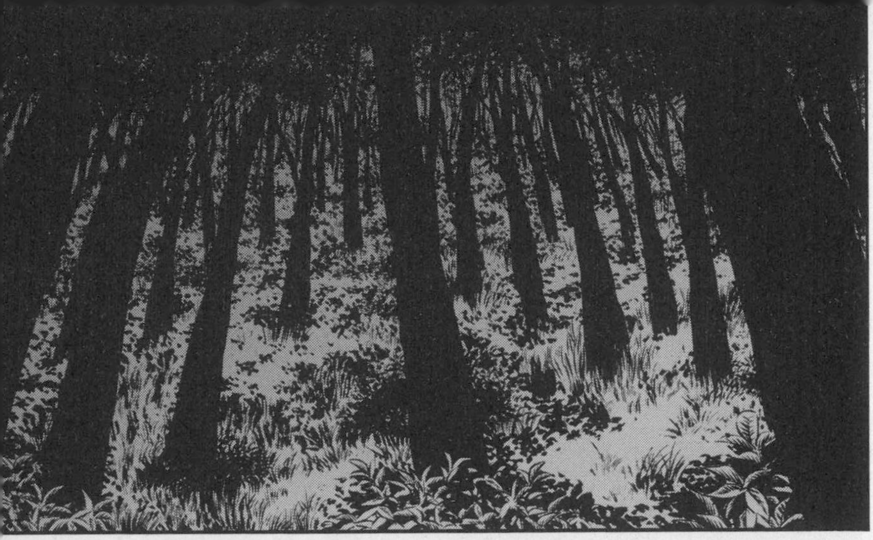

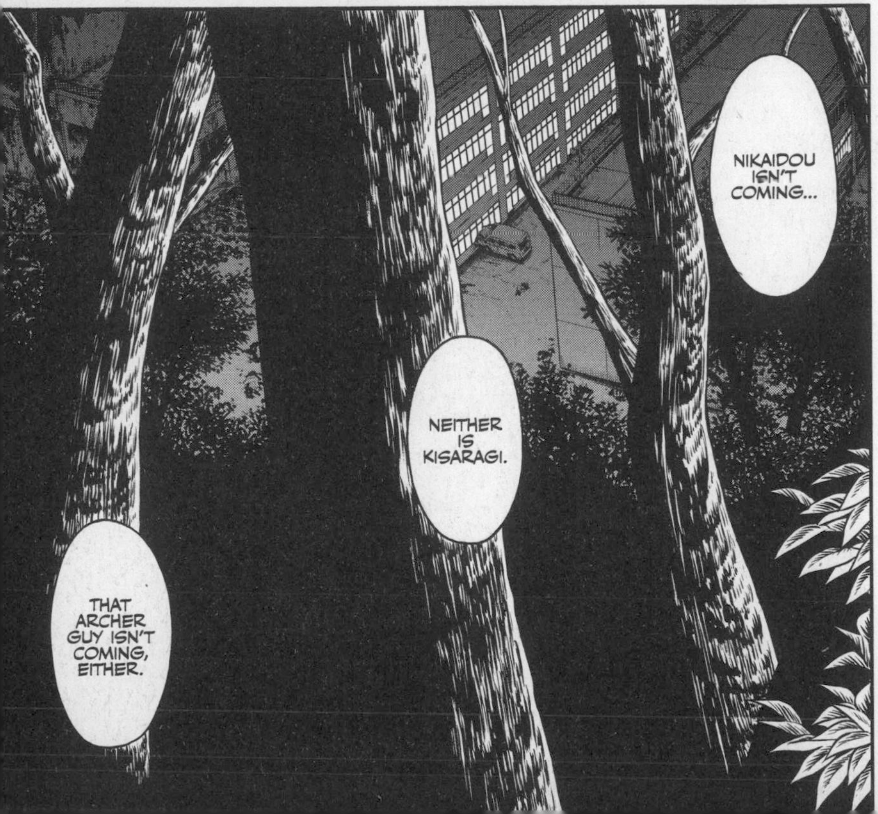
NIKAIDOU ISN'T COMING...
NEITHER IS KISARAGI.
THAT ARCHER GUY ISN'T COMING, EITHER.

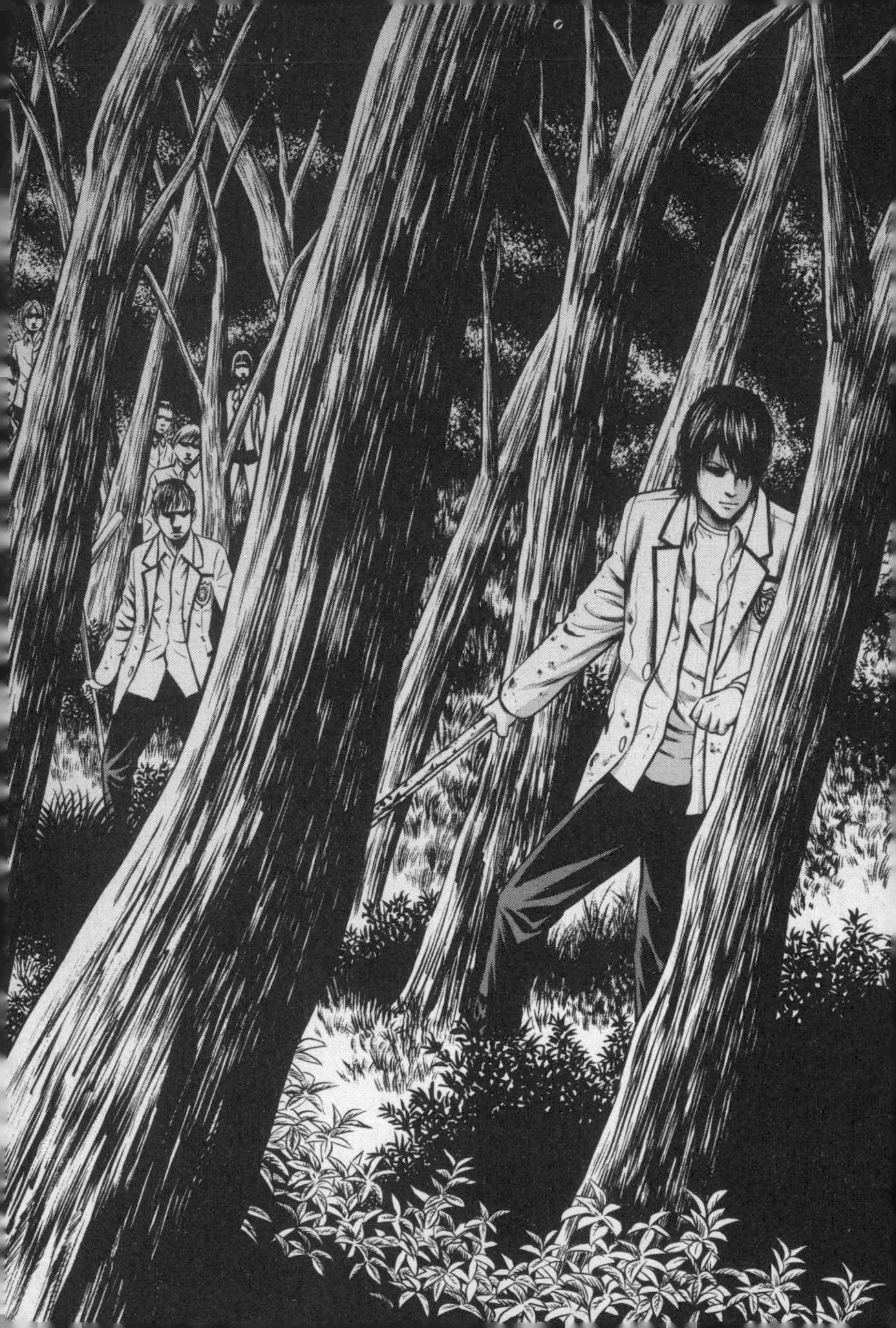

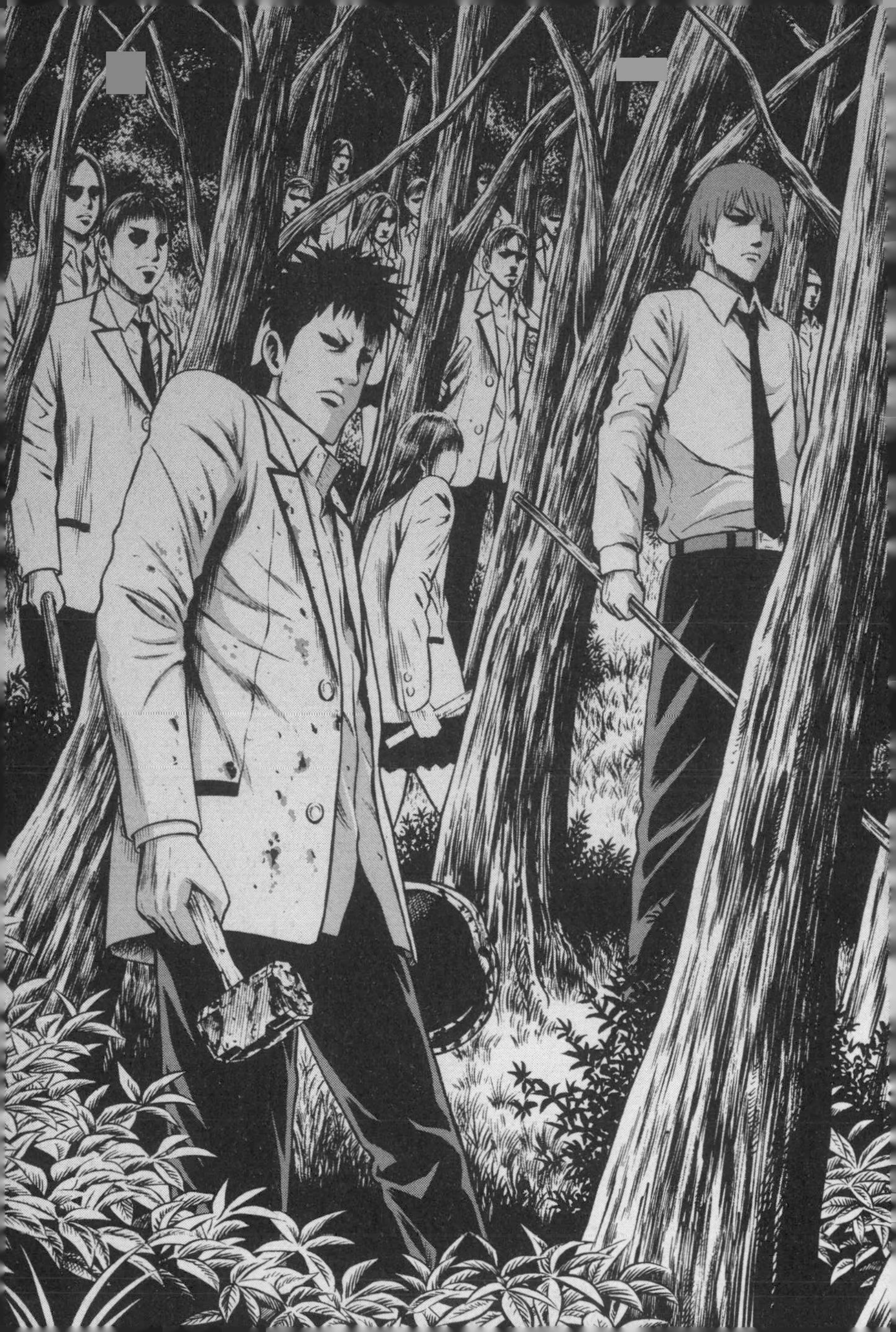

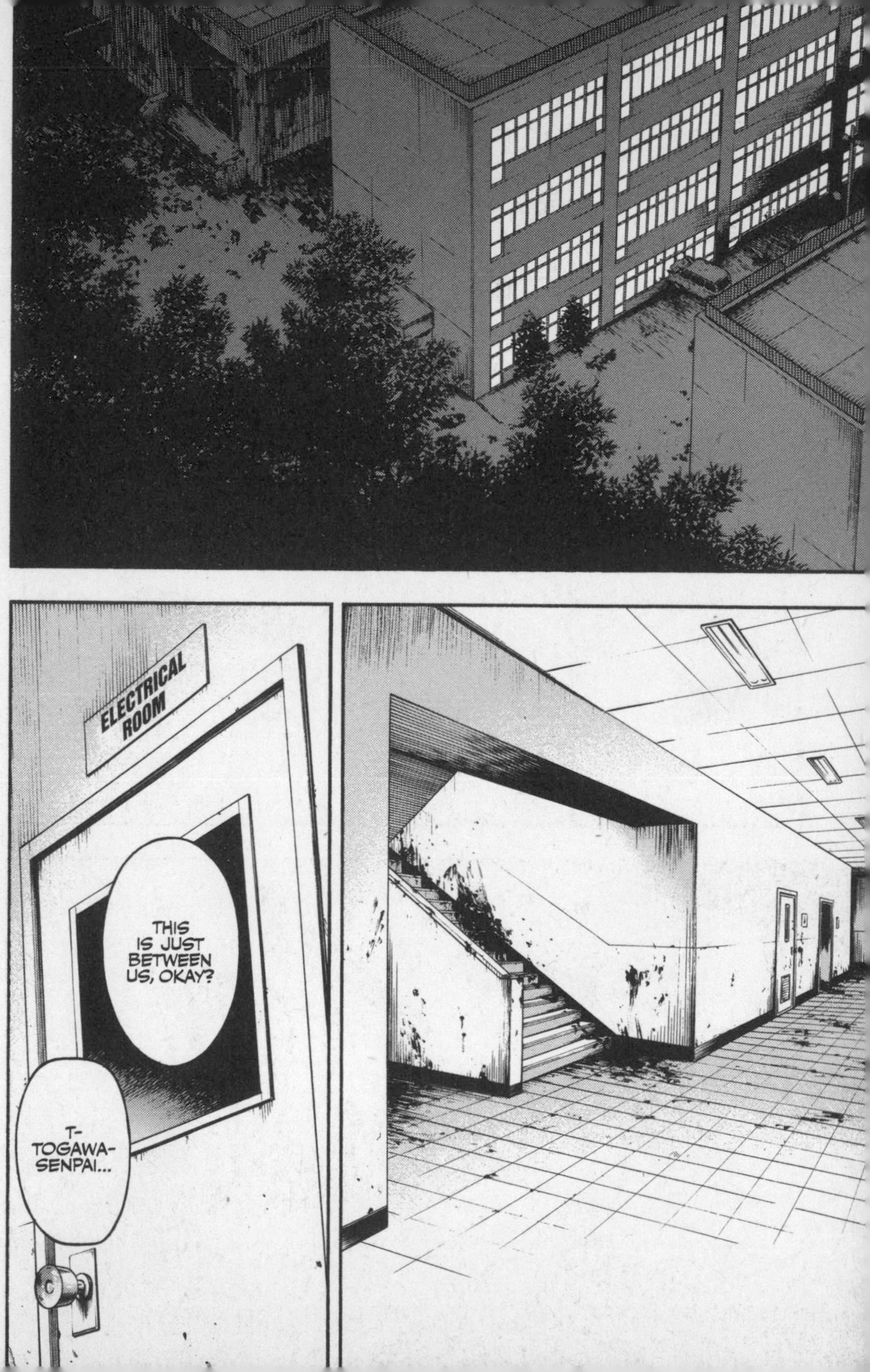
ELECTRICAL ROOM
THIS IS JUST BETWEEN US, OKAY?
T-TOGAWA-SENPAI...

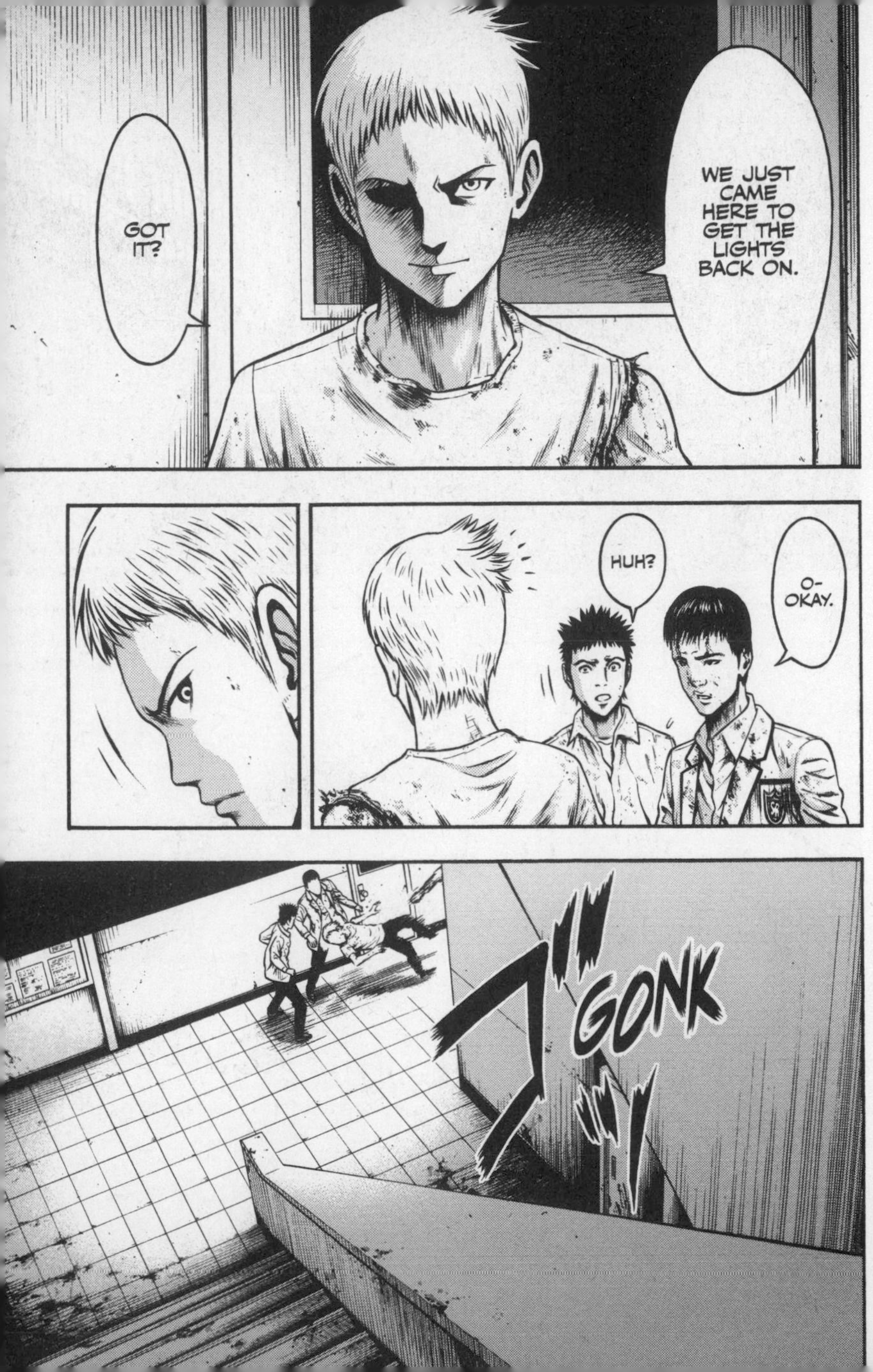
WE JUST CAME HERE TO GET THE LIGHTS BACK ON.
GOT IT?
O-OKAY.
HUH?
GONK

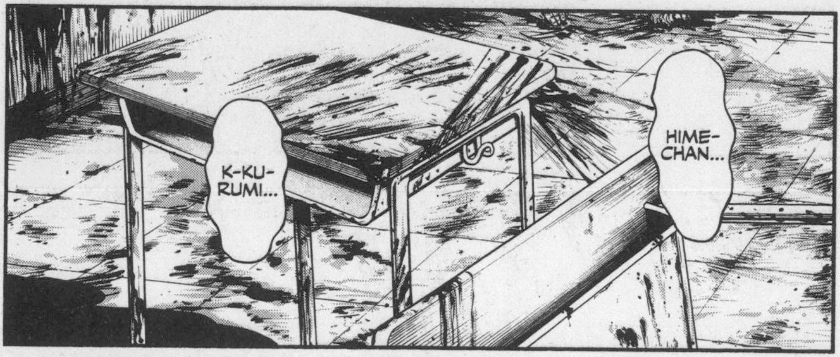
HIME-CHAN...
K-KURUMI...
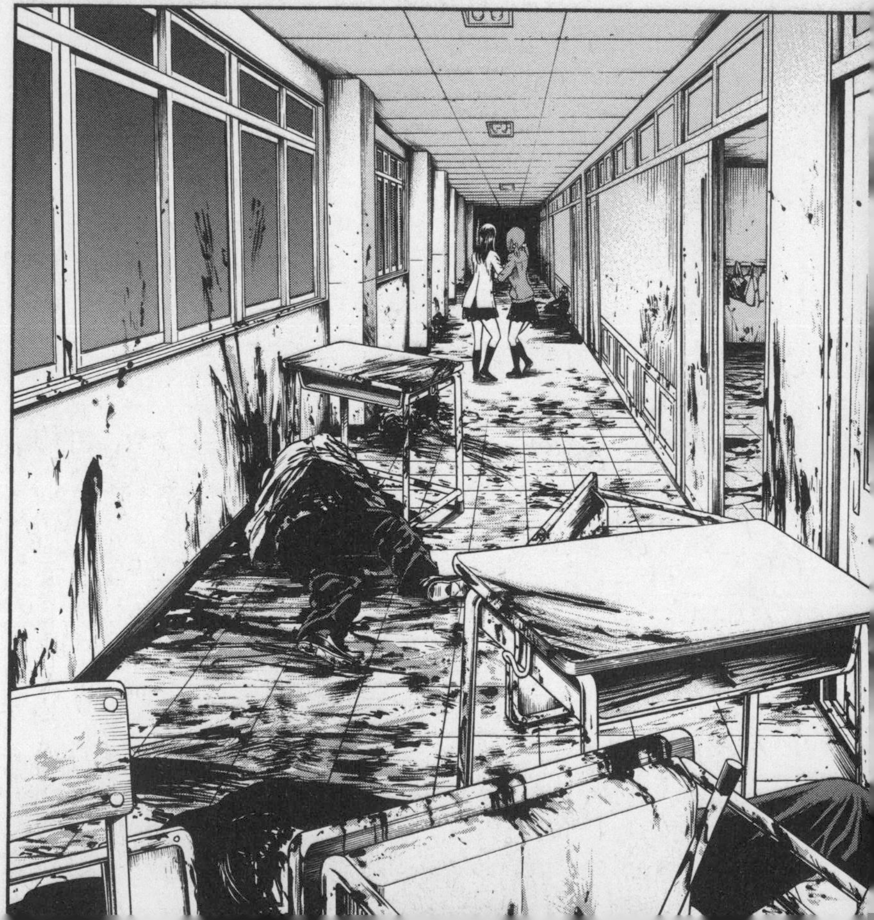

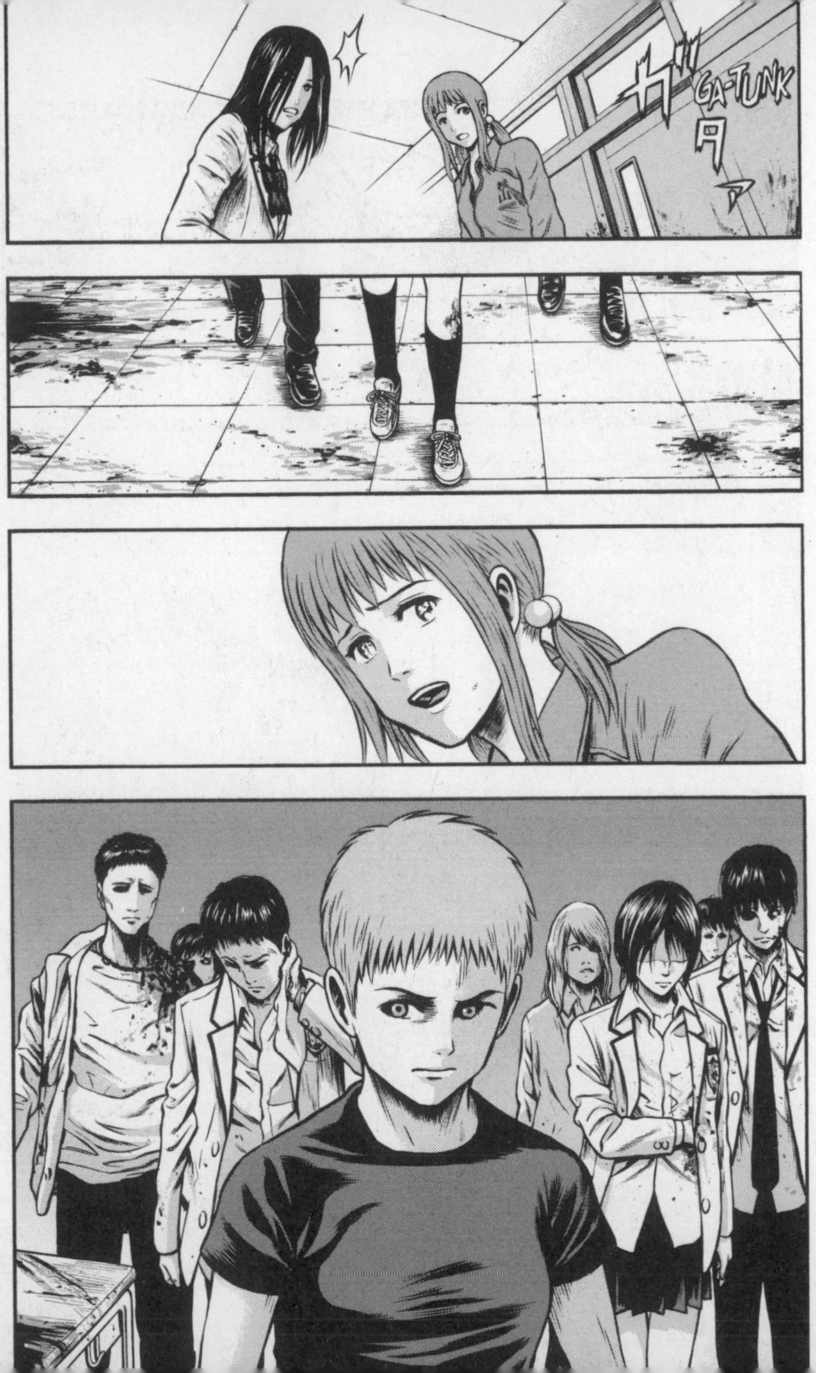
GA-TUNK

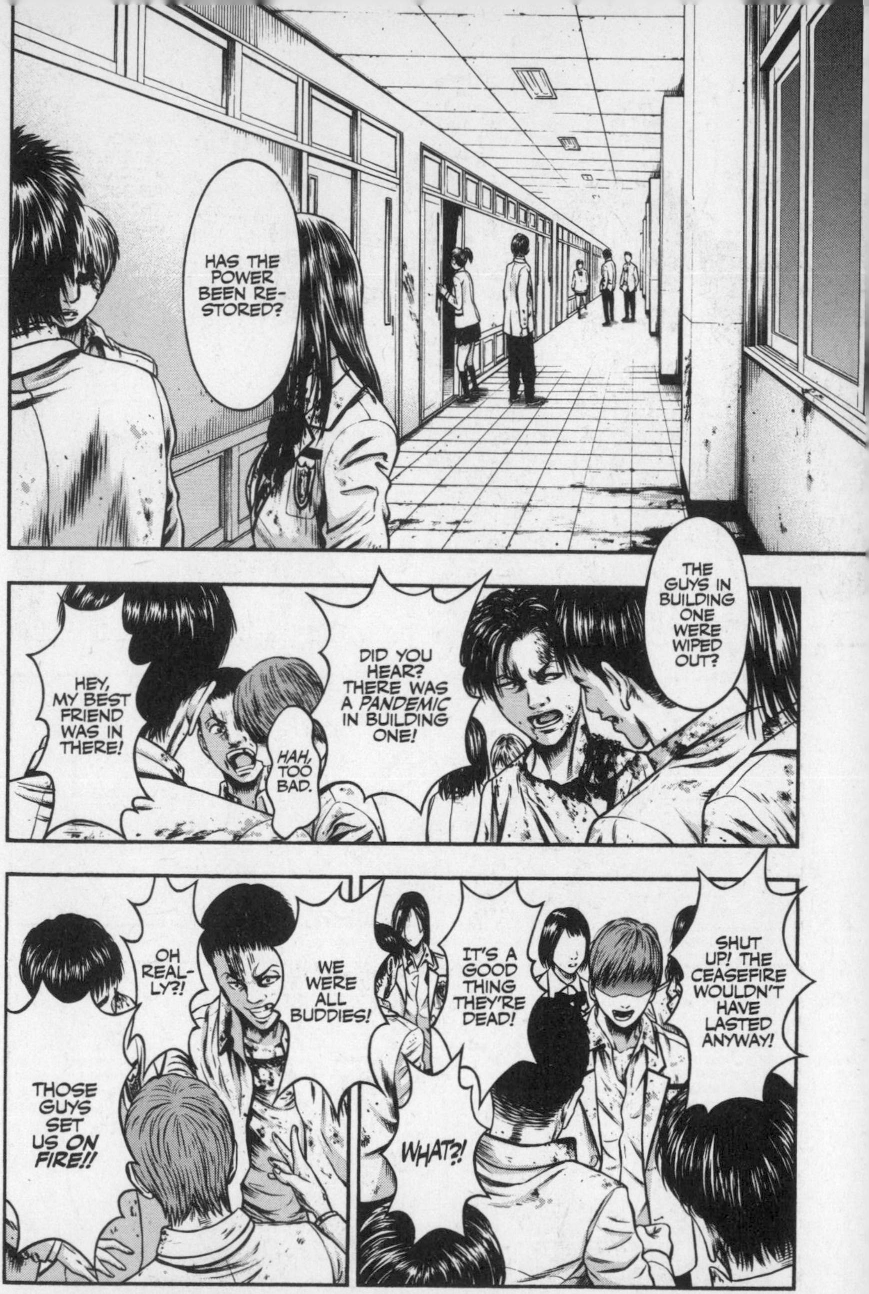
HAS THE POWER BEEN RE-STORED?
THE GUYS IN BUILDING ONE WERE WIPED OUT?
DID YOU HEAR? THERE WAS A *PANDEMIC* IN BUILDING ONE!
HEY, MY BEST FRIEND WAS IN THERE!
HAH, TOO BAD.
SHUT UP! THE CEASEFIRE WOULDN'T HAVE LASTED ANYWAY!
IT'S A GOOD THING THEY'RE DEAD!
WHAT?!
WE WERE ALL BUDDIES!
OH REAL-LY?!
THOSE GUYS SET US *ON FIRE!!*

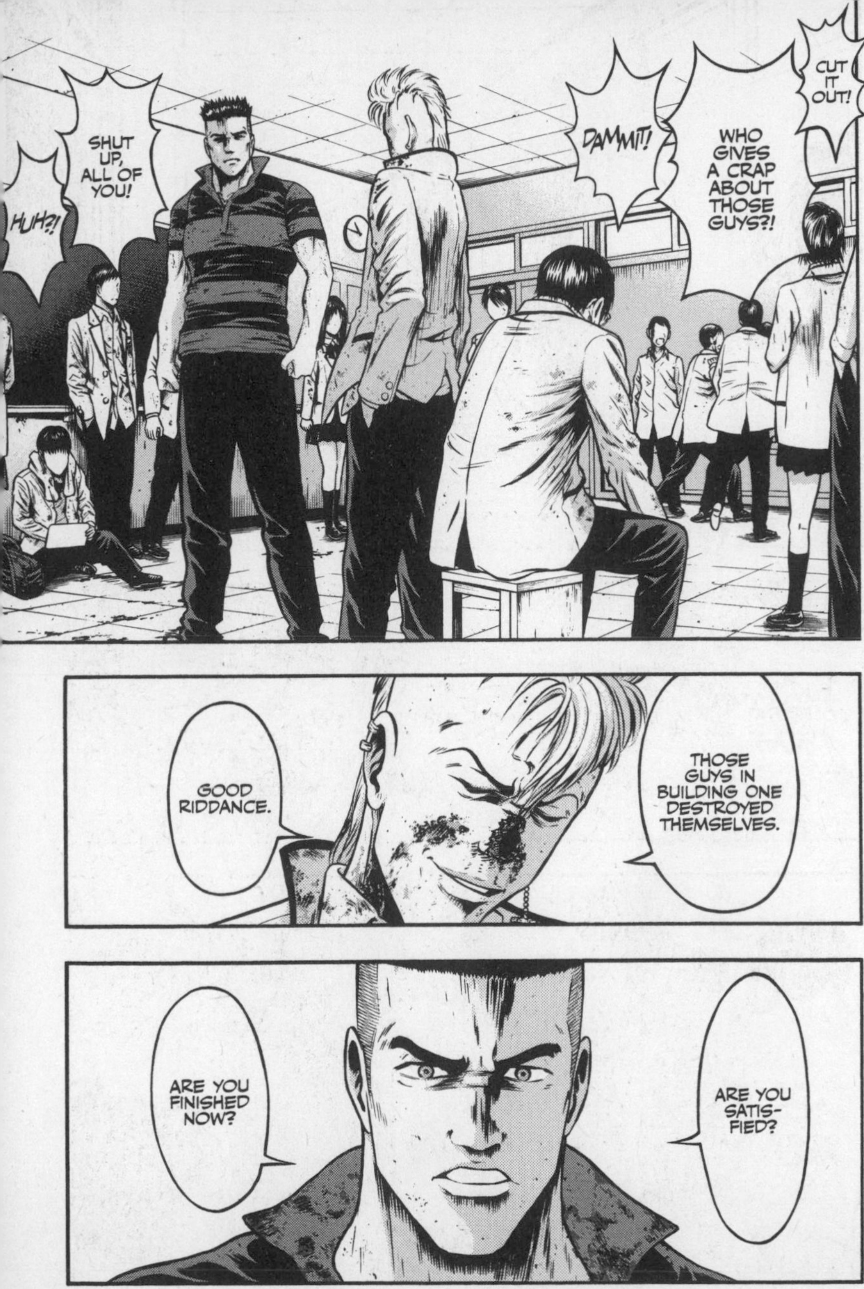
CUT IT OUT!
WHO GIVES A CRAP ABOUT THOSE GUYS?!
DAMMIT!
SHUT UP, ALL OF YOU!
HUH?!
THOSE GUYS IN BUILDING ONE DESTROYED THEMSELVES.
GOOD RIDDANCE.
ARE YOU SATIS-FIED?
ARE YOU FINISHED NOW?

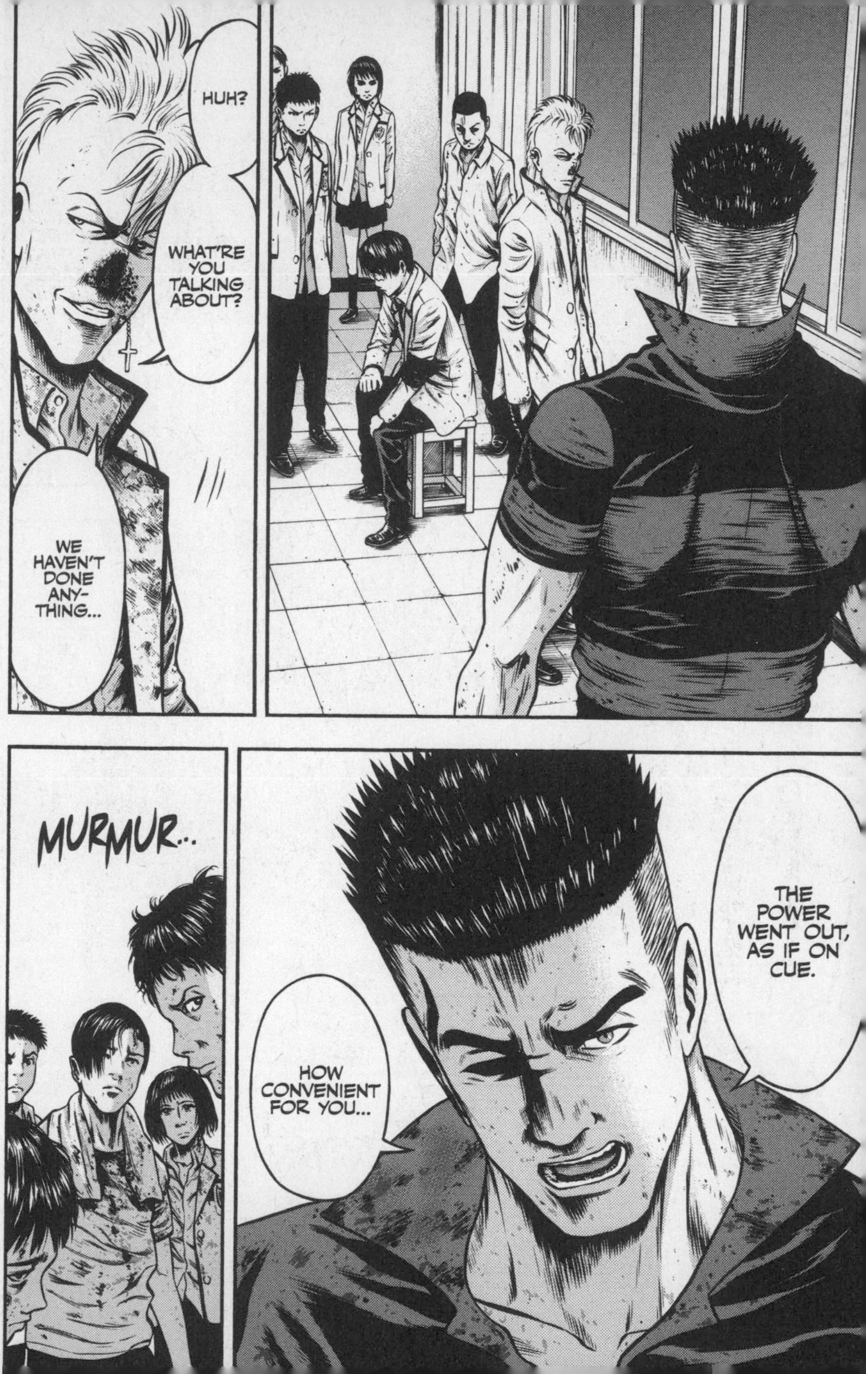
HUH?
WHAT'RE YOU TALKING ABOUT?
WE HAVEN'T DONE ANY-THING...
THE POWER WENT OUT, AS IF ON CUE.
HOW CONVENIENT FOR YOU...
MURMUR...

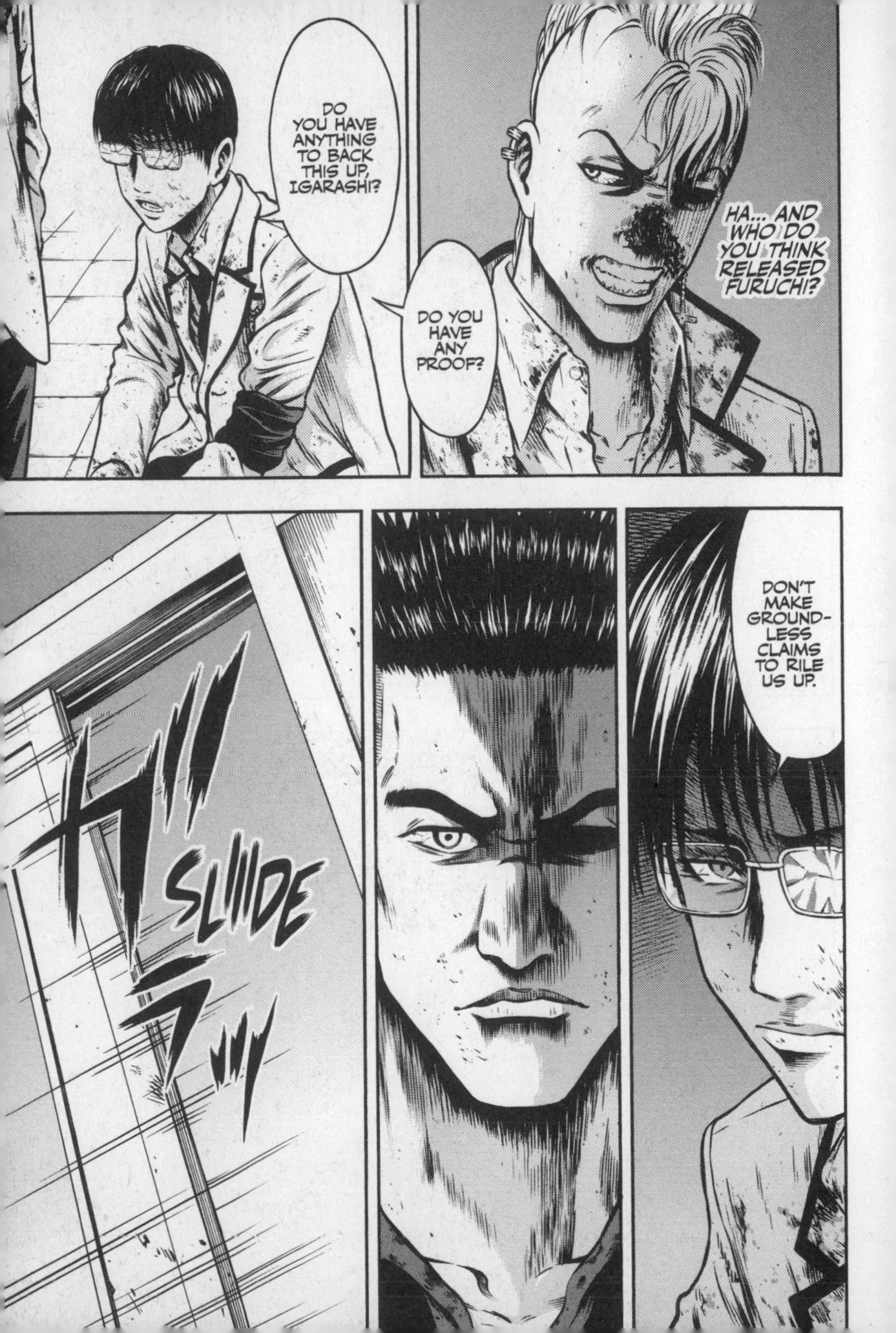
HA... AND WHO DO YOU THINK RELEASED FURUCHI!?
DO YOU HAVE ANY PROOF?
DO YOU HAVE ANYTHING TO BACK THIS UP, IGARASHI!?
DON'T MAKE GROUNDLESS CLAIMS TO RILE US UP.
SLIIDE

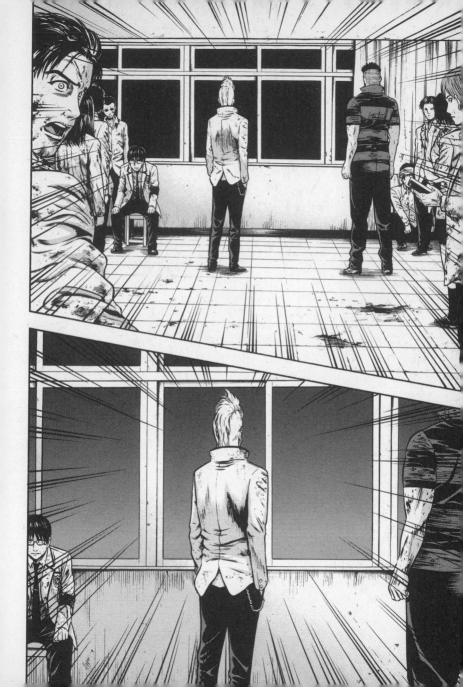

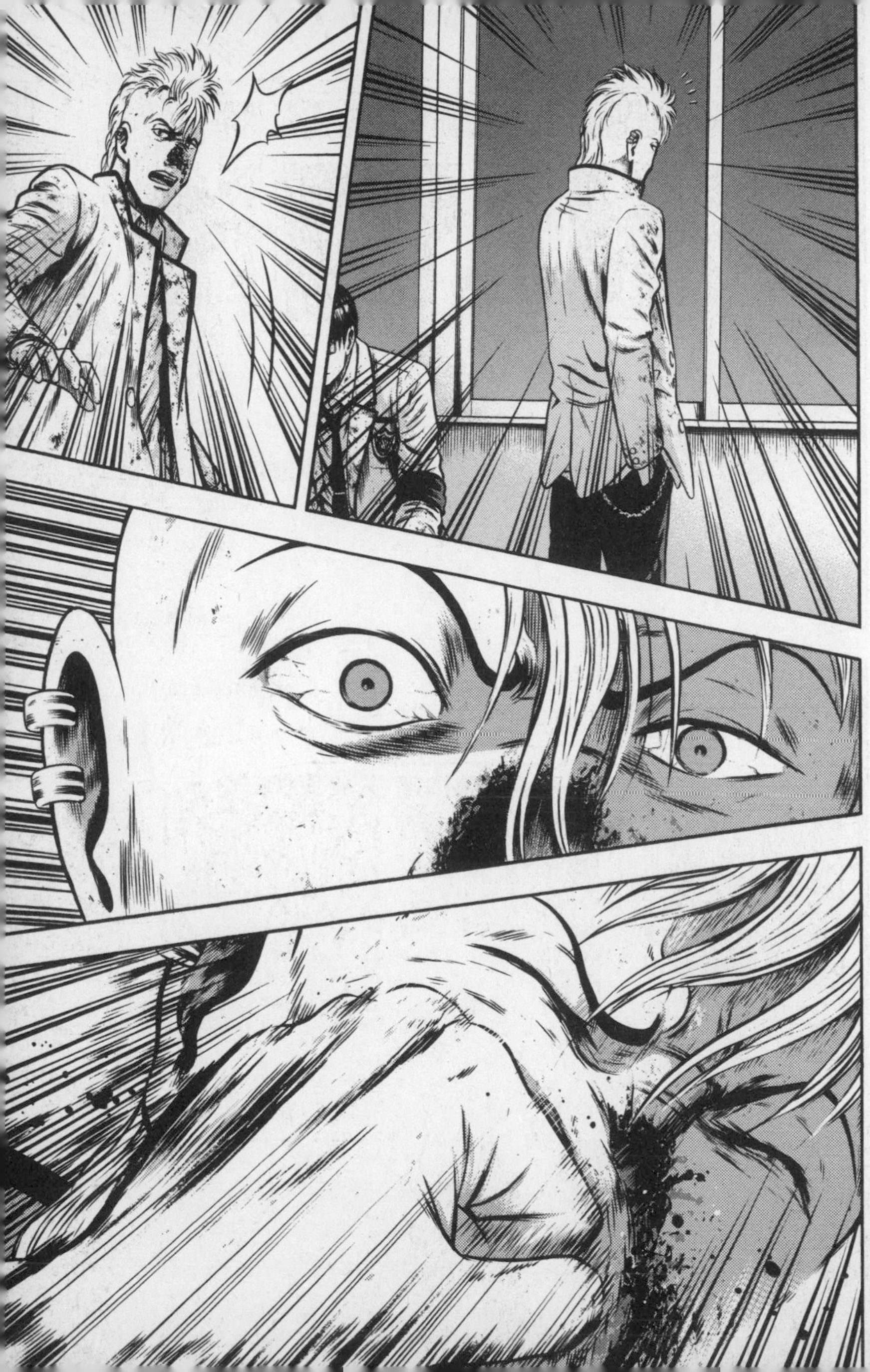

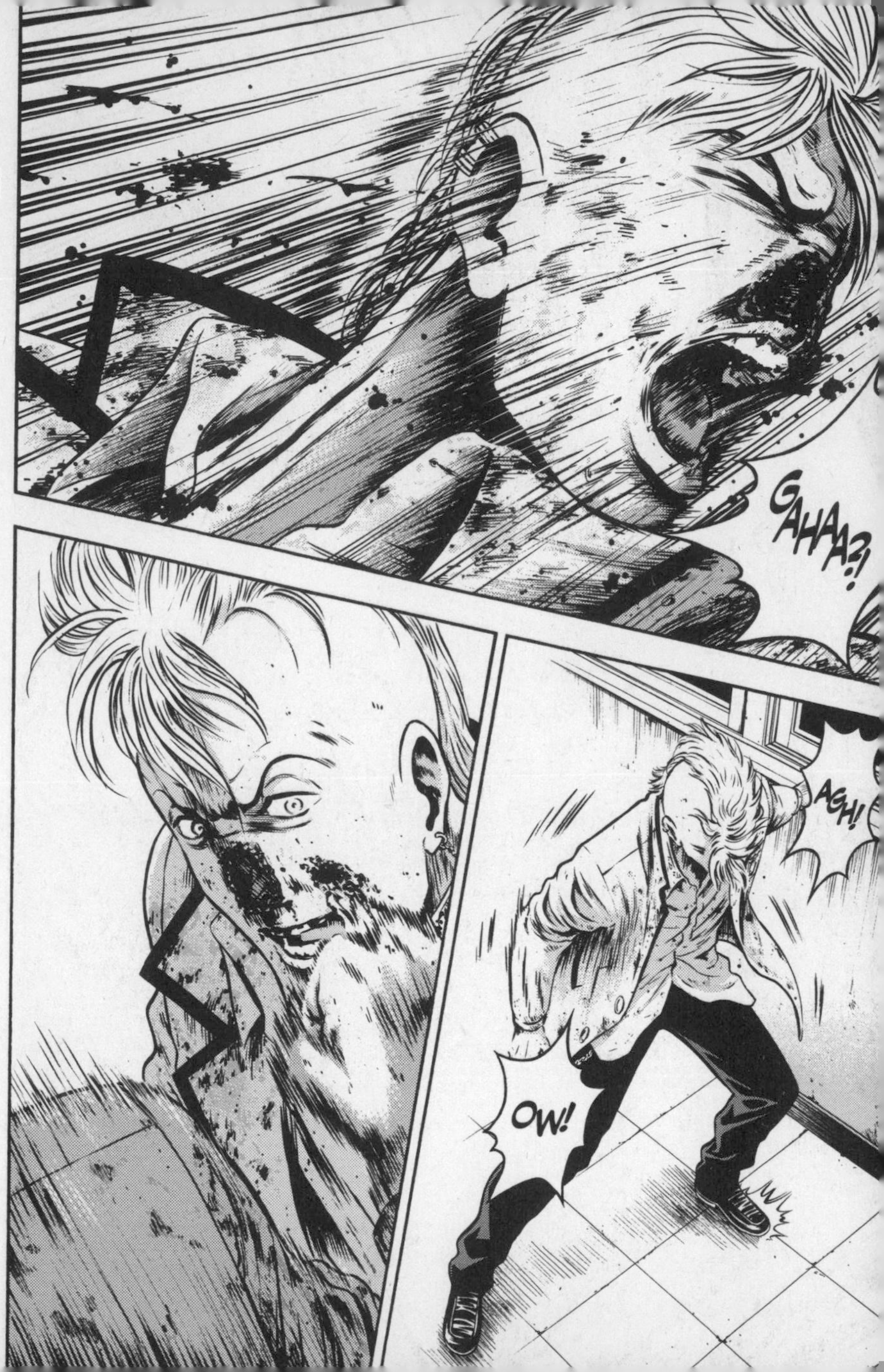
GAHAA?!
AGH!
OW!

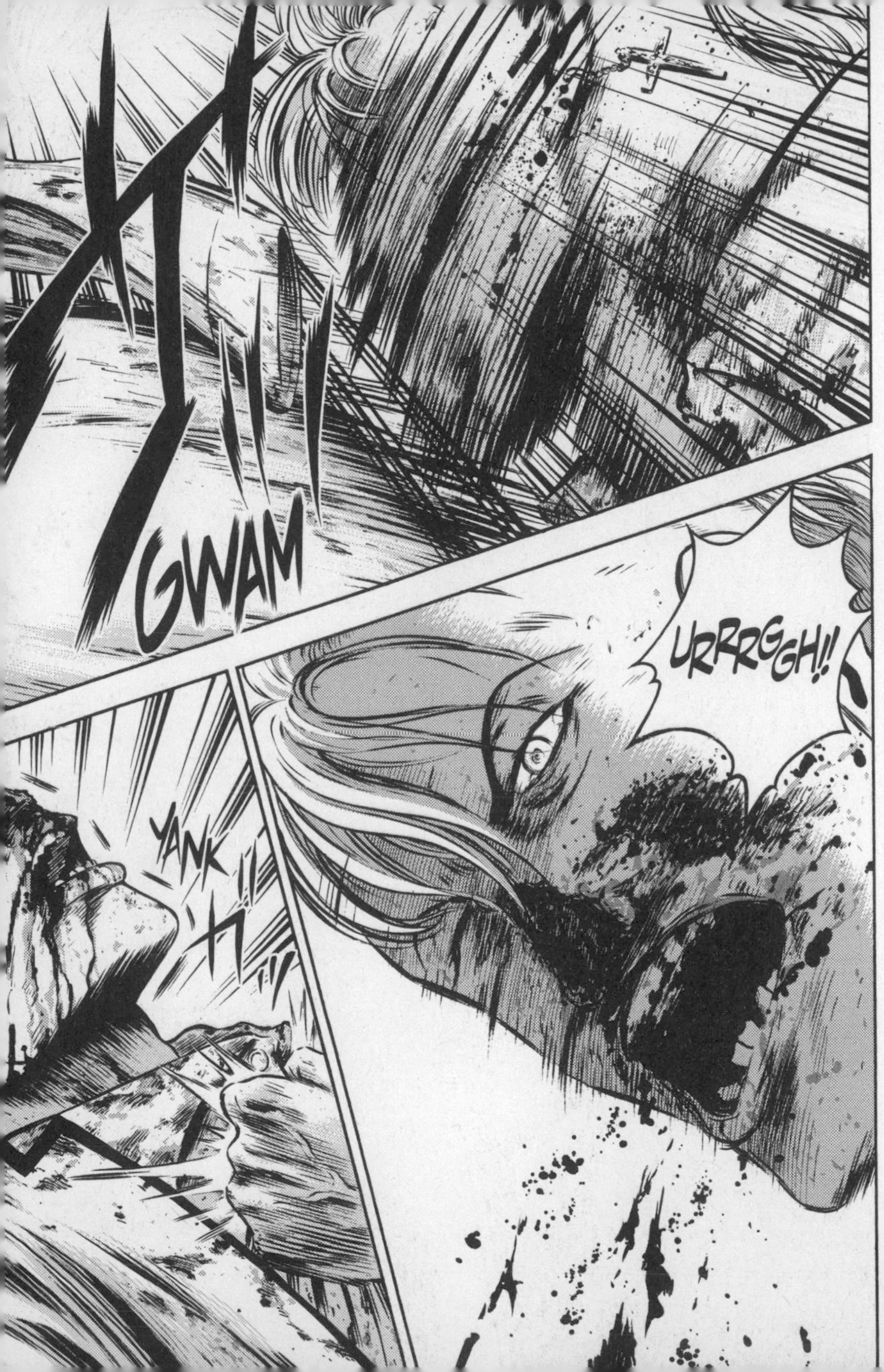
GWAM
URRRGGH!!
YANK

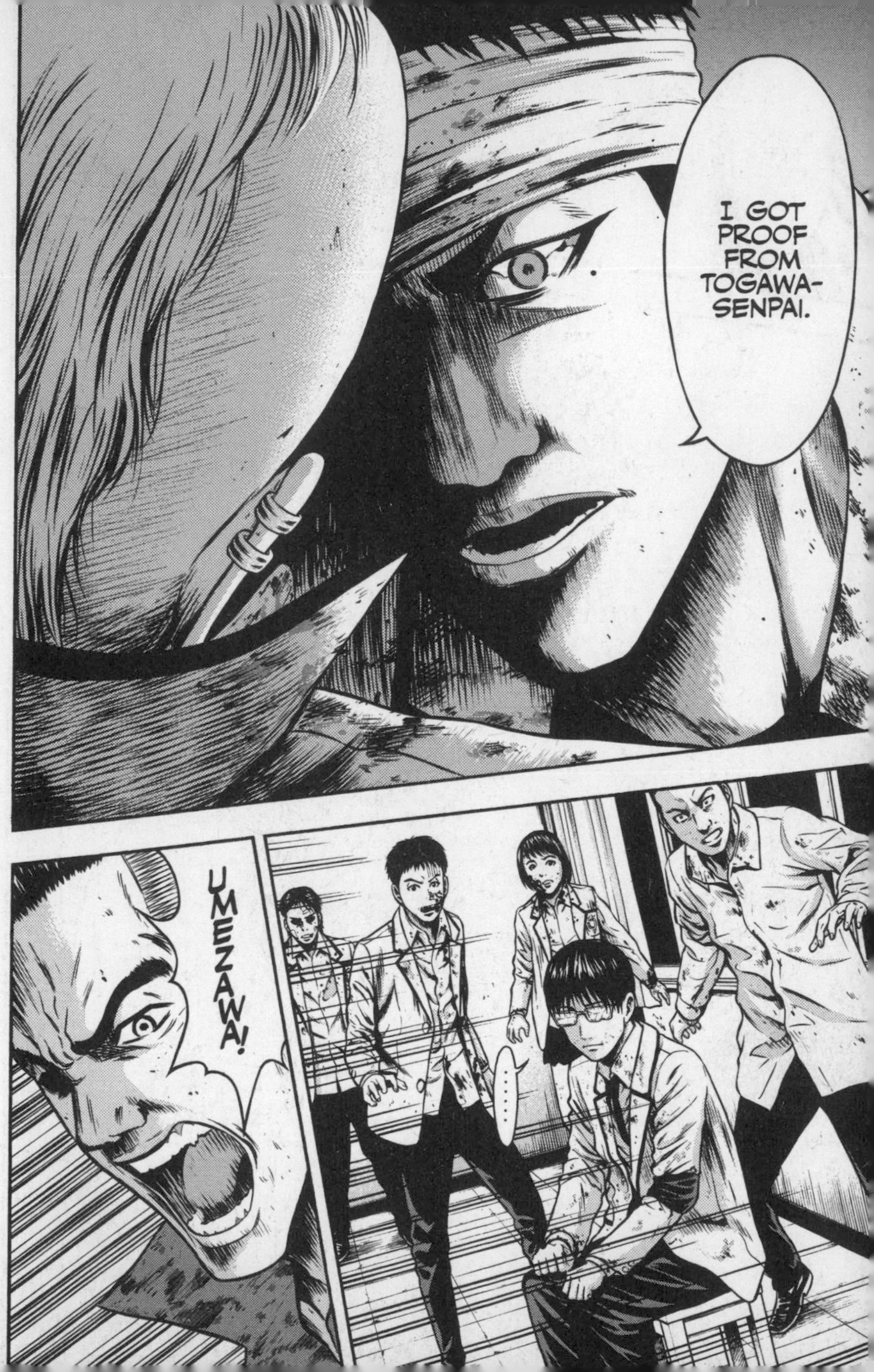
I GOT PROOF FROM TOGAWA-SENPAI.
...
UMEZAWA!

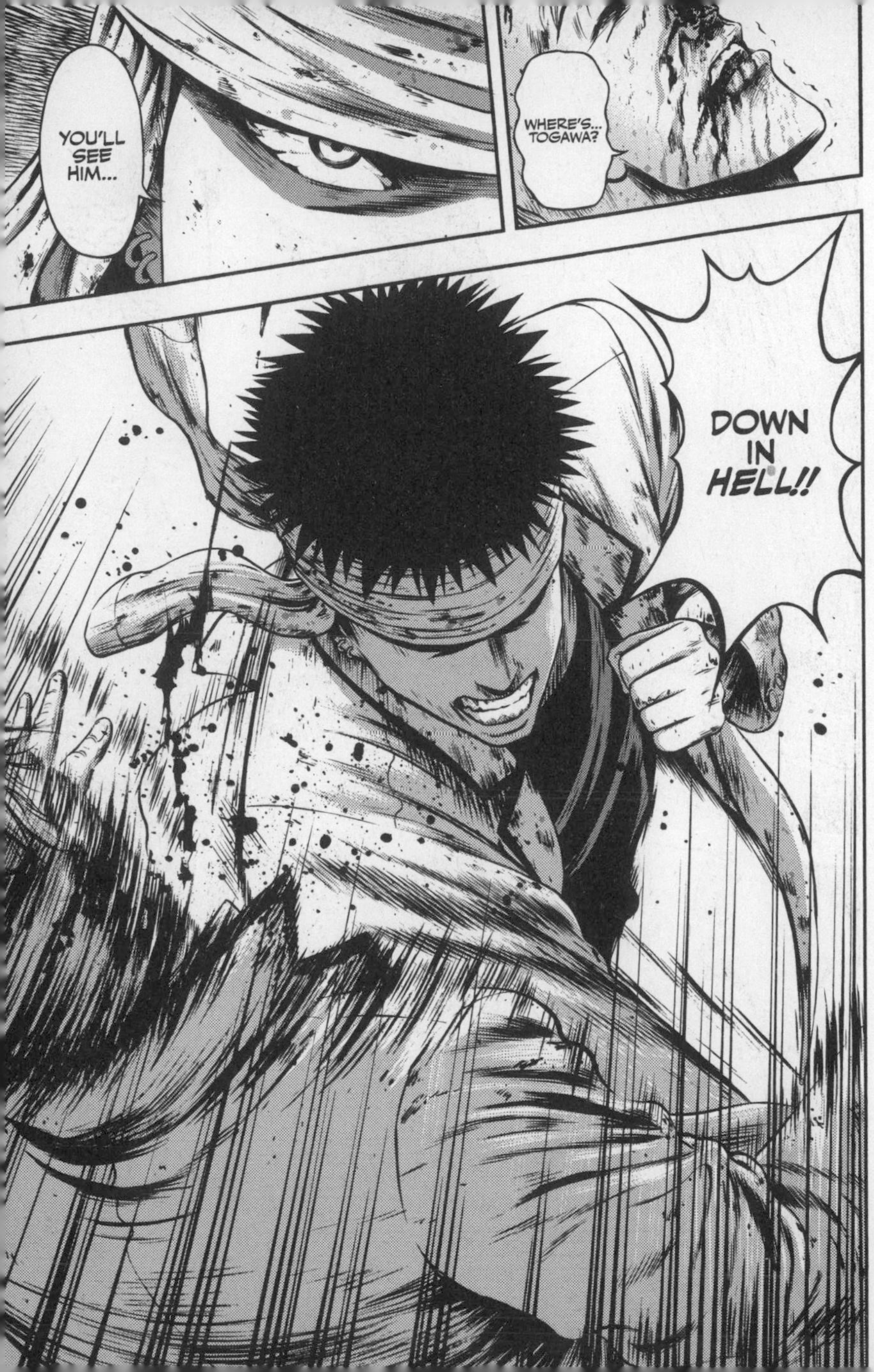
WHERE'S... TOGAWA?
YOU'LL SEE HIM...
DOWN IN HELL!!

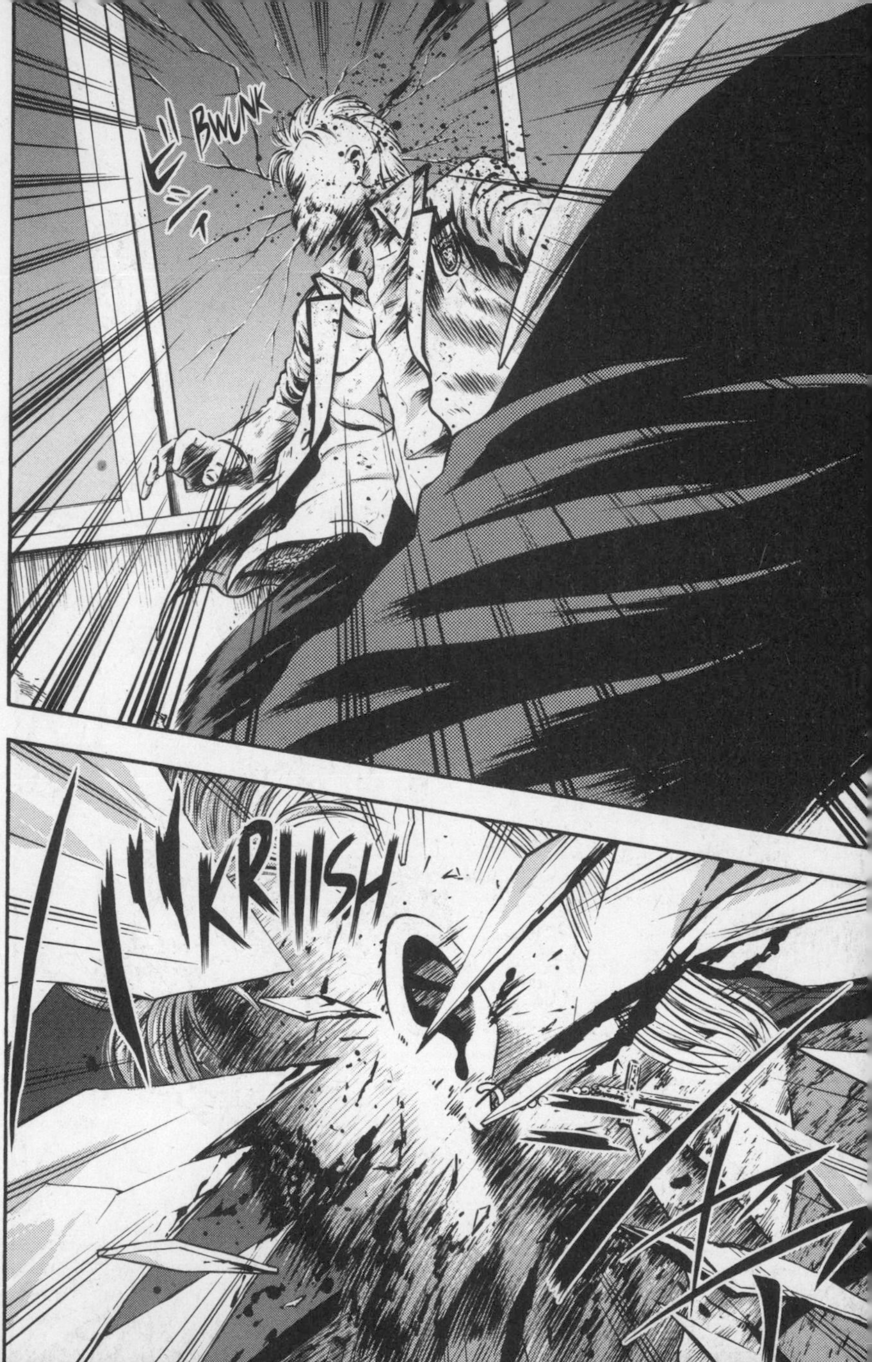
BWUNK
KRIIISH

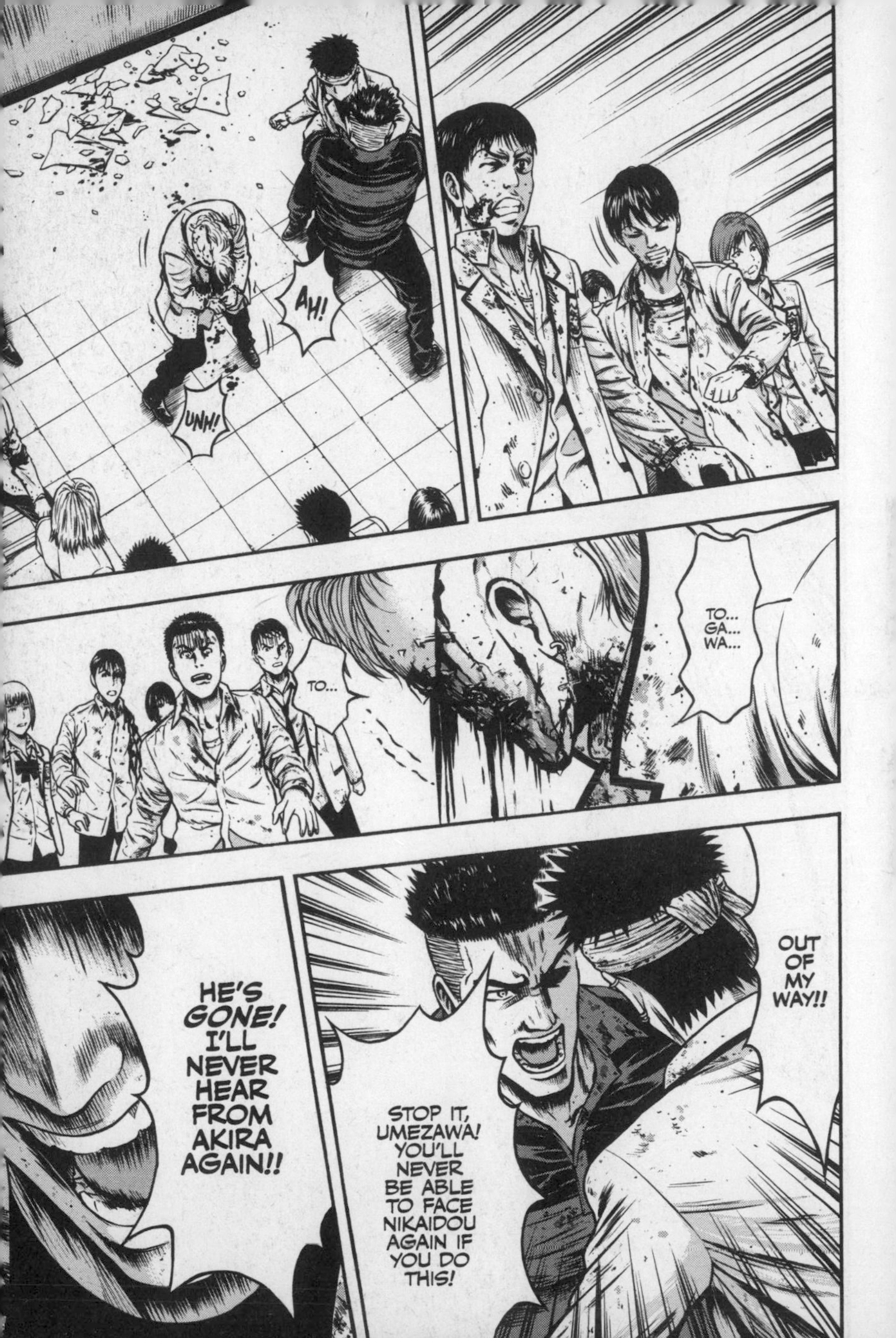
AH!
UNH!
TO... GA... WA...
TO...
OUT OF MY WAY!!
STOP IT, UMEZAWA! YOU'LL NEVER BE ABLE TO FACE NIKAIDOU AGAIN IF YOU DO THIS!
HE'S GONE! I'LL NEVER HEAR FROM AKIRA AGAIN!!

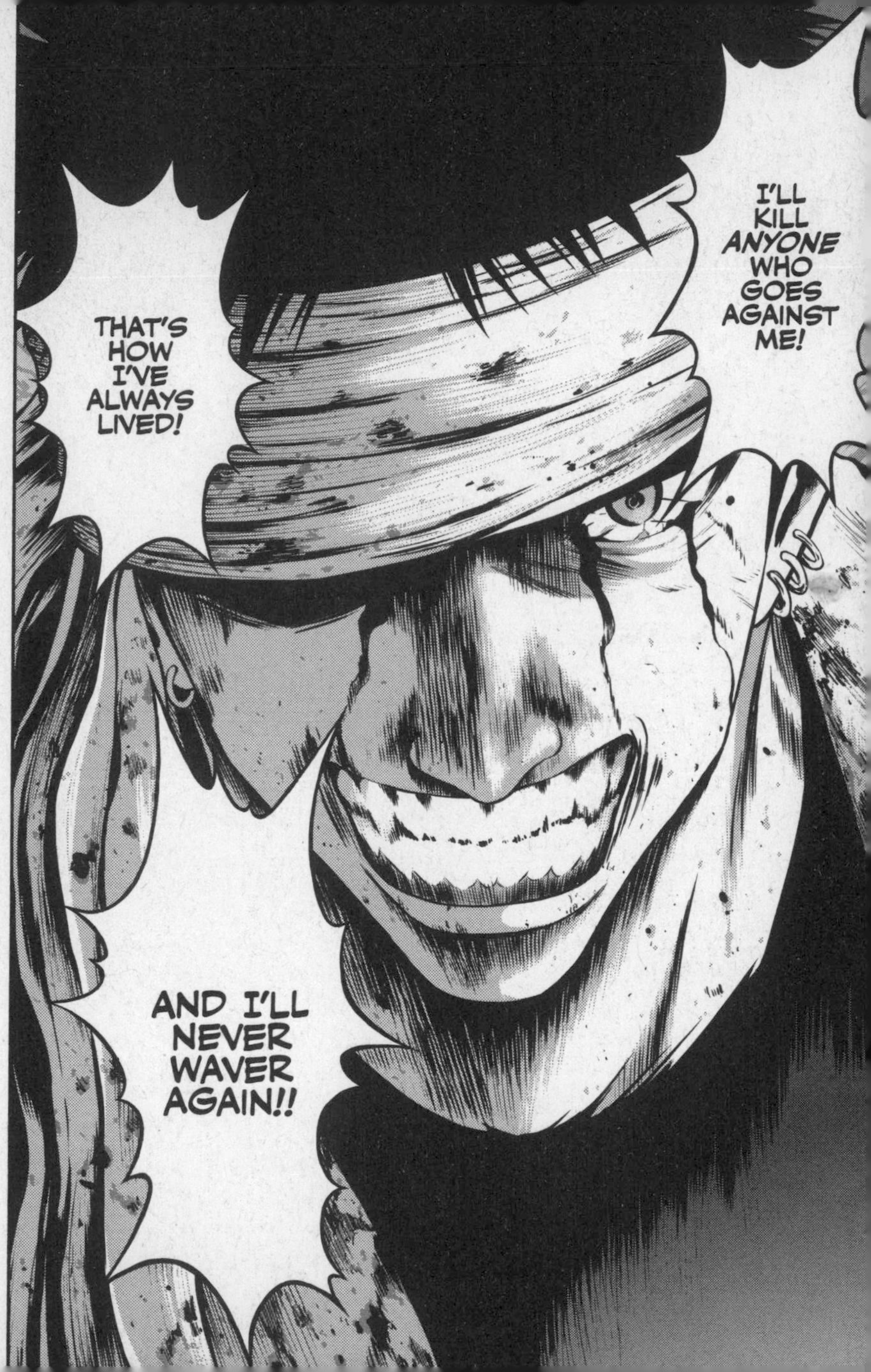
I'LL KILL ANYONE WHO GOES AGAINST ME!
THAT'S HOW I'VE ALWAYS LIVED!
AND I'LL NEVER WAVER AGAIN!!

HOUR OF THE ZOMBIE

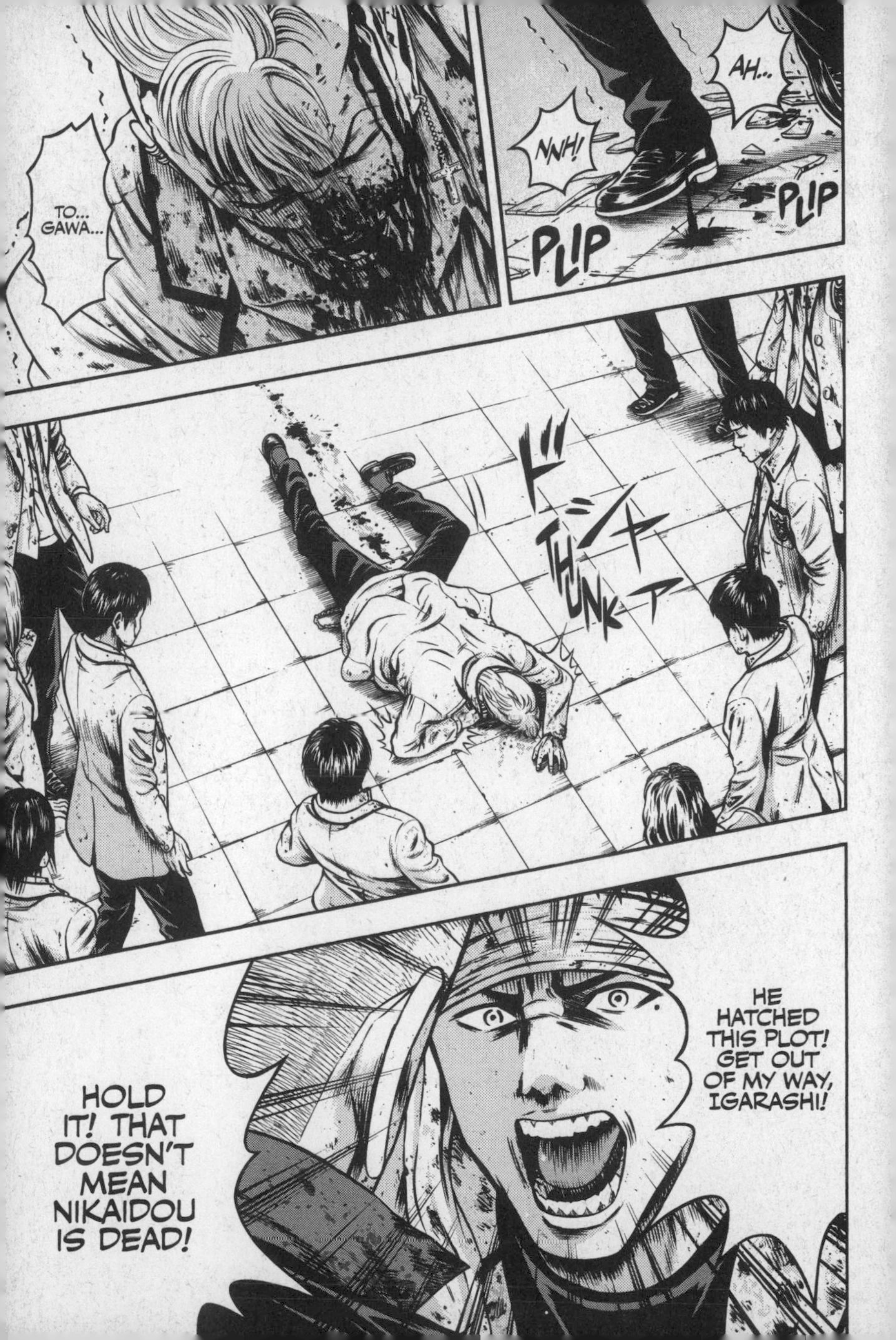
AH...
NNH!
PLIP
PLIP
TO... GAWA...
ドシャ
THUNK
HE HATCHED THIS PLOT! GET OUT OF MY WAY, IGARASHI!
HOLD IT! THAT DOESN'T MEAN NIKAIDOU IS DEAD!

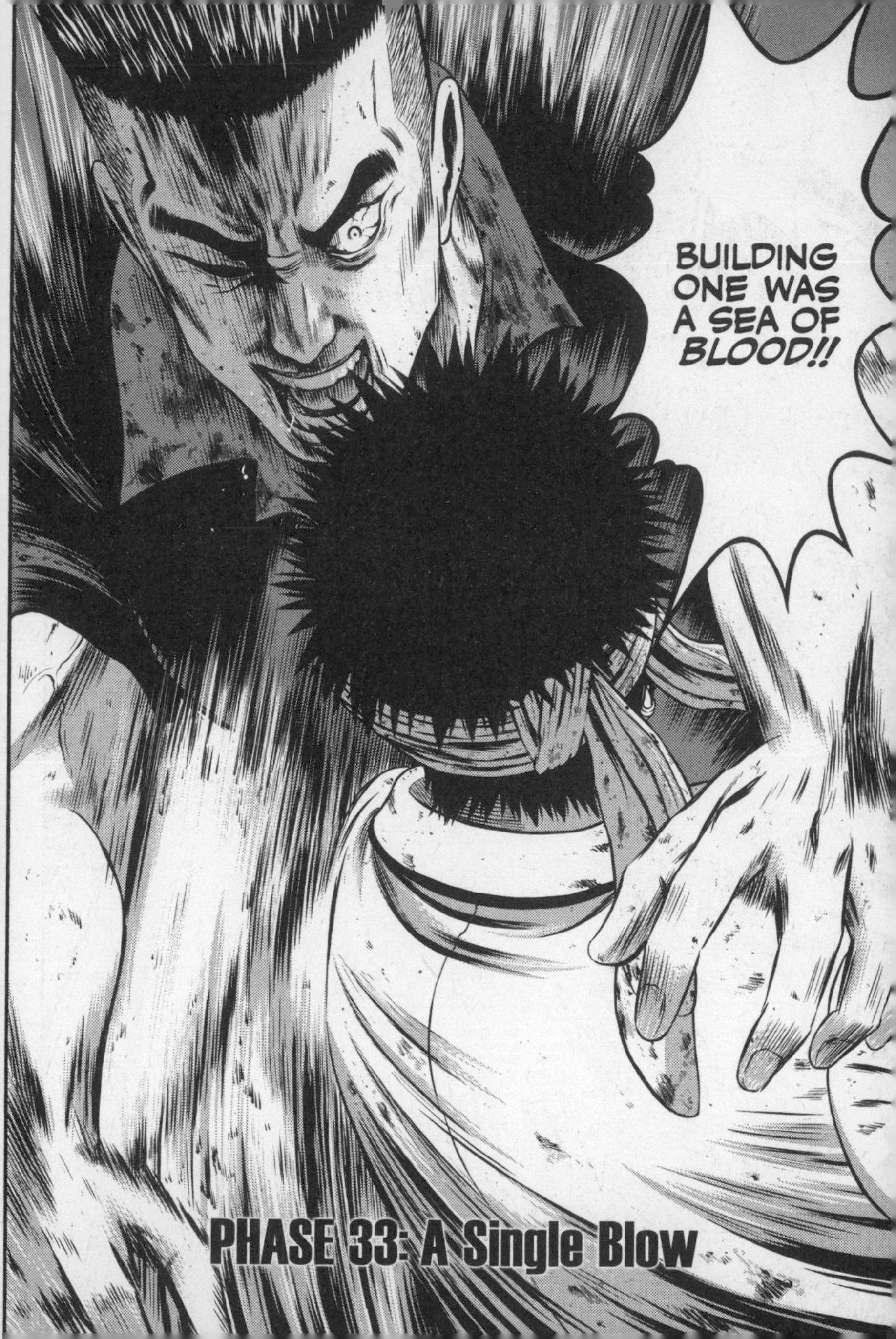
BUILDING ONE WAS A SEA OF BLOOD!!
PHASE 33: A Single Blow

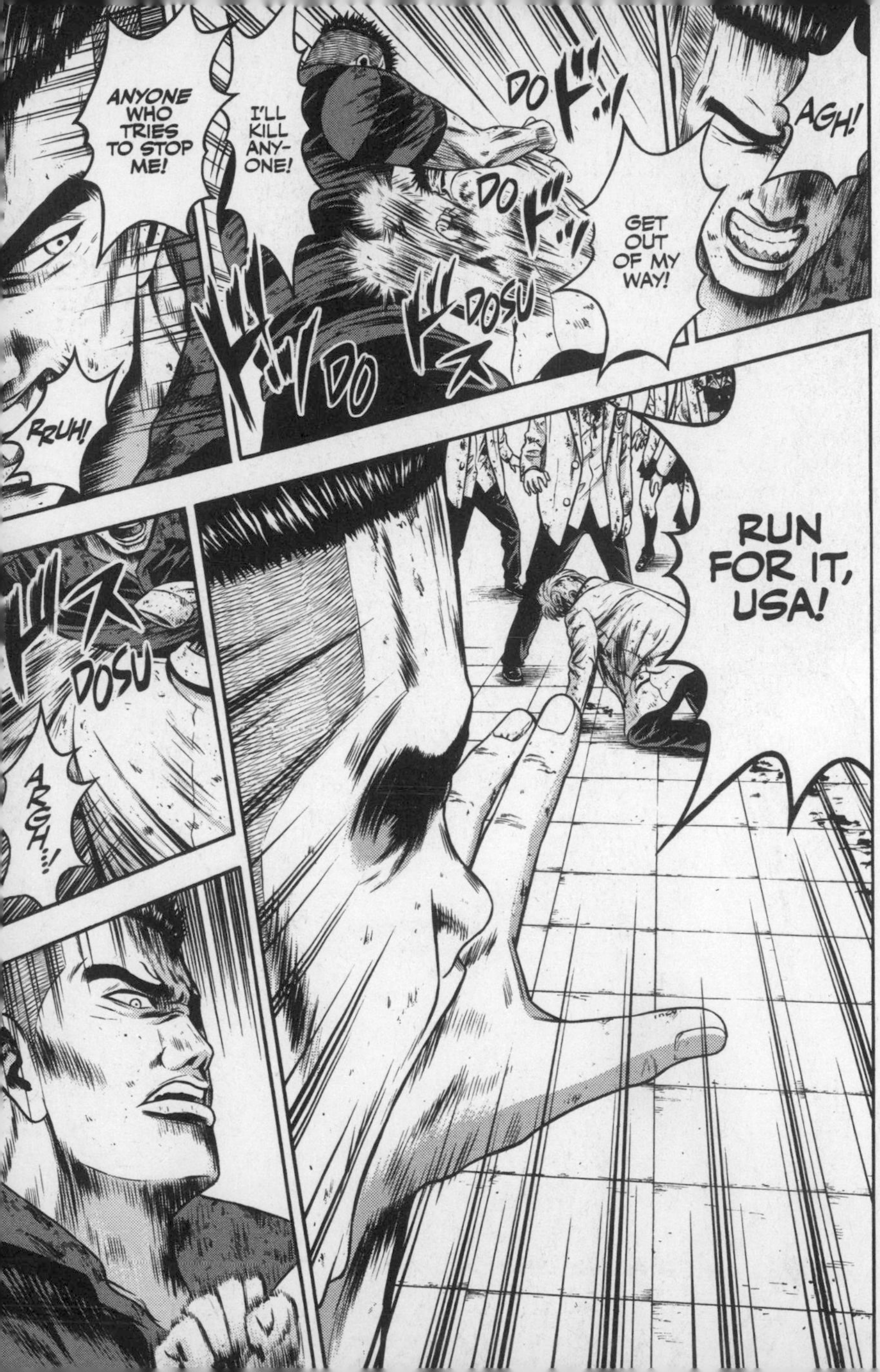
AGH!
GET OUT OF MY WAY!
DO ド
DO ド
I'LL KILL ANY-ONE!
ANYONE WHO TRIES TO STOP ME!
DOSU ドス
DO ド
RRUH!
RUN FOR IT, USA!
DOSU ドス
ARGH..!

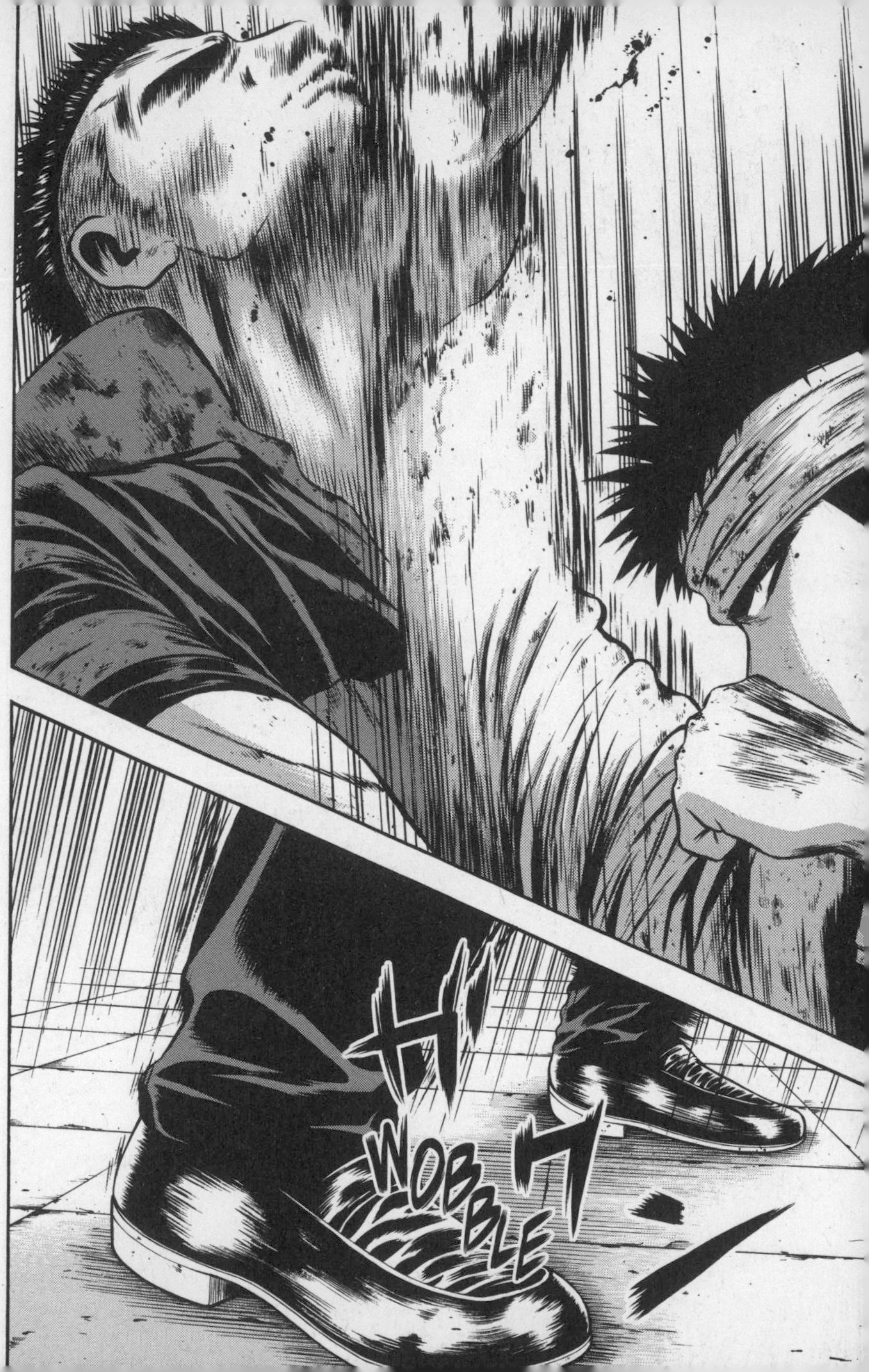
WOBBLE

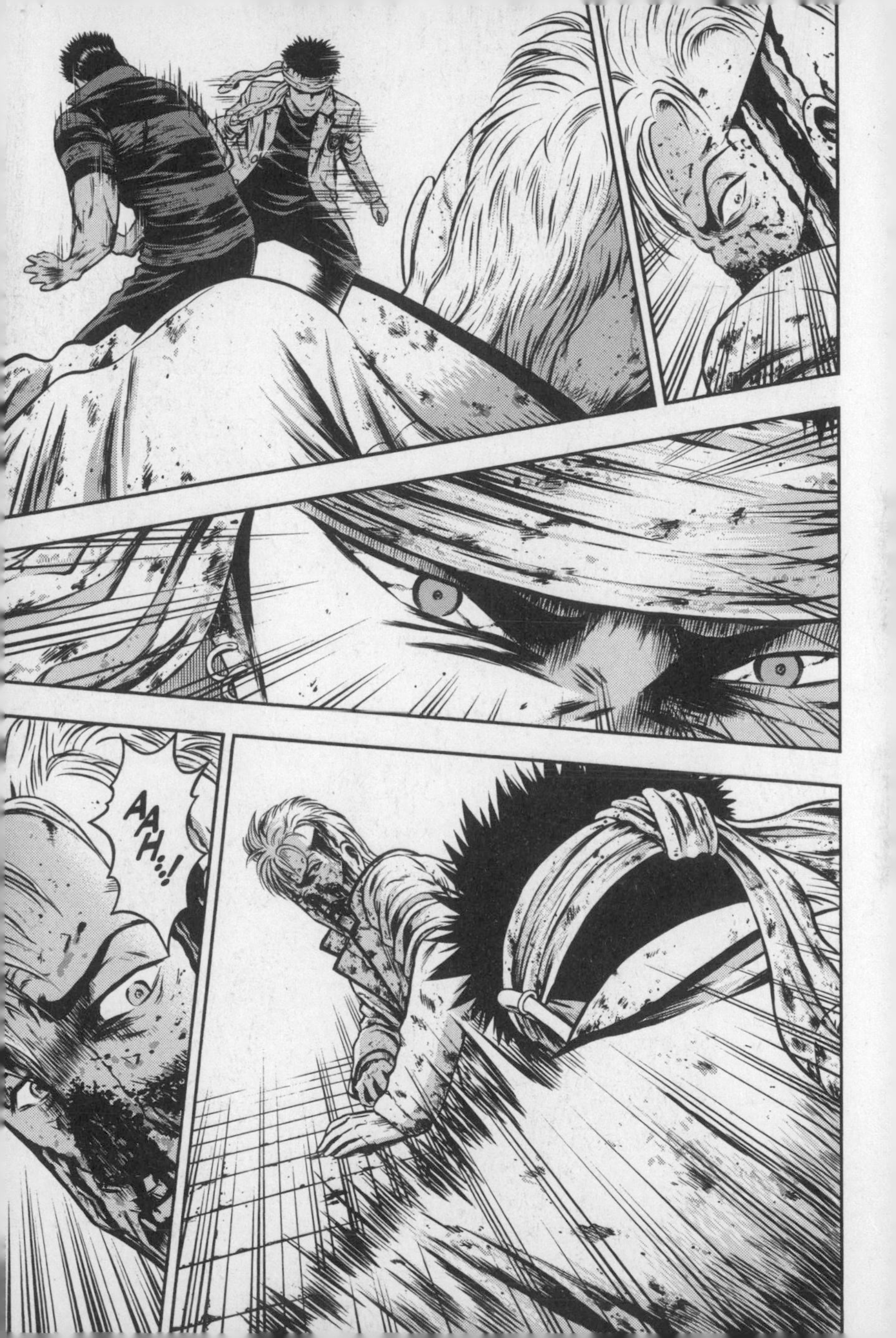
AAH...!

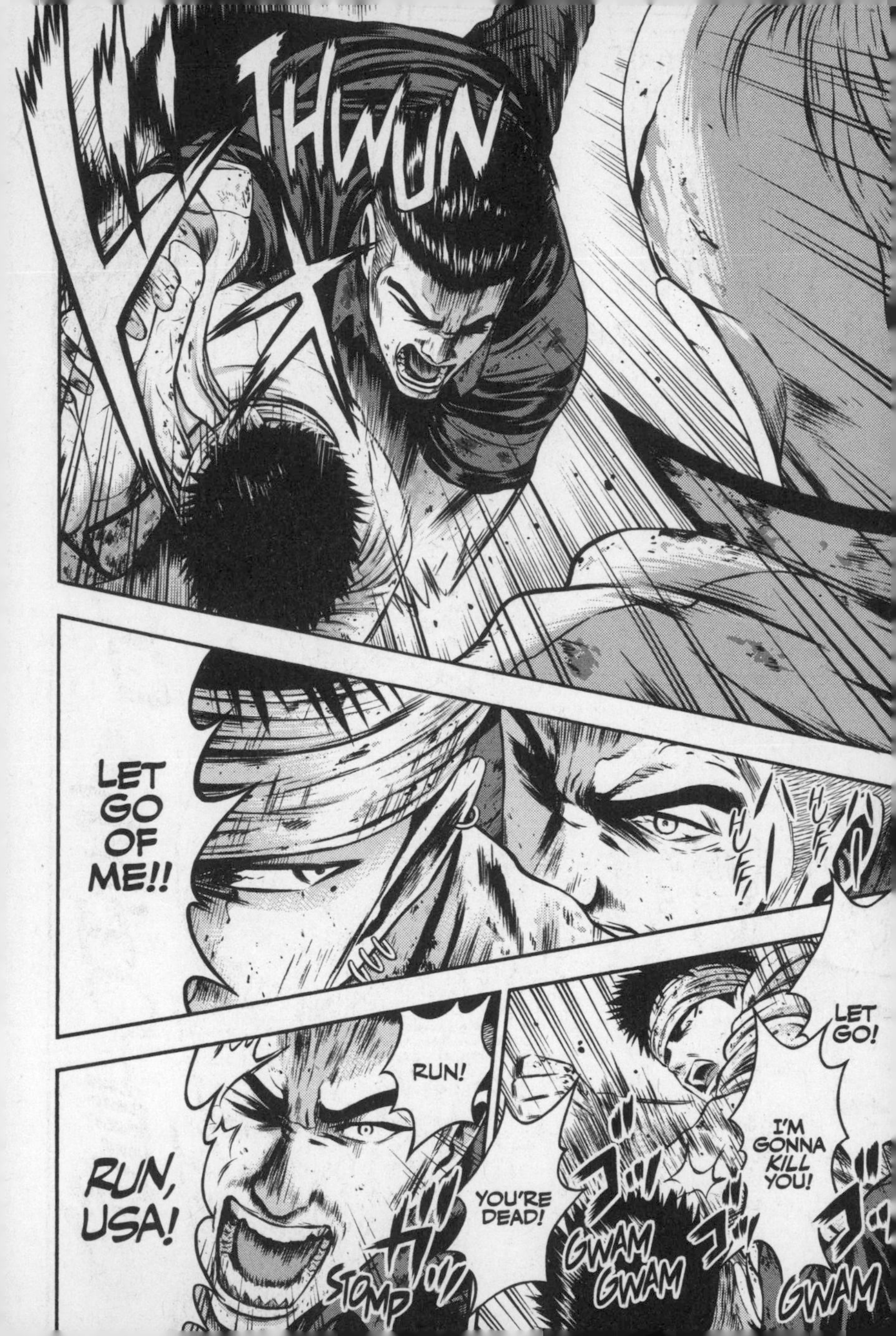
THWUN
HUFF HUFF
LET GO OF ME!!
LET GO!
I'M GONNA KILL YOU!
GWAM
GWAM GWAM
YOU'RE DEAD!
STOMP
RUN!
RUN, USA!

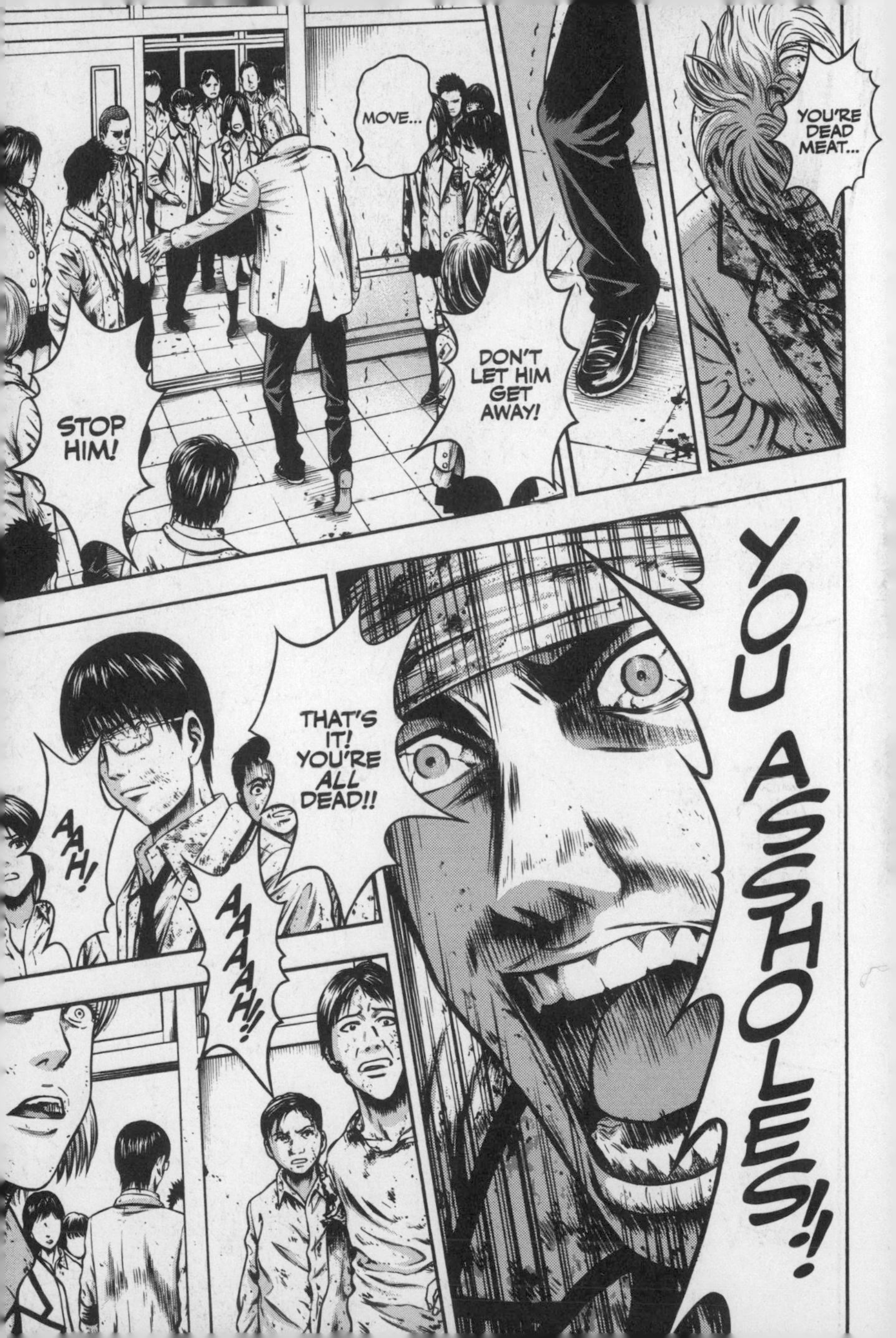
YOU'RE DEAD MEAT...
DON'T LET HIM GET AWAY!
MOVE...
STOP HIM!
YOU ASSHOLES!!
THAT'S IT! YOU'RE *ALL* DEAD!!
AAAAH!!
AAH!

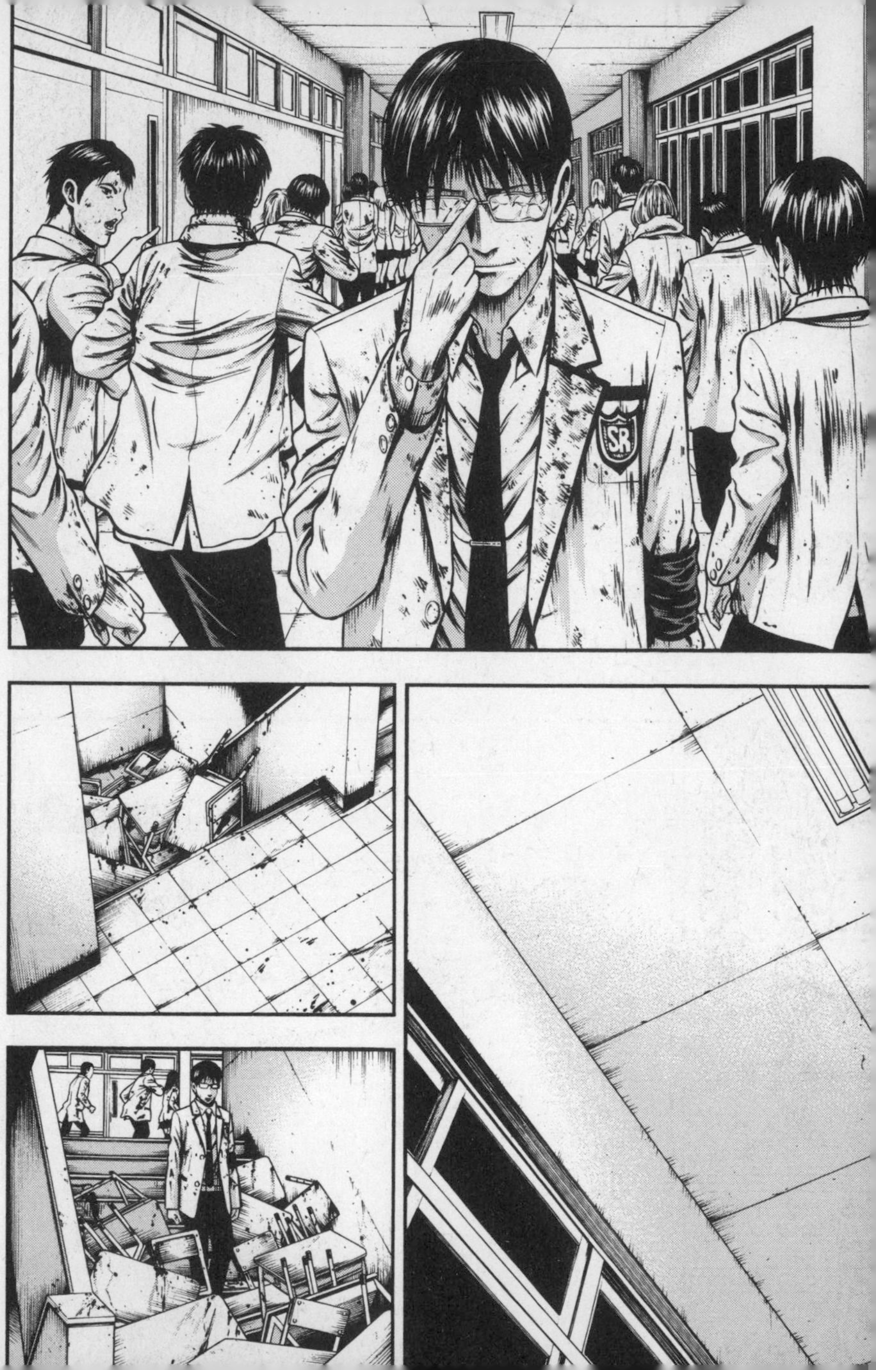
SR

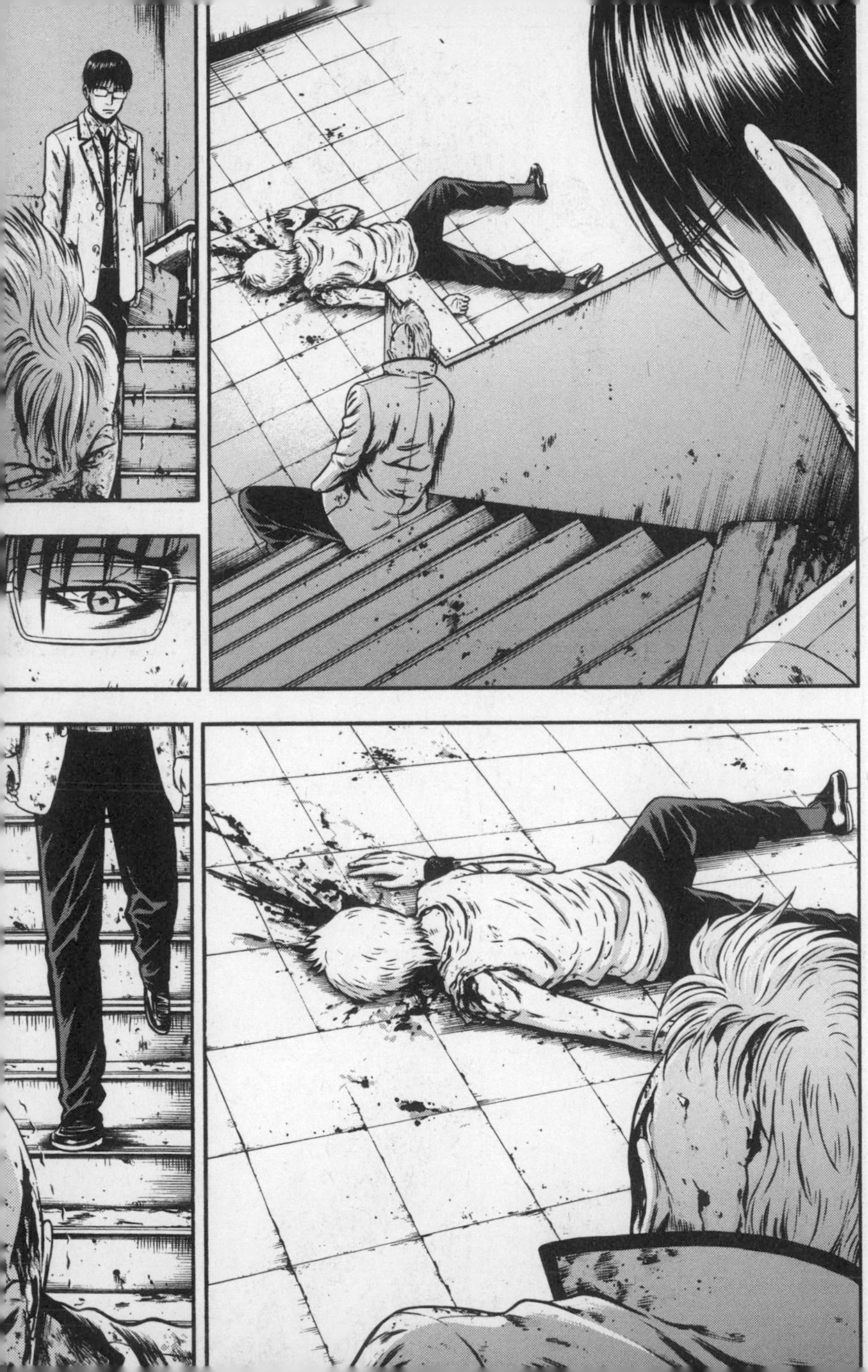

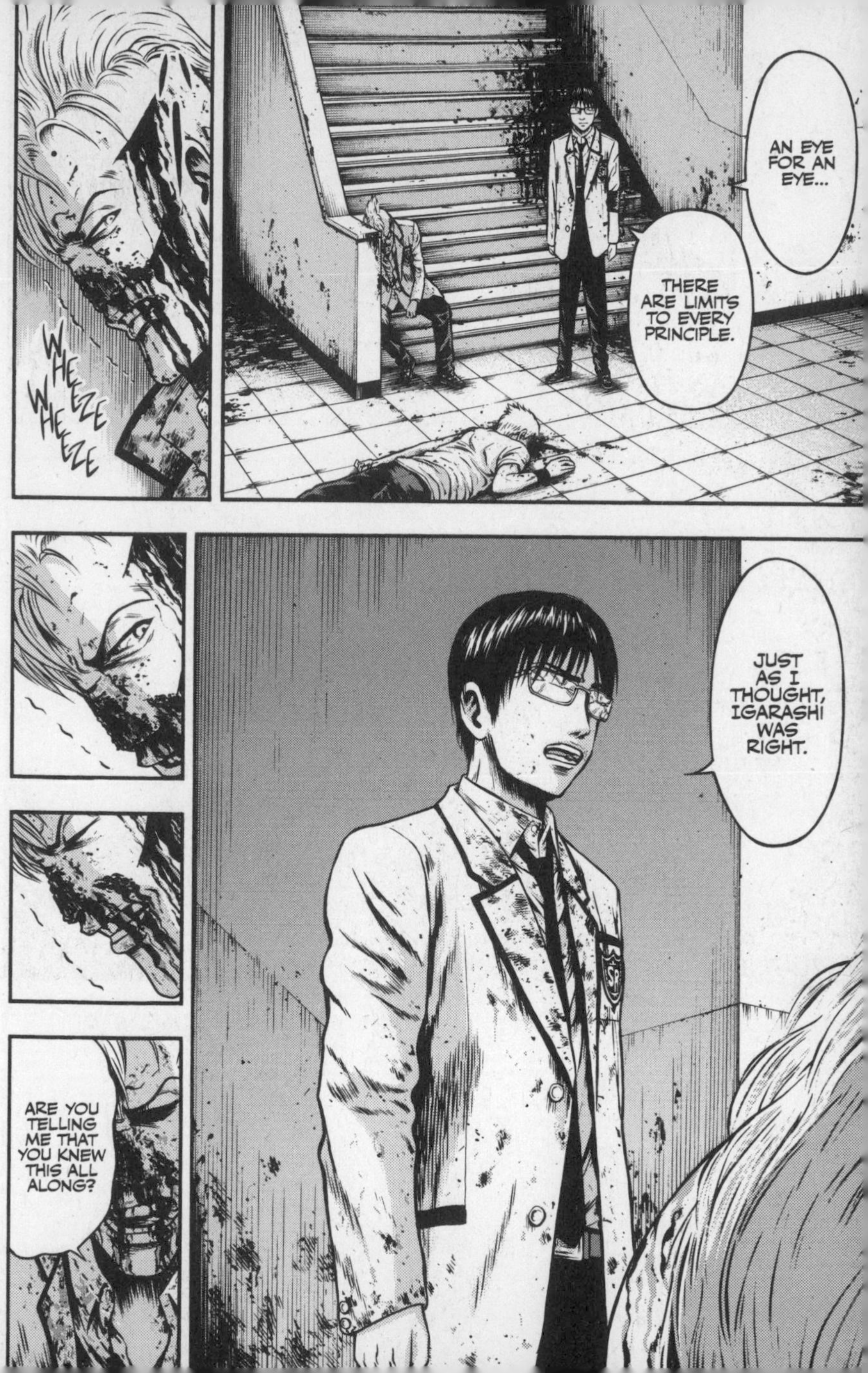
AN EYE FOR AN EYE...
THERE ARE LIMITS TO EVERY PRINCIPLE.
WHEEZE WHEEZE
JUST AS I THOUGHT, IGARASHI WAS RIGHT.
ARE YOU TELLING ME THAT YOU KNEW THIS ALL ALONG?

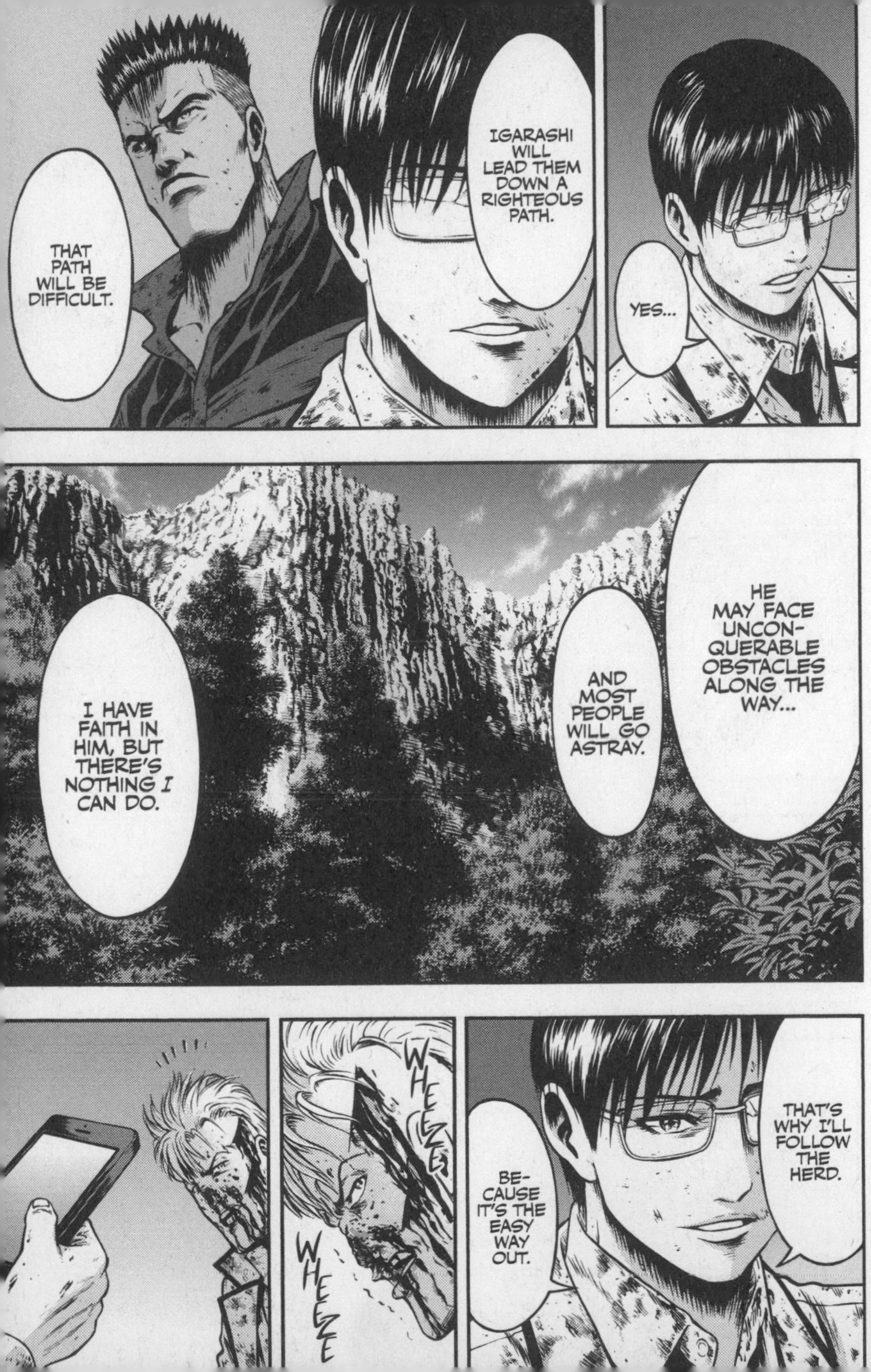
YES...
IGARASHI WILL LEAD THEM DOWN A RIGHTEOUS PATH.
THAT PATH WILL BE DIFFICULT.
HE MAY FACE UNCON-QUERABLE OBSTACLES ALONG THE WAY...
AND MOST PEOPLE WILL GO ASTRAY.
I HAVE FAITH IN HIM, BUT THERE'S NOTHING *I* CAN DO.
THAT'S WHY I'LL FOLLOW THE HERD.
BE-CAUSE IT'S THE EASY WAY OUT.
WHEEZE
WHEEZE

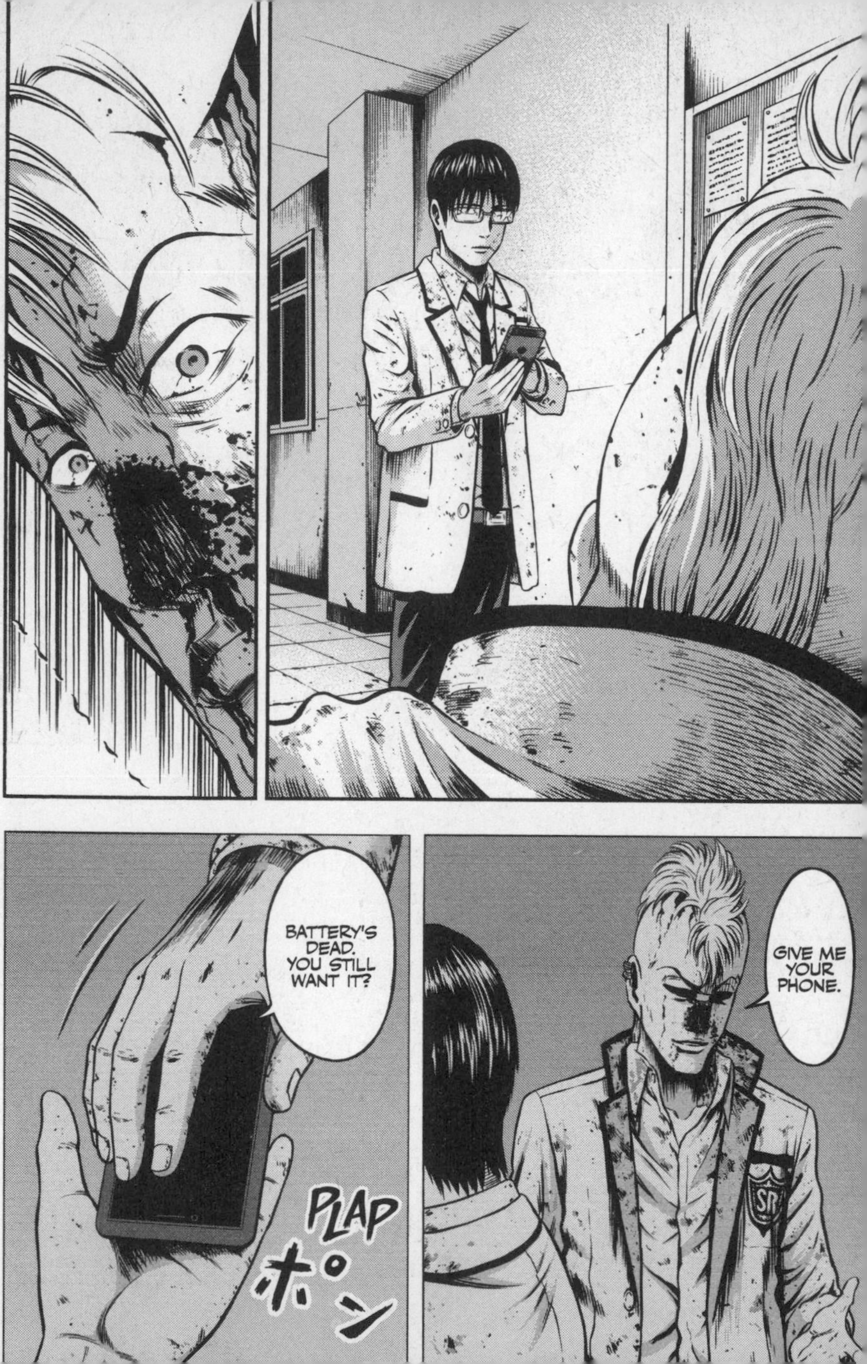
GIVE ME YOUR PHONE.
BATTERY'S DEAD. YOU STILL WANT IT?
PLAP
ポン

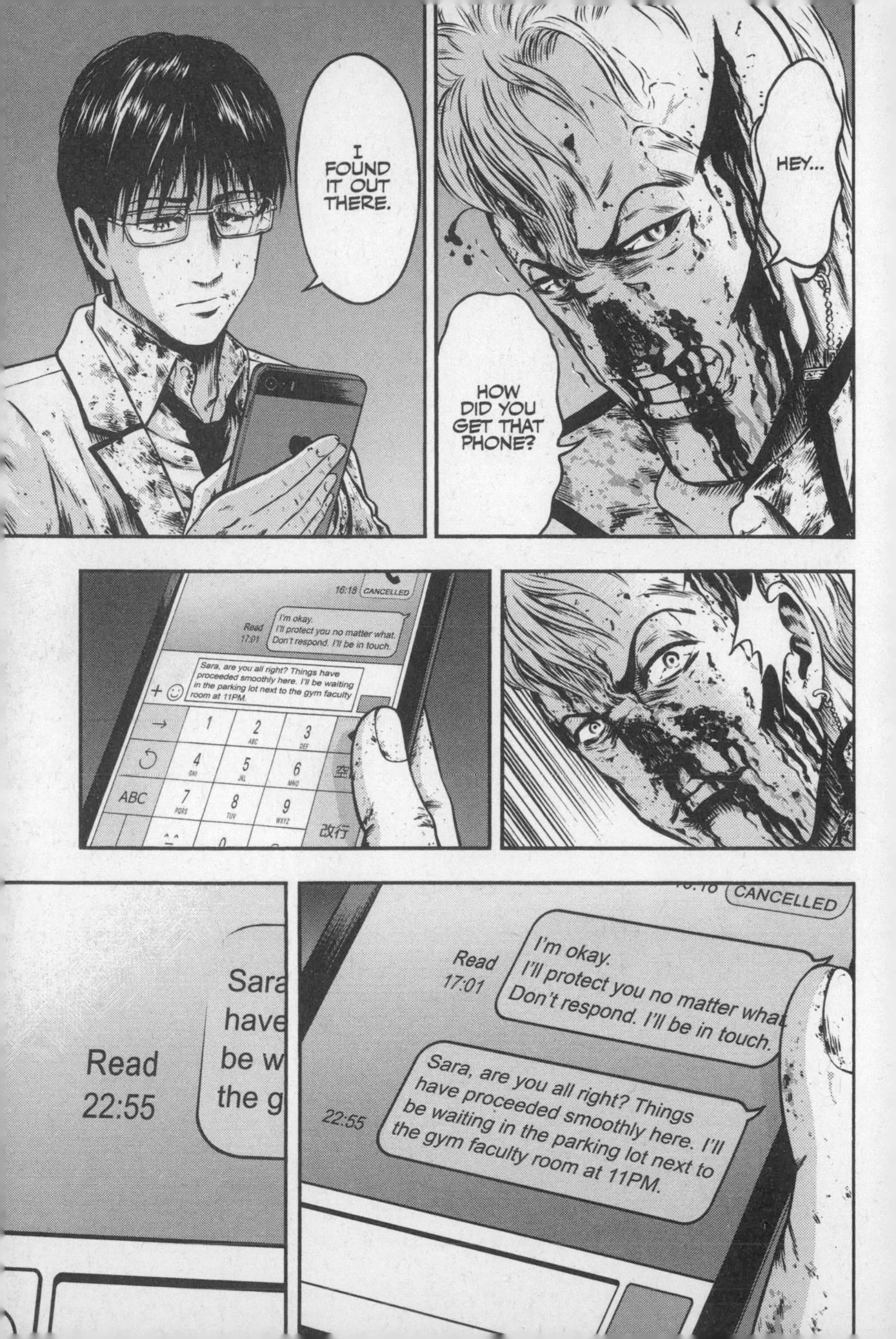
HEY...
HOW DID YOU GET THAT PHONE?
I FOUND IT OUT THERE.
16:18 CANCELLED
Read 17:01
I'm okay. I'll protect you no matter what. Don't respond. I'll be in touch.
Sara, are you all right? Things have proceeded smoothly here. I'll be waiting in the parking lot next to the gym faculty room at 11PM.
CANCELLED
Read 17:01
I'm okay. I'll protect you no matter what. Don't respond. I'll be in touch.
22:55
Sara, are you all right? Things have proceeded smoothly here. I'll be waiting in the parking lot next to the gym faculty room at 11PM.
Read 22:55

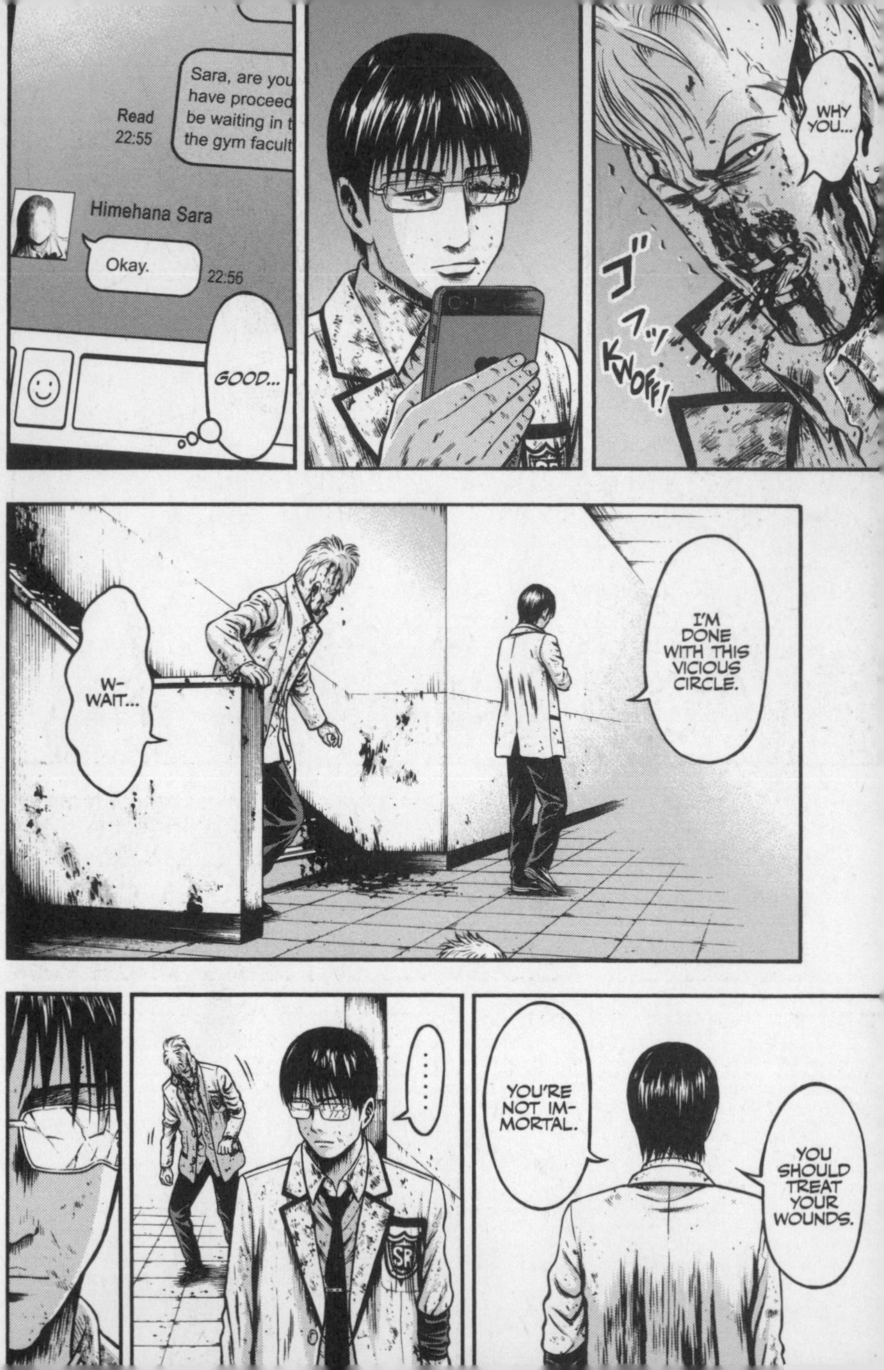

WHY YOU...
ゴフッ
KWOFF!
Sara, are you
have proceed
be waiting in t
the gym facult
Read
22:55
Himehana Sara
Okay.
22:56
GOOD...
I'M DONE WITH THIS VICIOUS CIRCLE.
W- WAIT...
YOU SHOULD TREAT YOUR WOUNDS.
YOU'RE NOT IM- MORTAL.
......

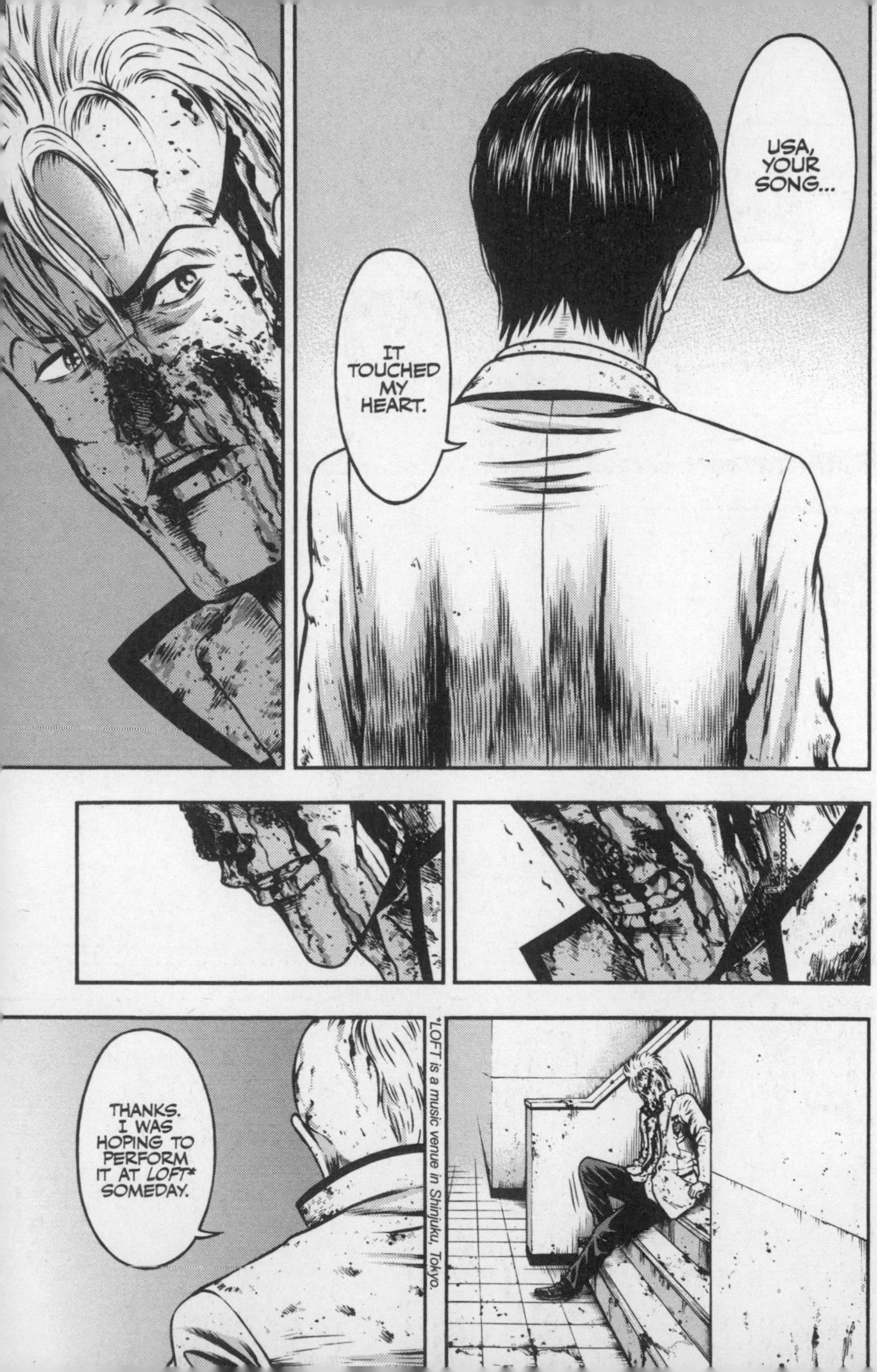
USA, YOUR SONG...
IT TOUCHED MY HEART.
THANKS. I WAS HOPING TO PERFORM IT AT LOFT* SOMEDAY.
*LOFT is a music venue in Shinjuku, Tokyo.

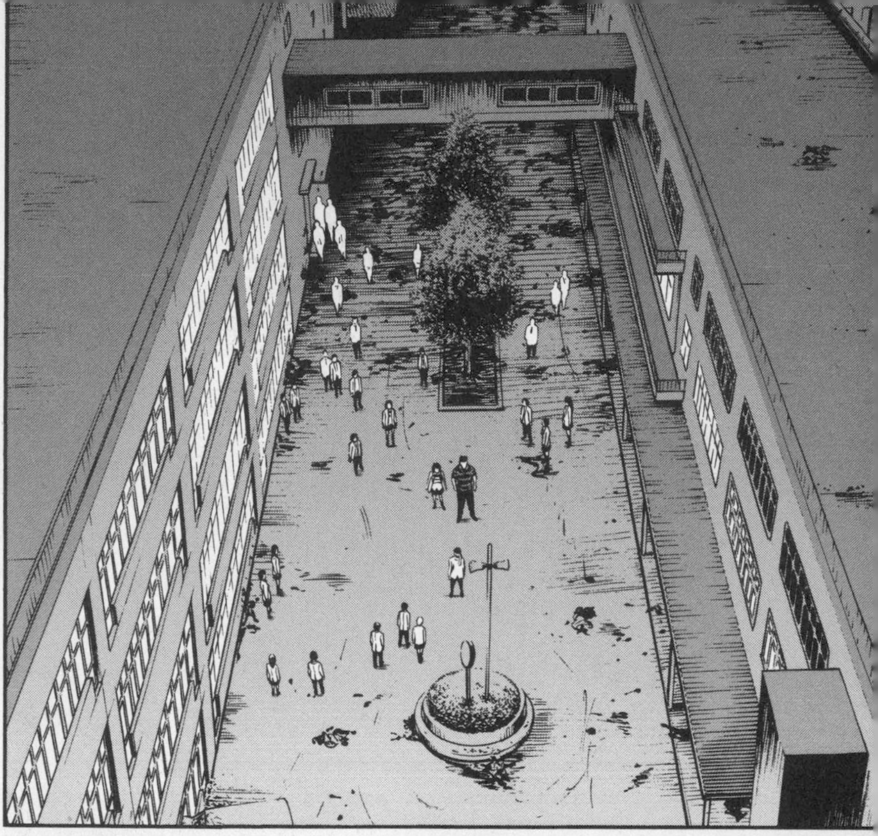
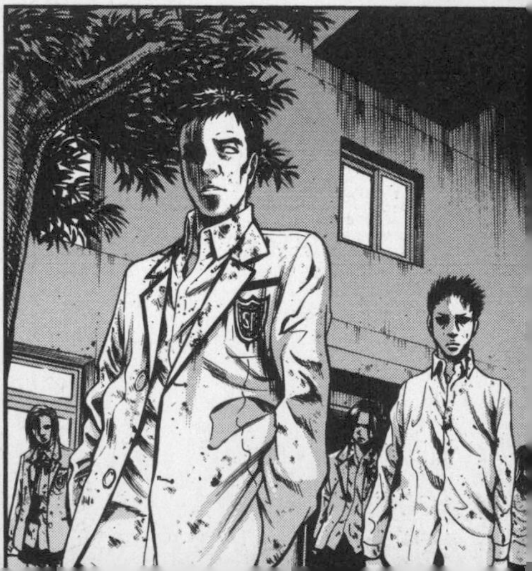
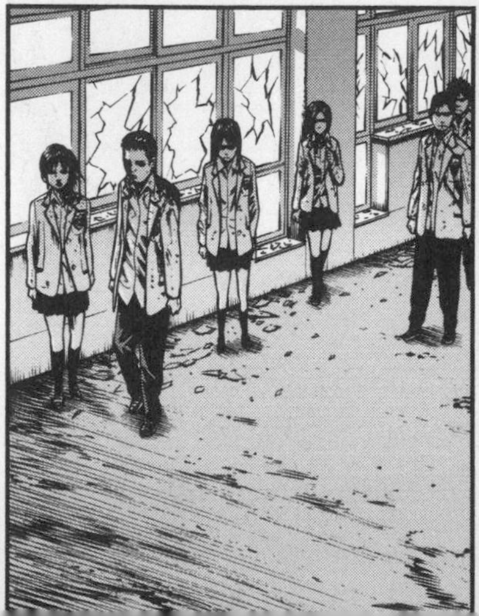

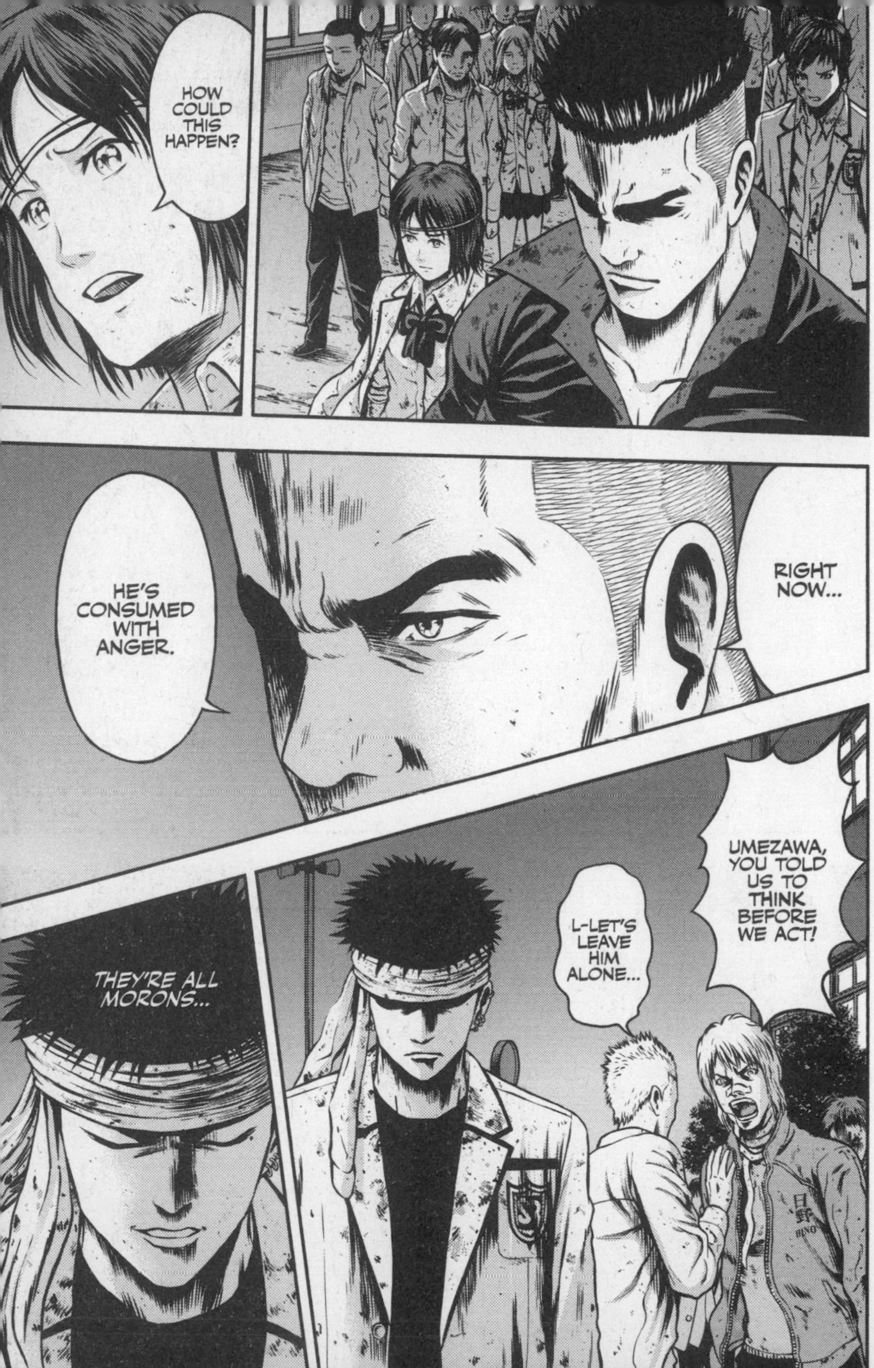
HOW COULD THIS HAPPEN?
RIGHT NOW...
HE'S CONSUMED WITH ANGER.
UMEZAWA, YOU TOLD US TO THINK BEFORE WE ACT!
L-LET'S LEAVE HIM ALONE...
THEY'RE ALL MORONS...

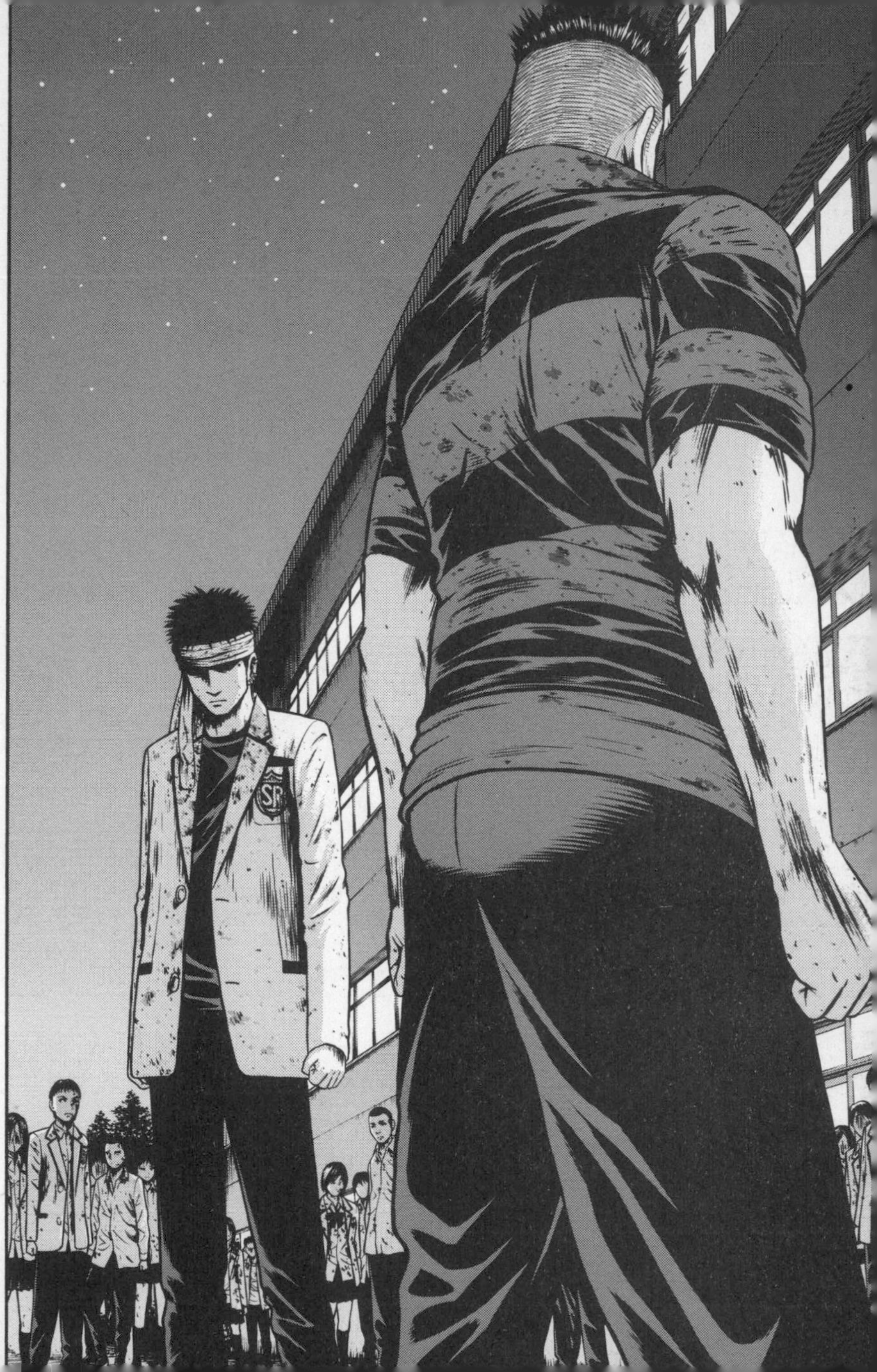

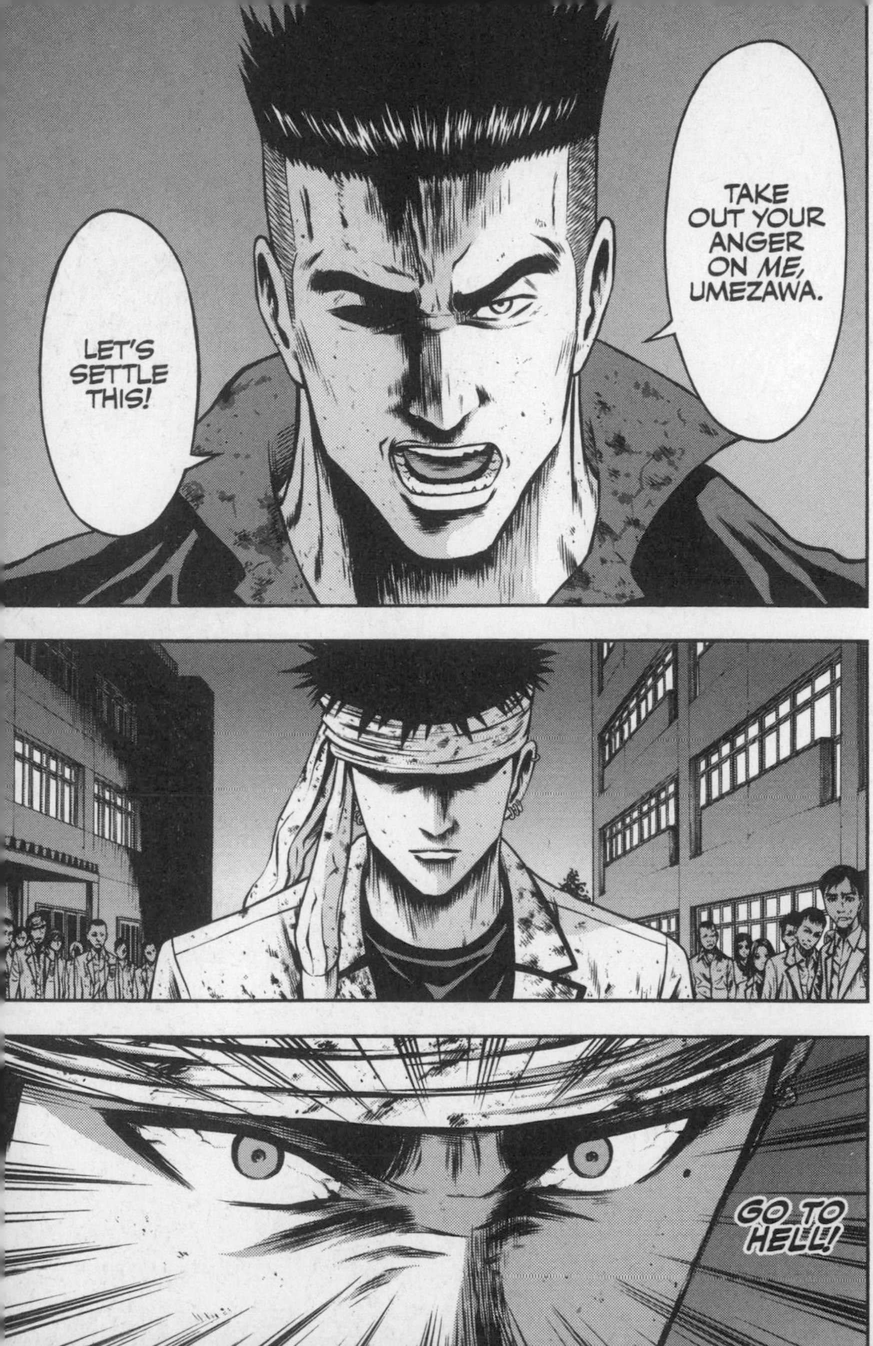
TAKE OUT YOUR ANGER ON *ME*, UMEZAWA.
LET'S SETTLE THIS!
GO TO HELL!

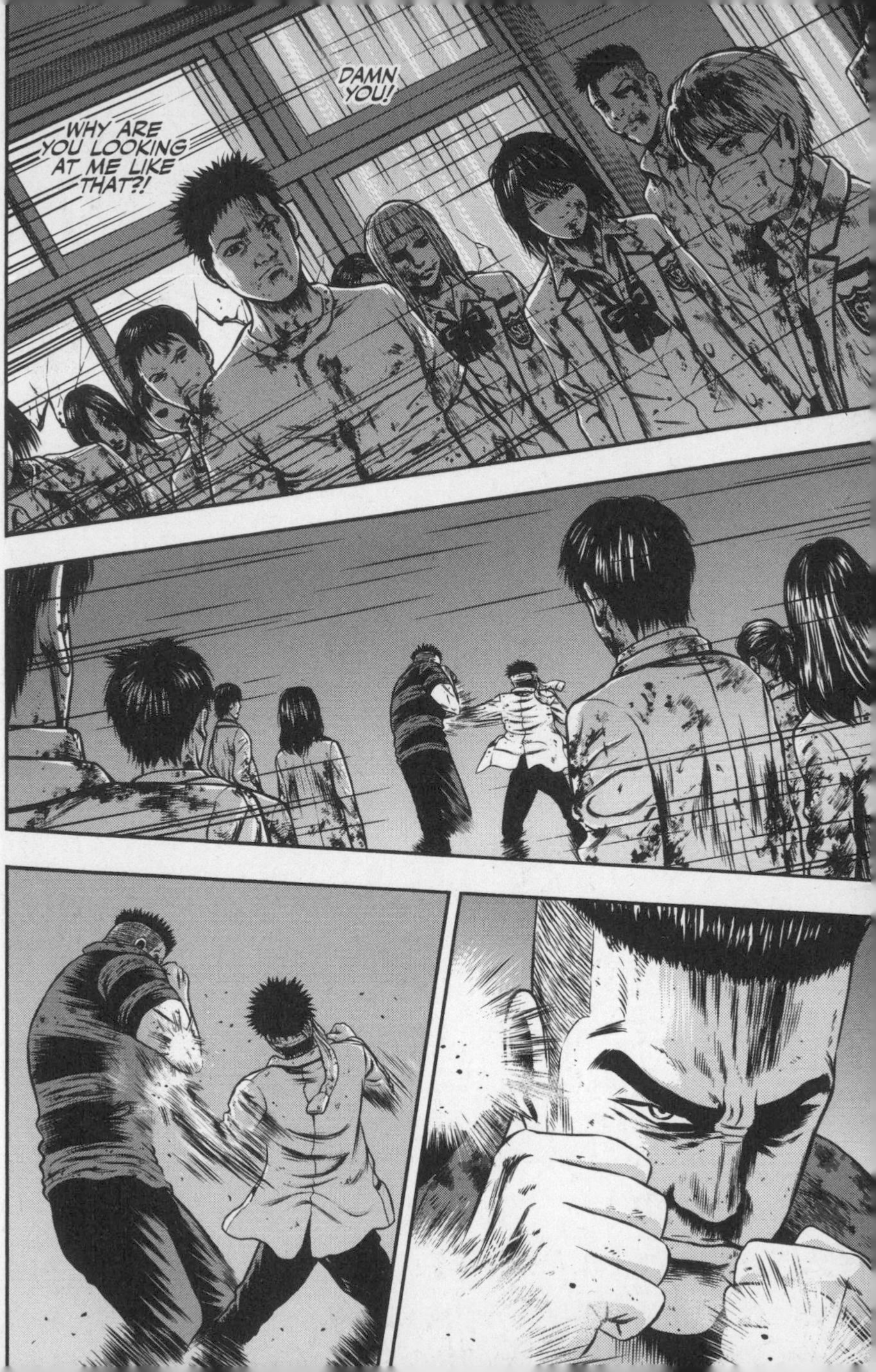
DAMN YOU!
WHY ARE YOU LOOKING AT ME LIKE THAT?!

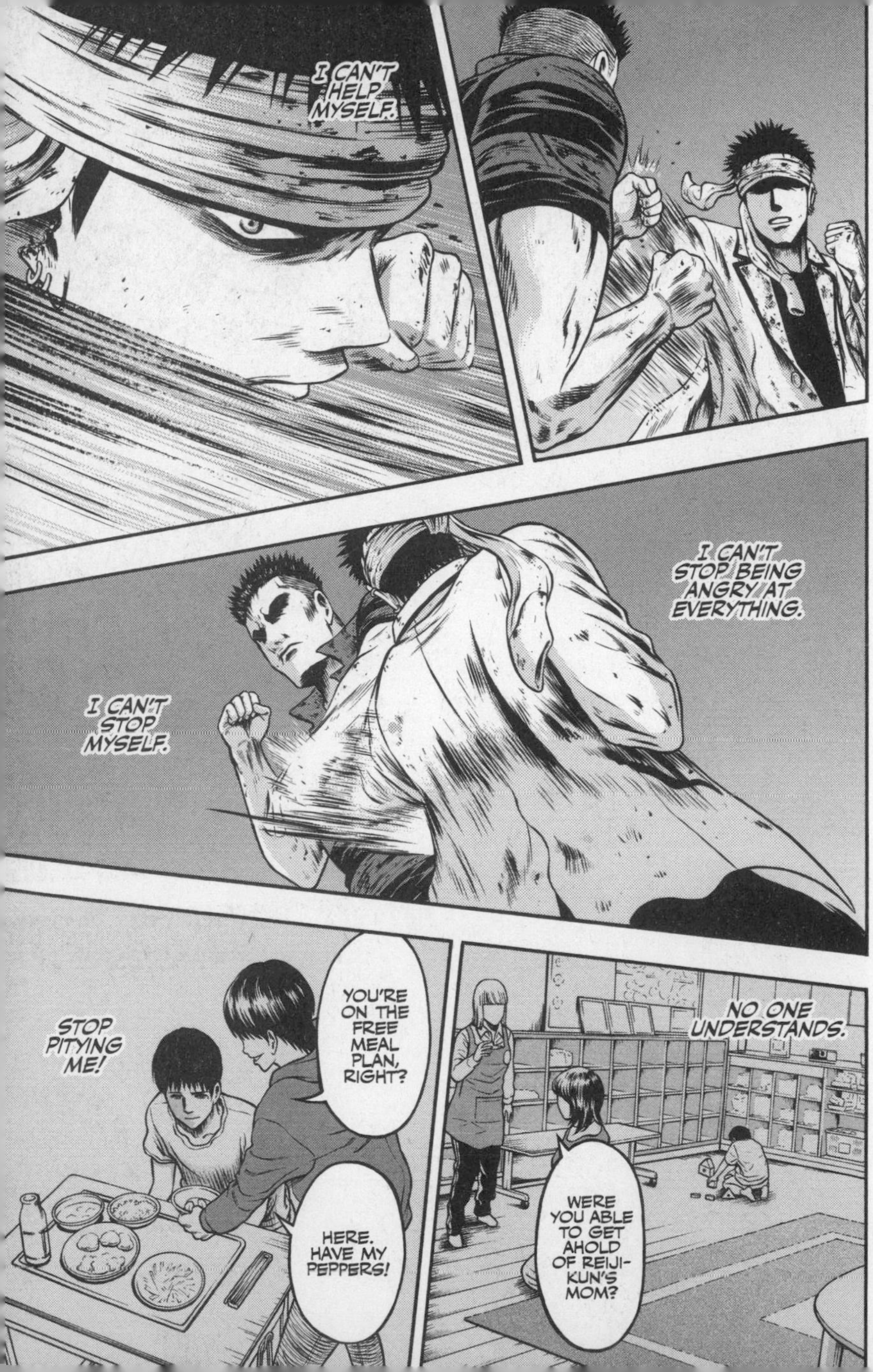
I CAN'T HELP MYSELF.
I CAN'T STOP BEING ANGRY AT EVERYTHING.
I CAN'T STOP MYSELF.
NO ONE UNDERSTANDS.
WERE YOU ABLE TO GET AHOLD OF REIJI-KUN'S MOM?
YOU'RE ON THE FREE MEAL PLAN, RIGHT?
STOP PITYING ME!
HERE. HAVE MY PEPPERS!

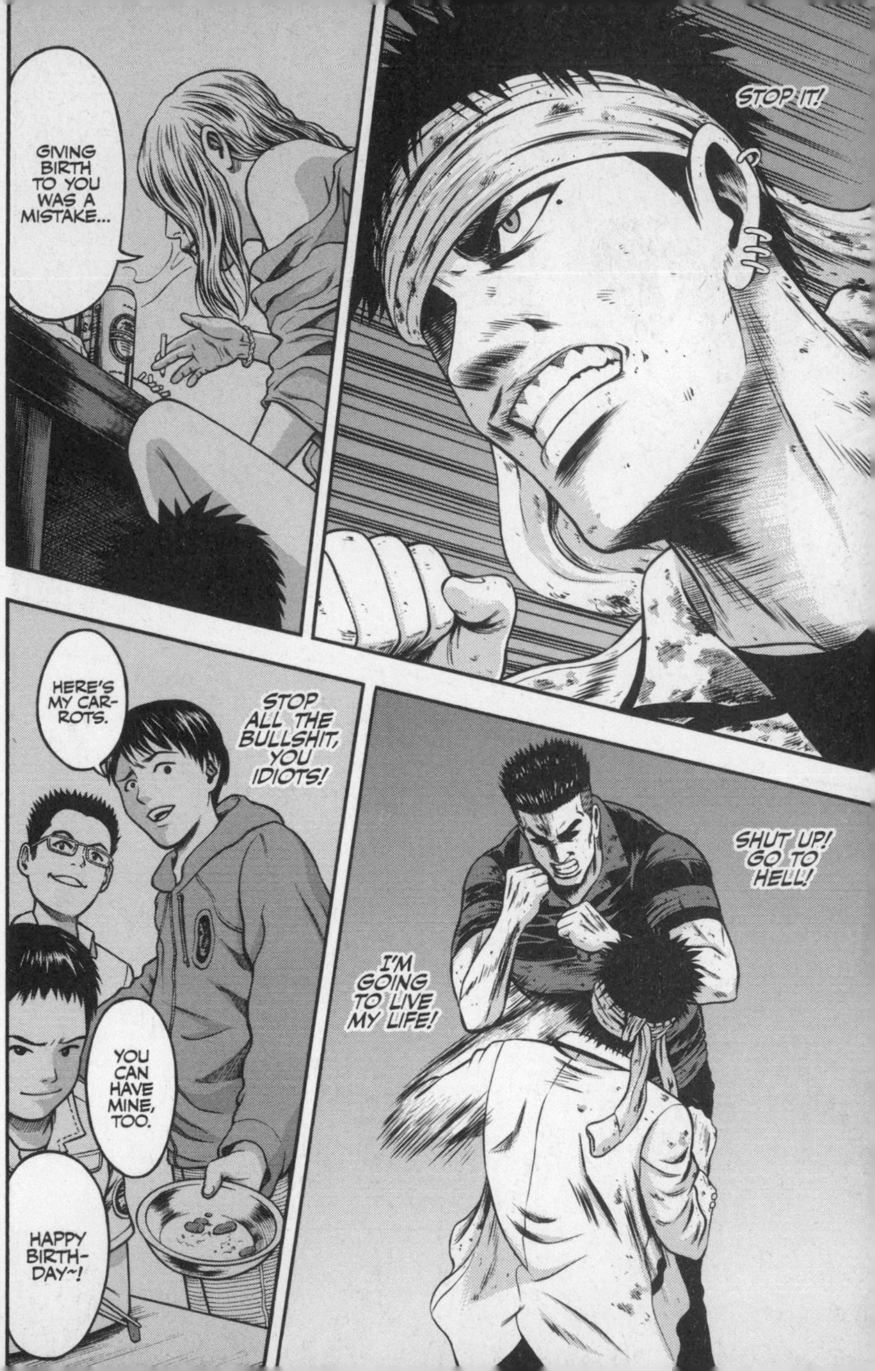
STOP IT!
GIVING BIRTH TO YOU WAS A MISTAKE...
SHUT UP! GO TO HELL!
I'M GOING TO LIVE MY LIFE!
STOP ALL THE BULLSHIT, YOU IDIOTS!
HERE'S MY CAR-ROTS.
YOU CAN HAVE MINE, TOO.
HAPPY BIRTH-DAY~!

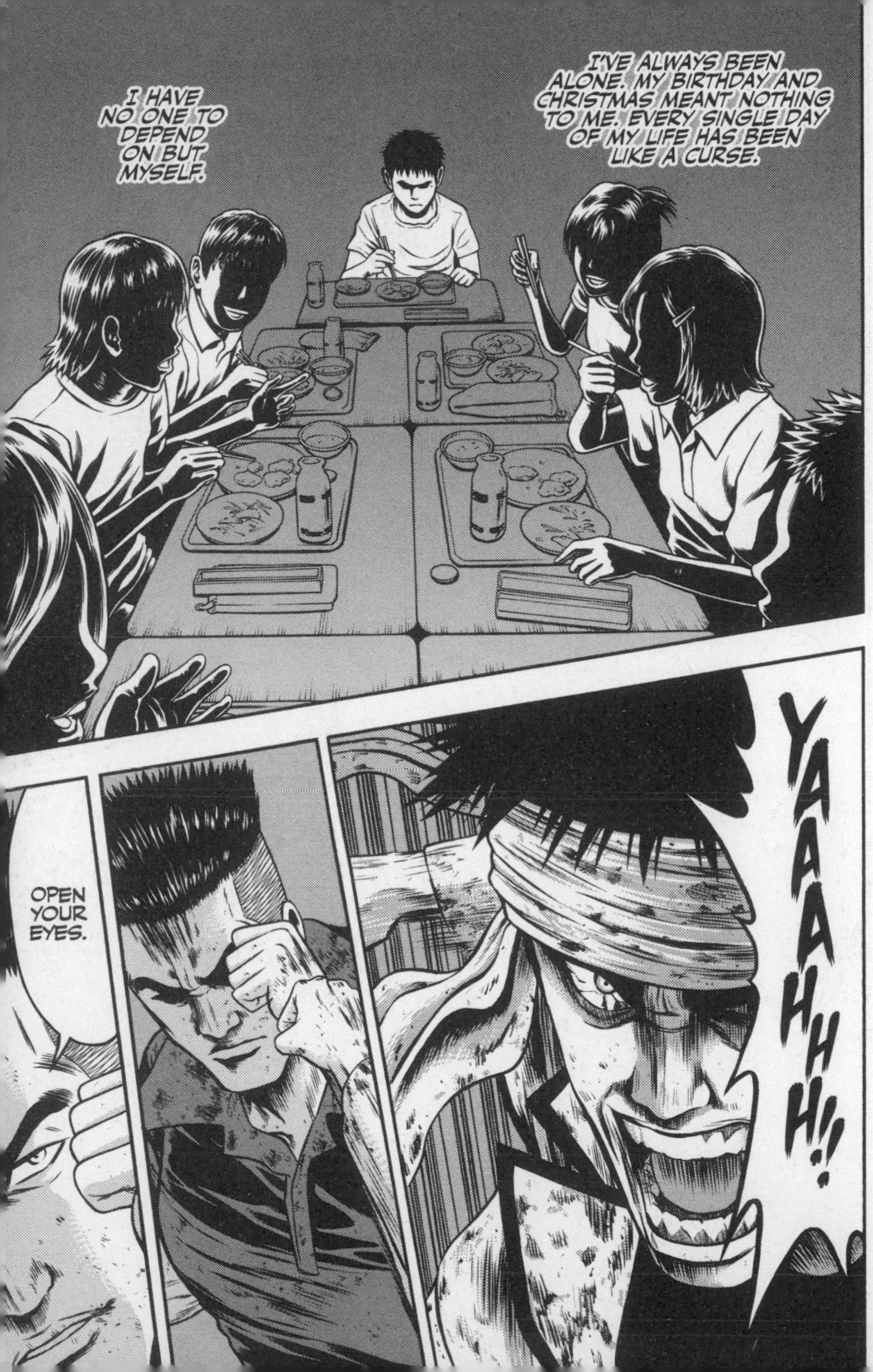
I'VE ALWAYS BEEN ALONE. MY BIRTHDAY AND CHRISTMAS MEANT NOTHING TO ME. EVERY SINGLE DAY OF MY LIFE HAS BEEN LIKE A CURSE.
I HAVE NO ONE TO DEPEND ON BUT MYSELF.
YAAAHHH!!
OPEN YOUR EYES.

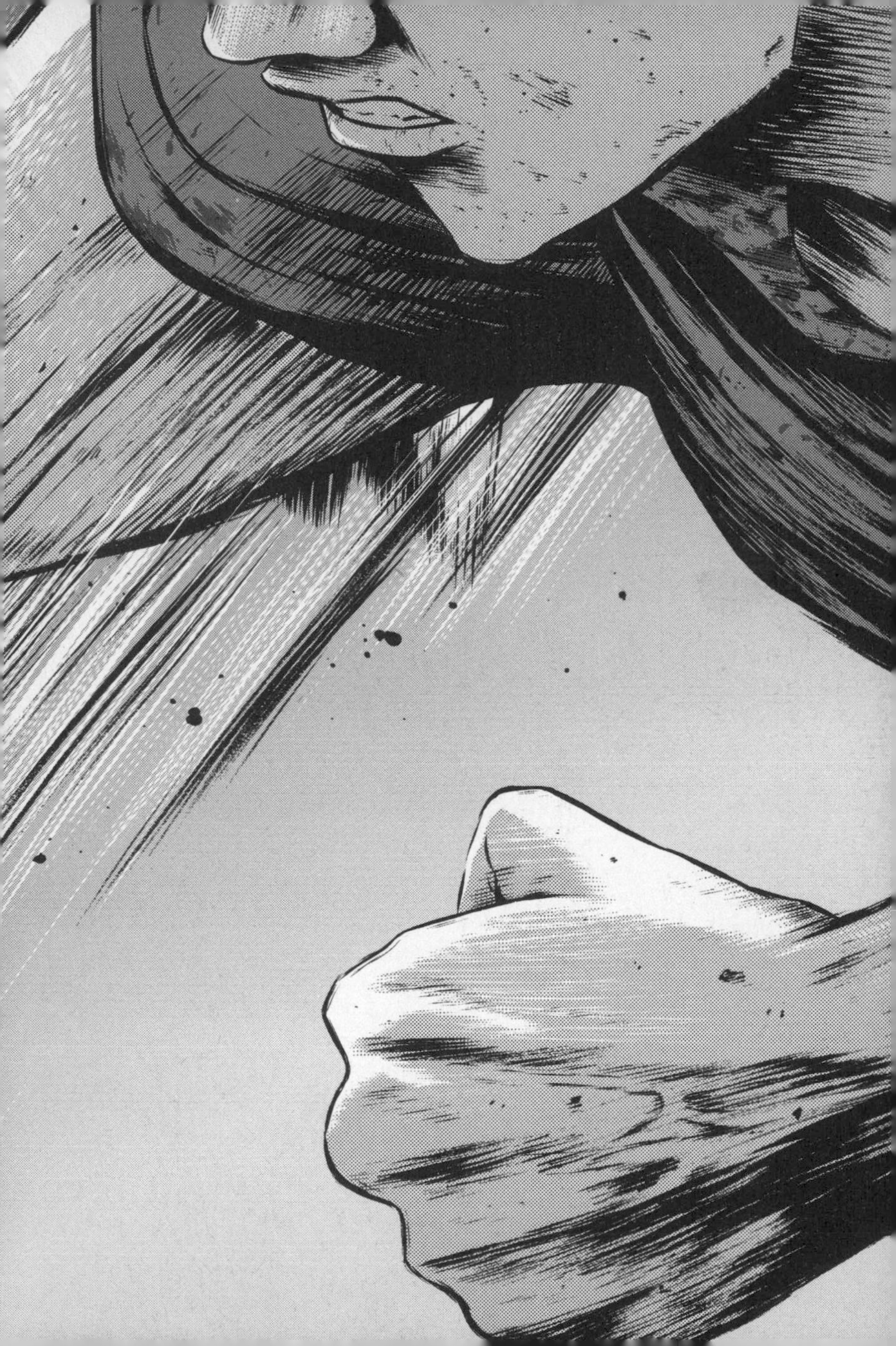

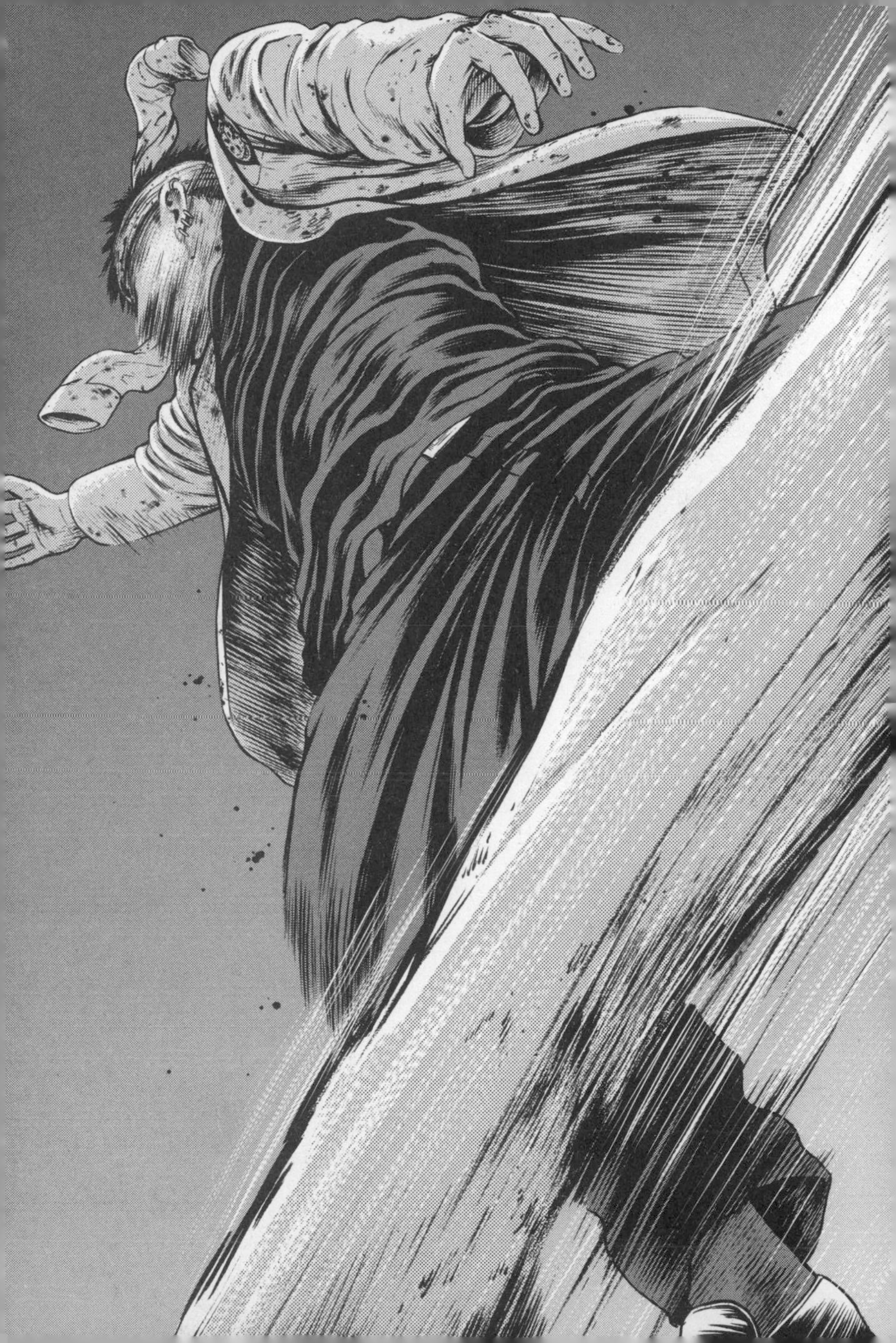

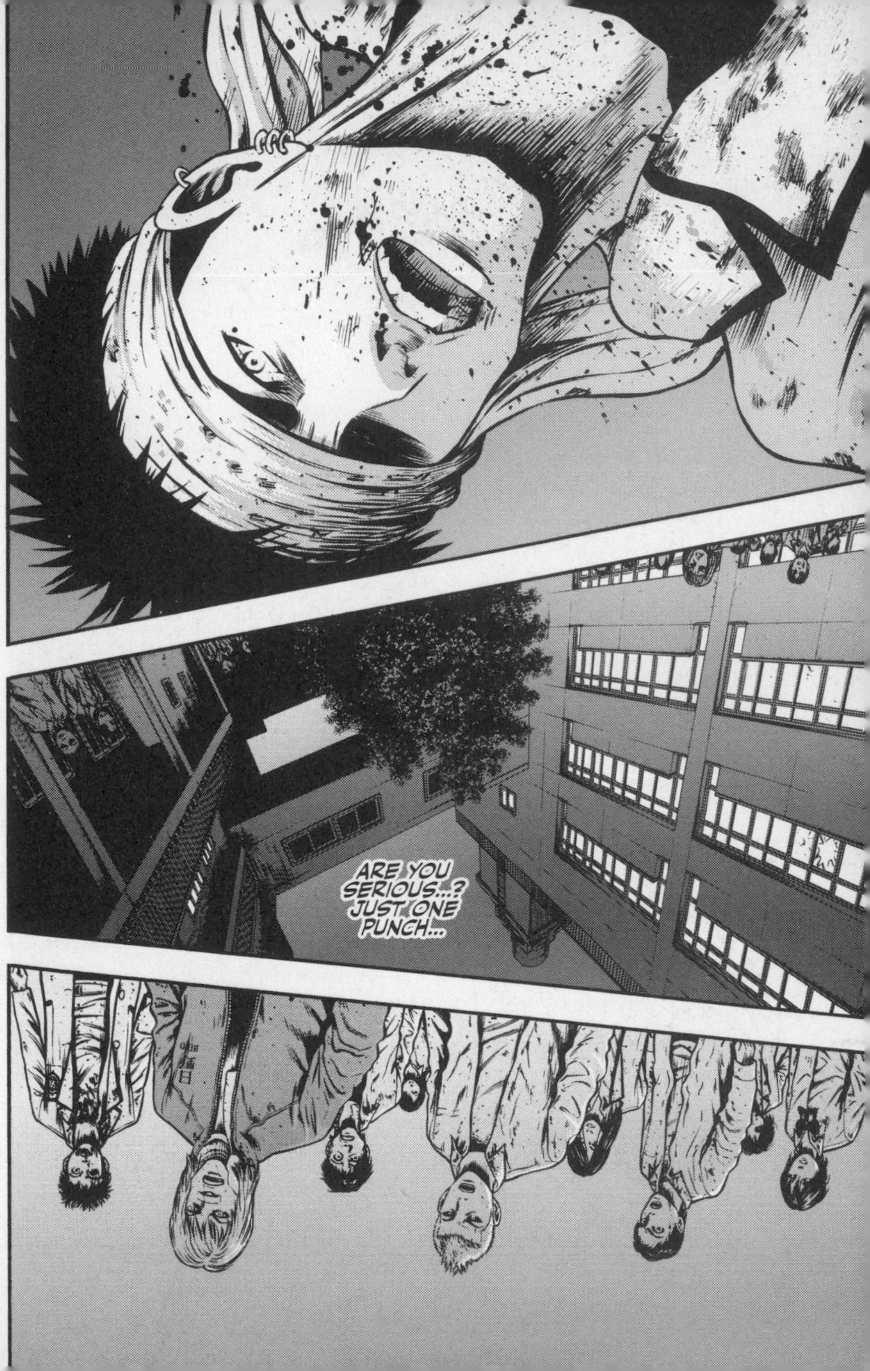
ARE YOU SERIOUS...? JUST ONE PUNCH...

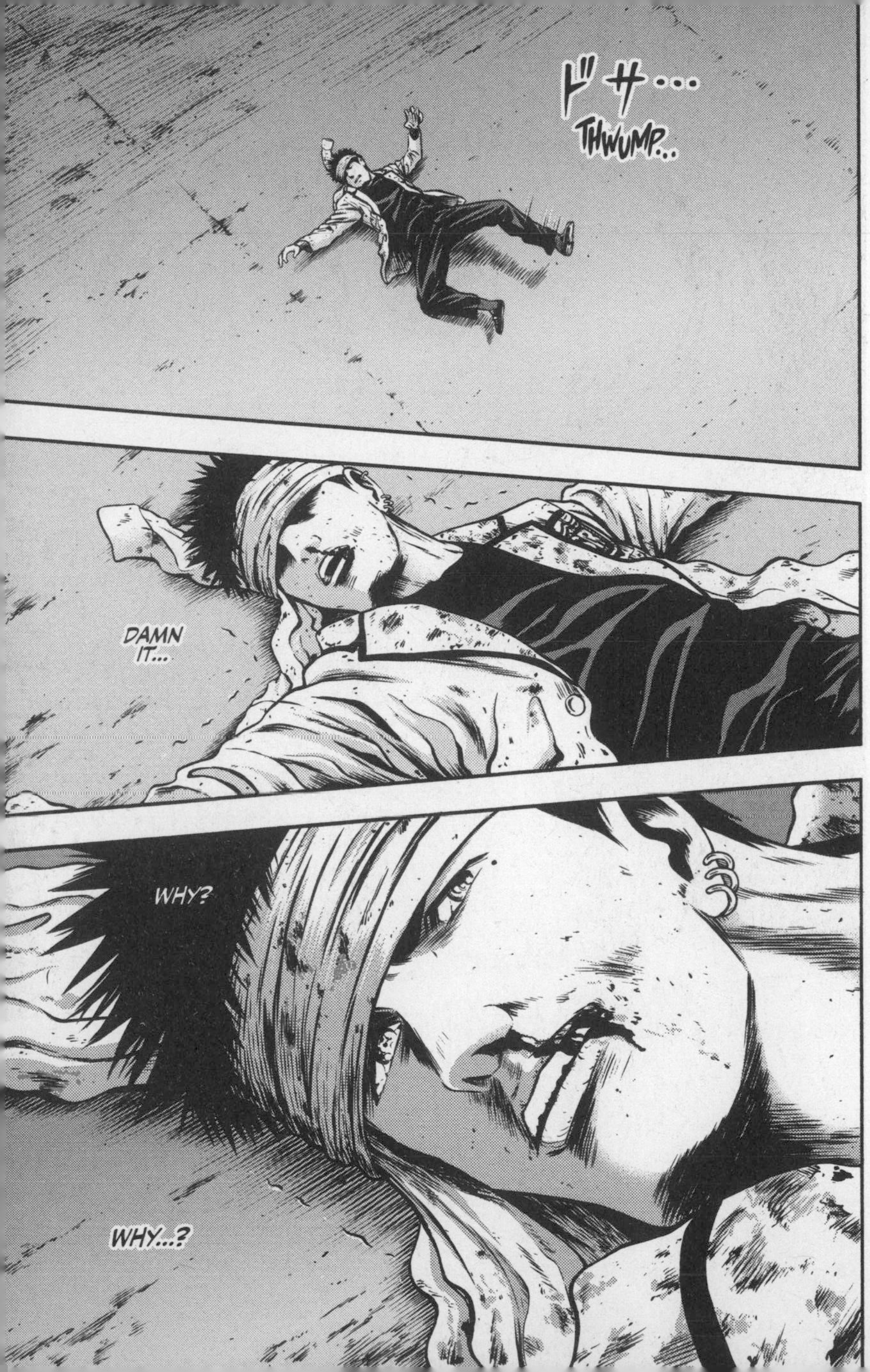
ドサ…
THWUMP...
DAMN IT...
WHY?
WHY...?

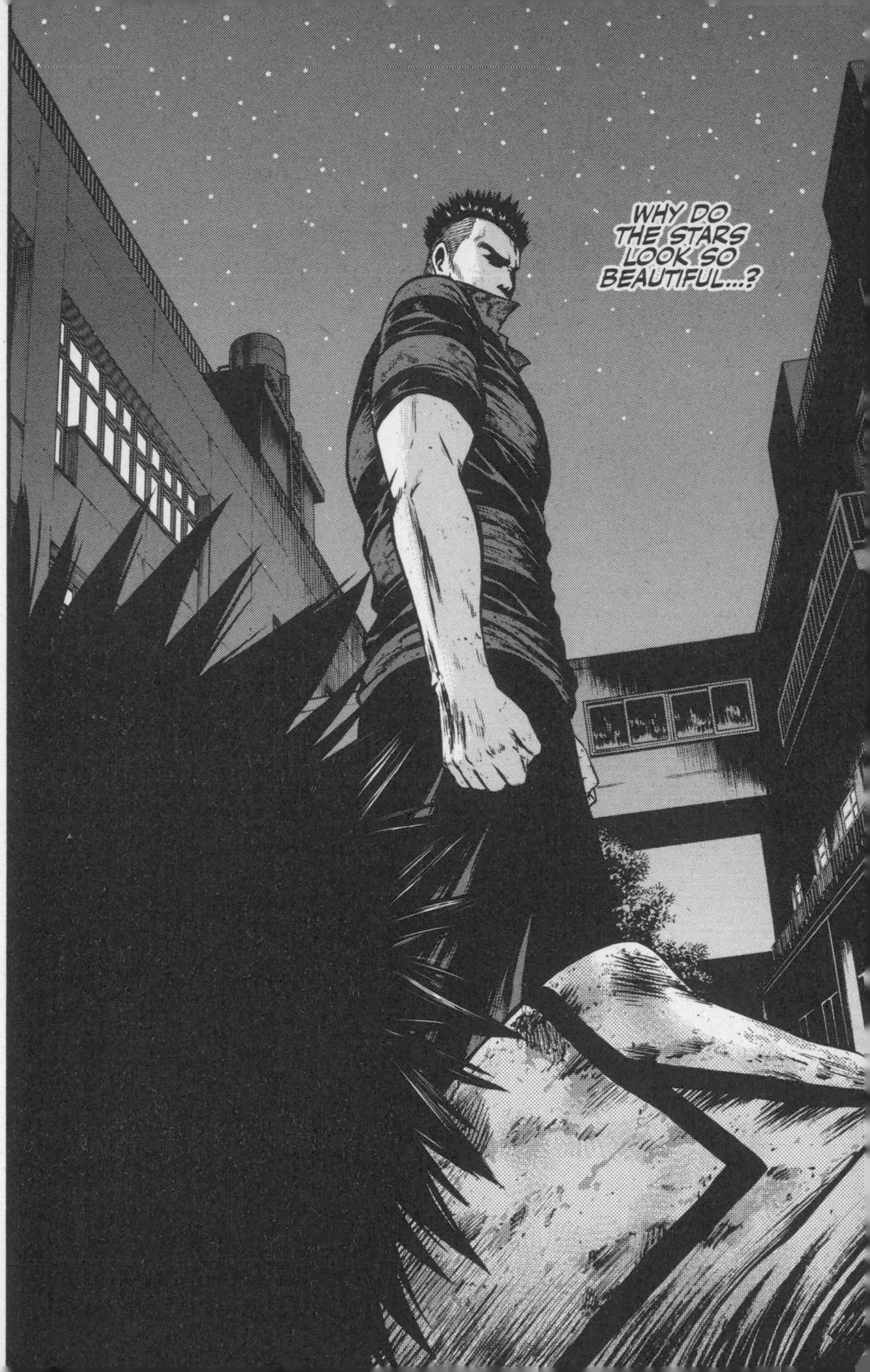
WHY DO THE STARS LOOK SO BEAUTIFUL...?

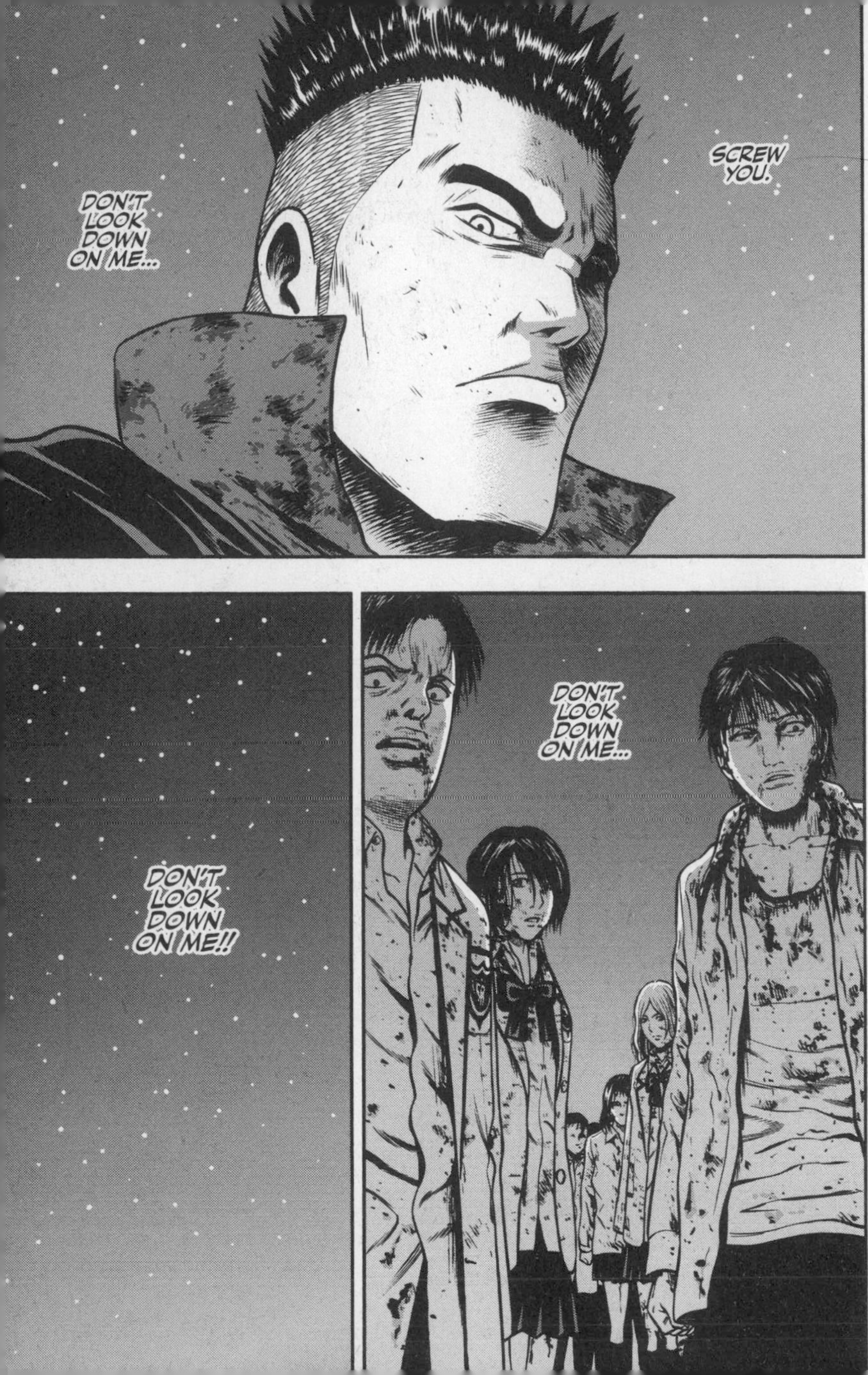
SCREW YOU.
DON'T LOOK DOWN ON ME...
DON'T LOOK DOWN ON ME...
DON'T LOOK DOWN ON ME!!

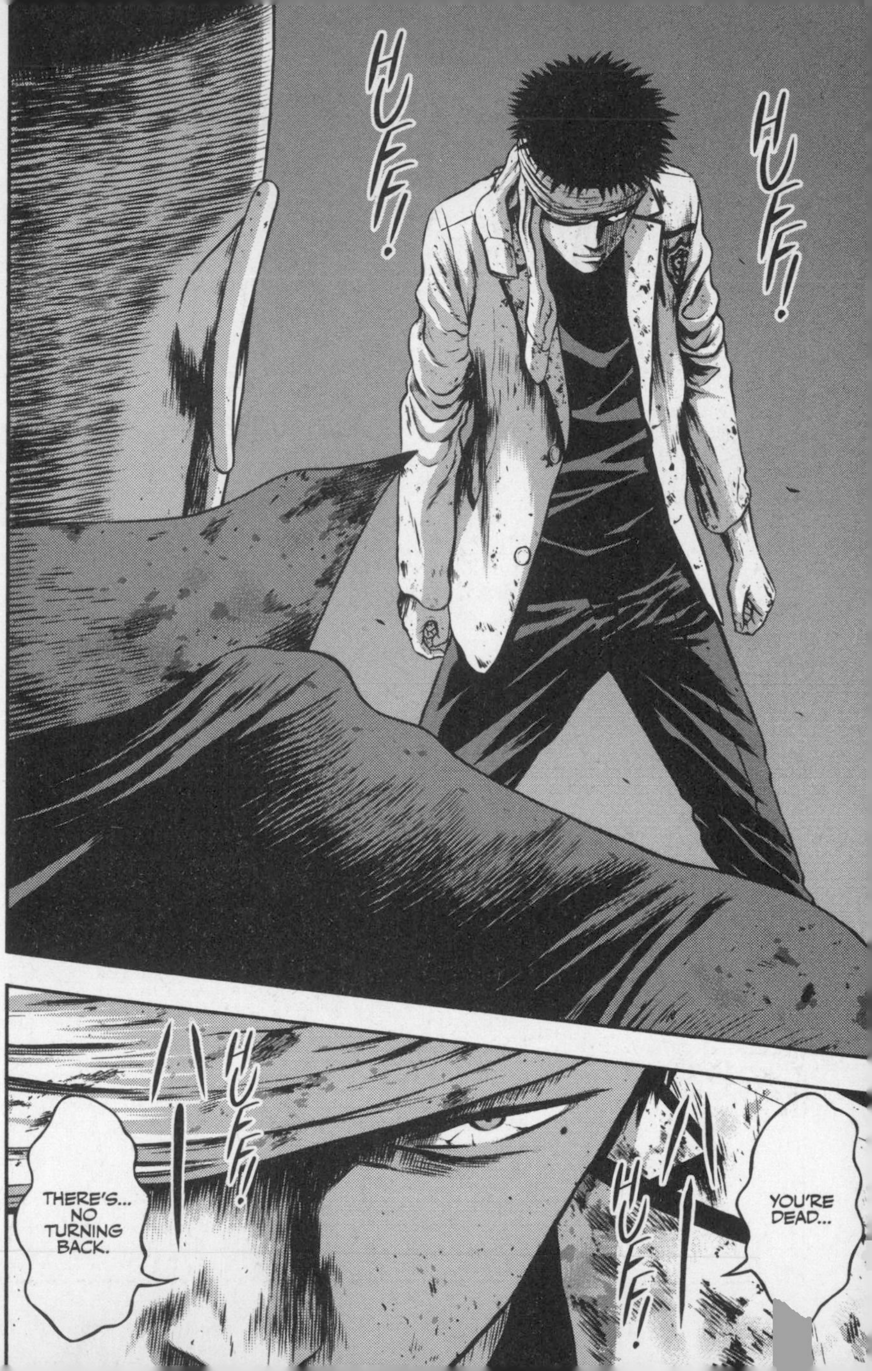
HUFF!
HUFF!
YOU'RE DEAD...
ハー
HUFF!
ハー
HUFF!
THERE'S... NO TURNING BACK.

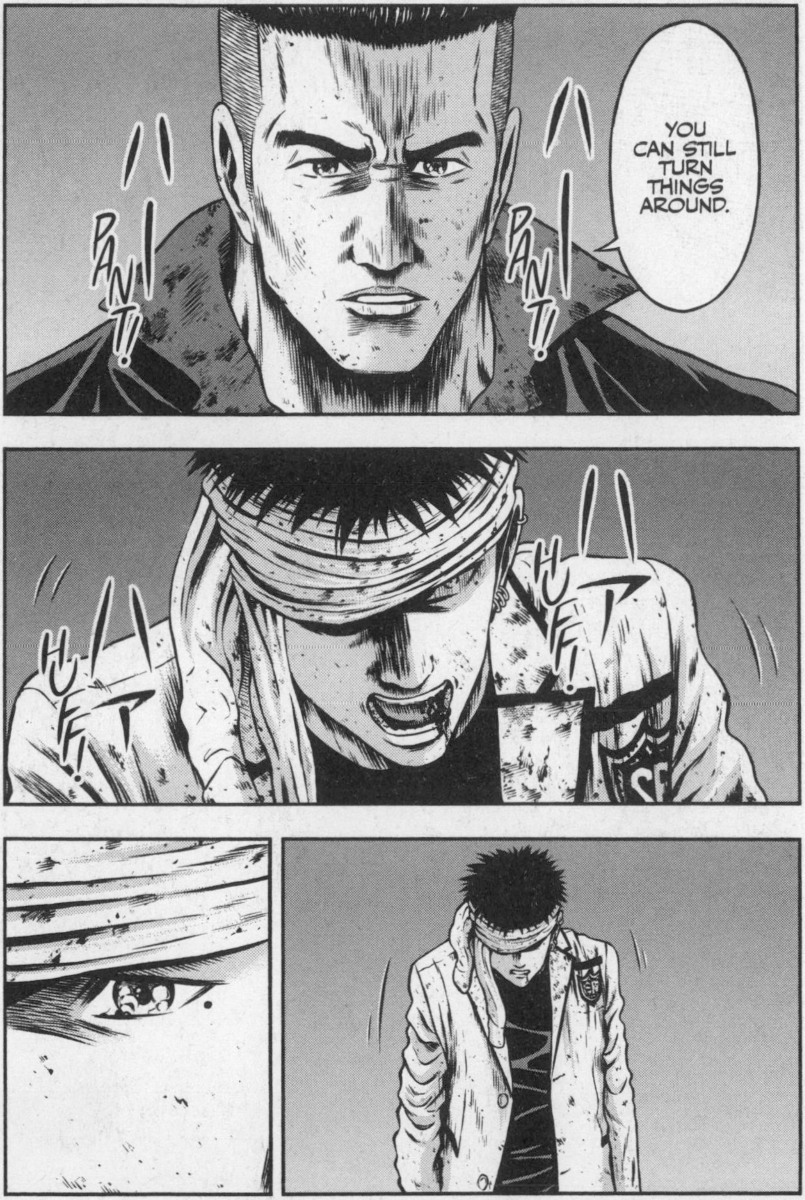
YOU CAN STILL TURN THINGS AROUND.
PANT!
PANT!
HUFF!
HUFF!

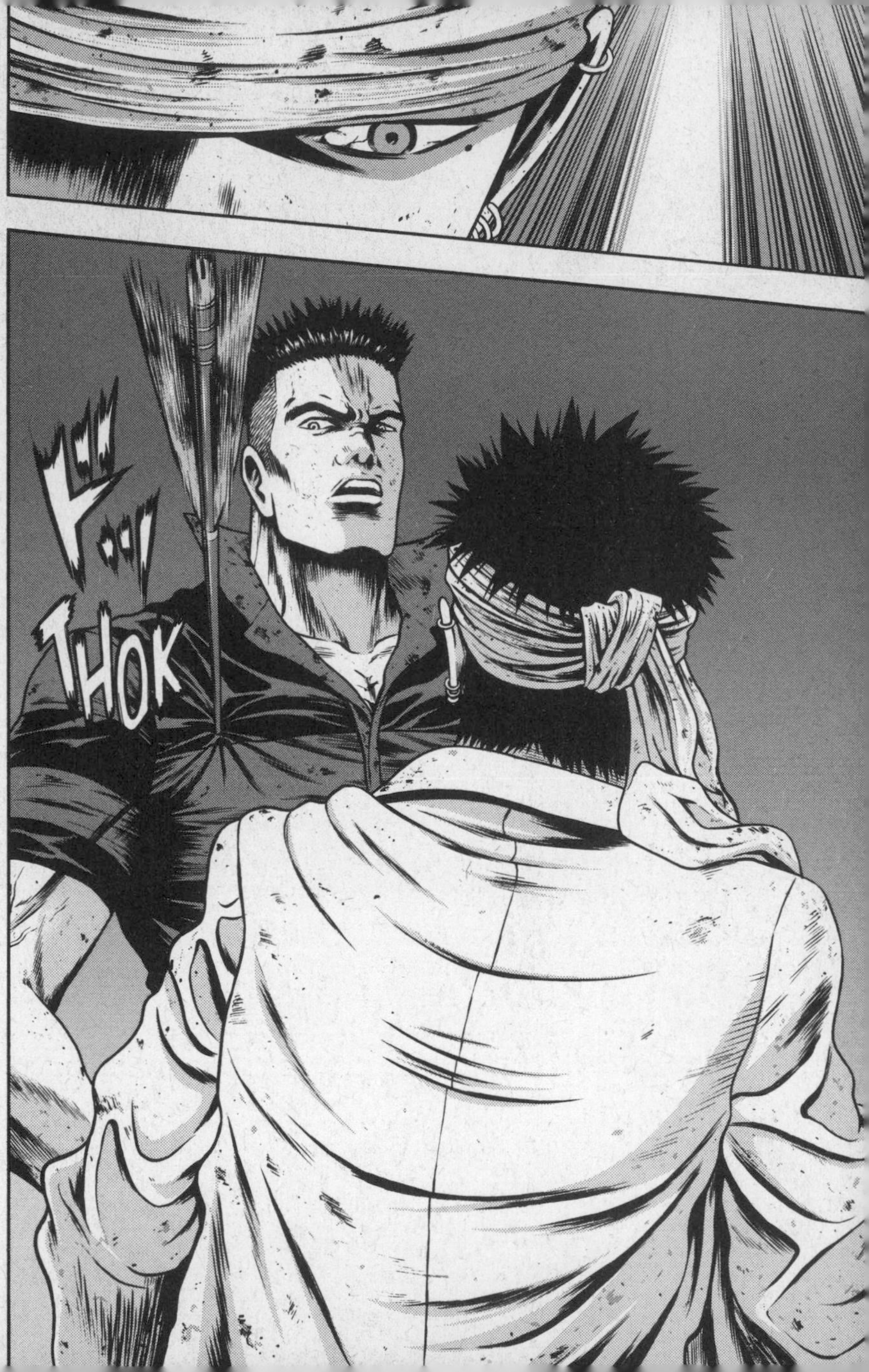
THOK

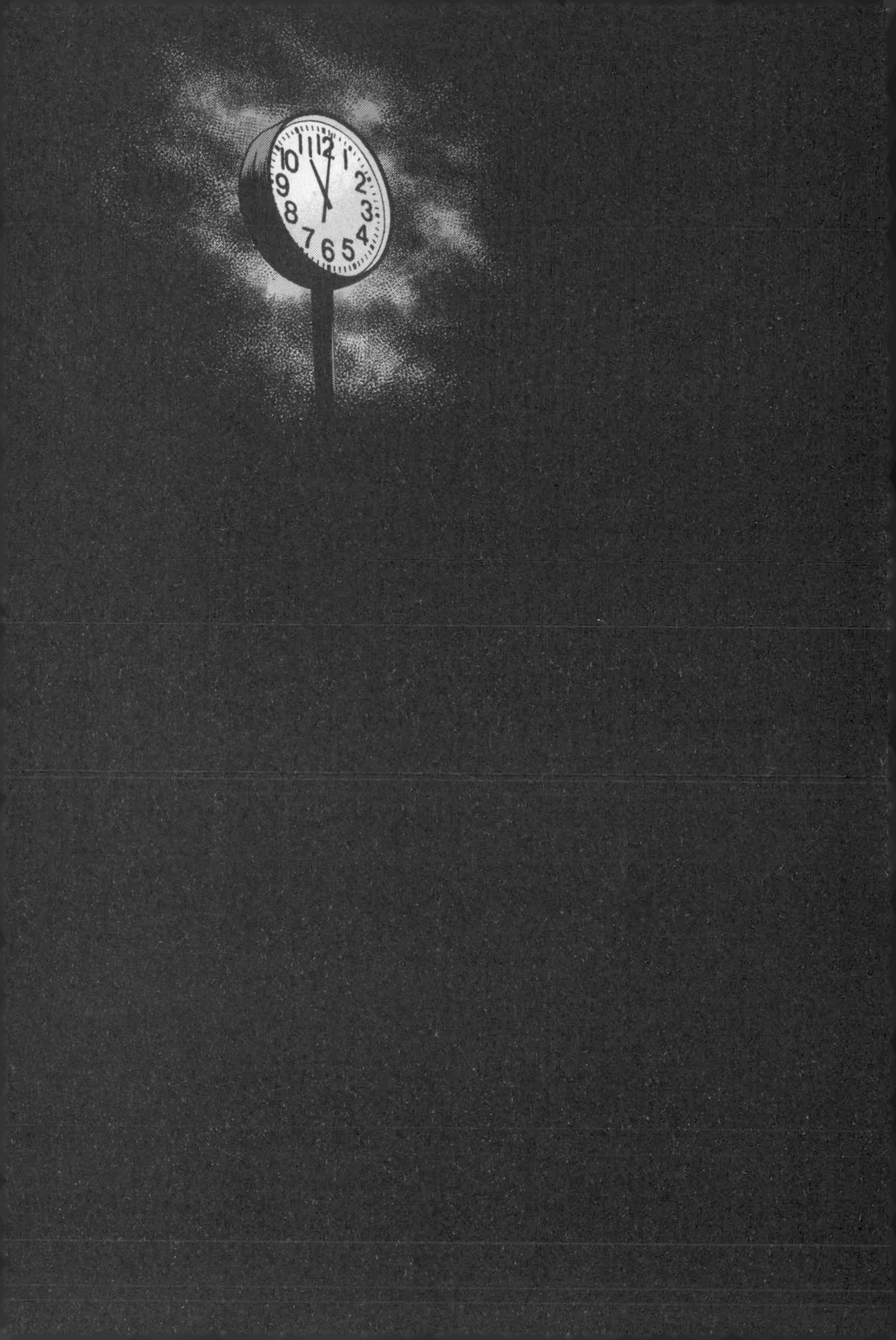

HOUR OF THE ZOMBIE

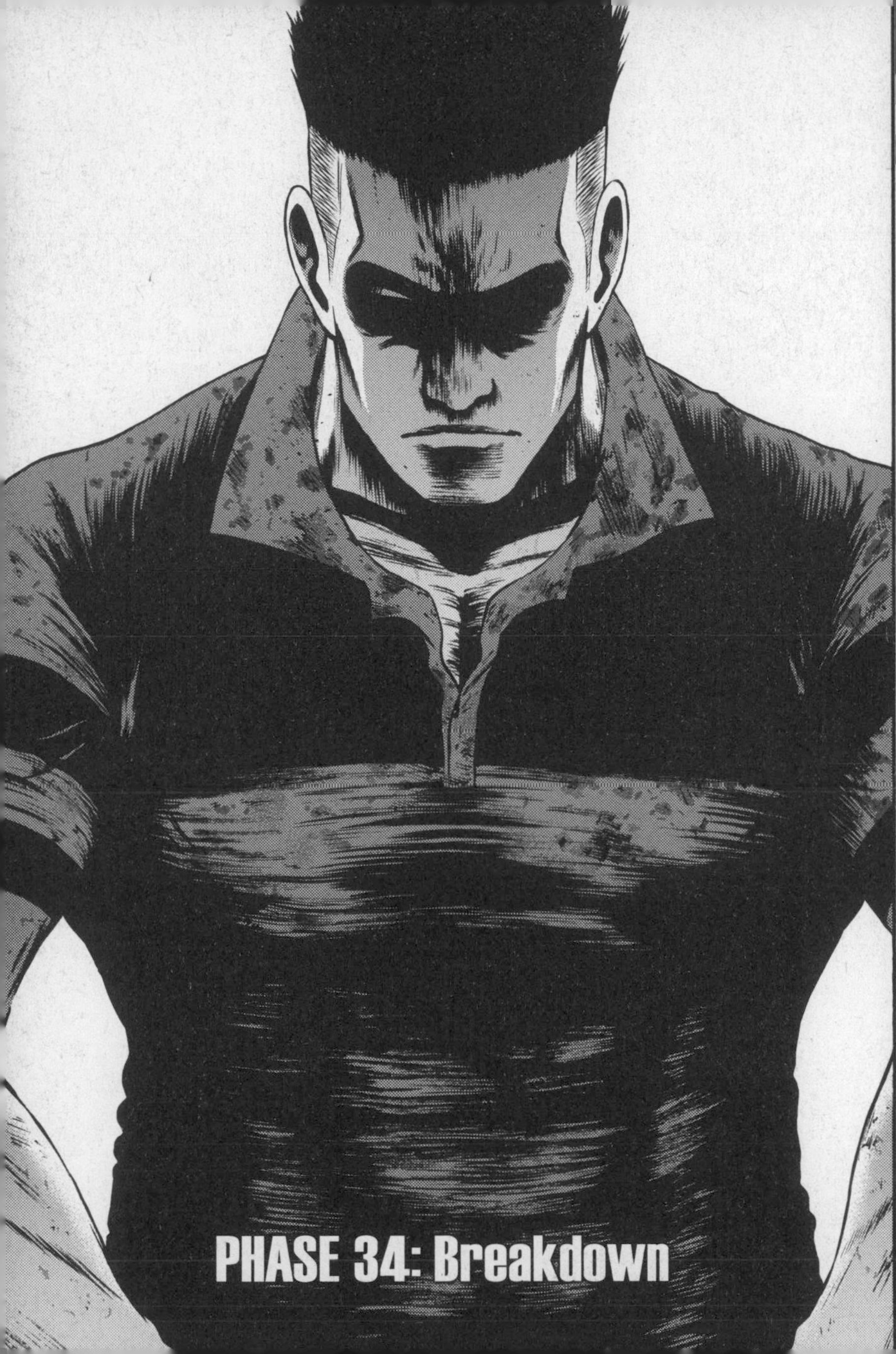
PHASE 34: Breakdown

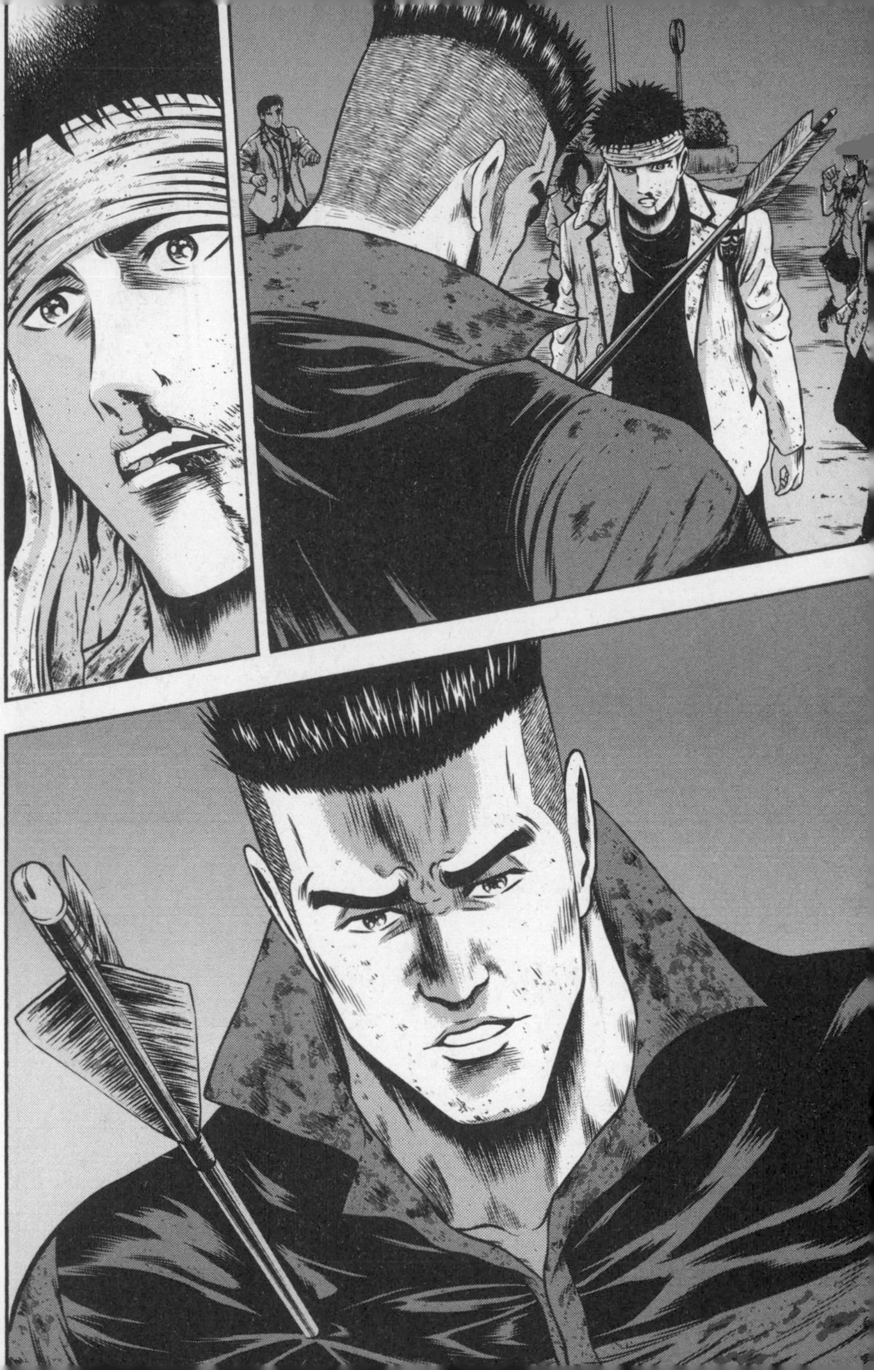

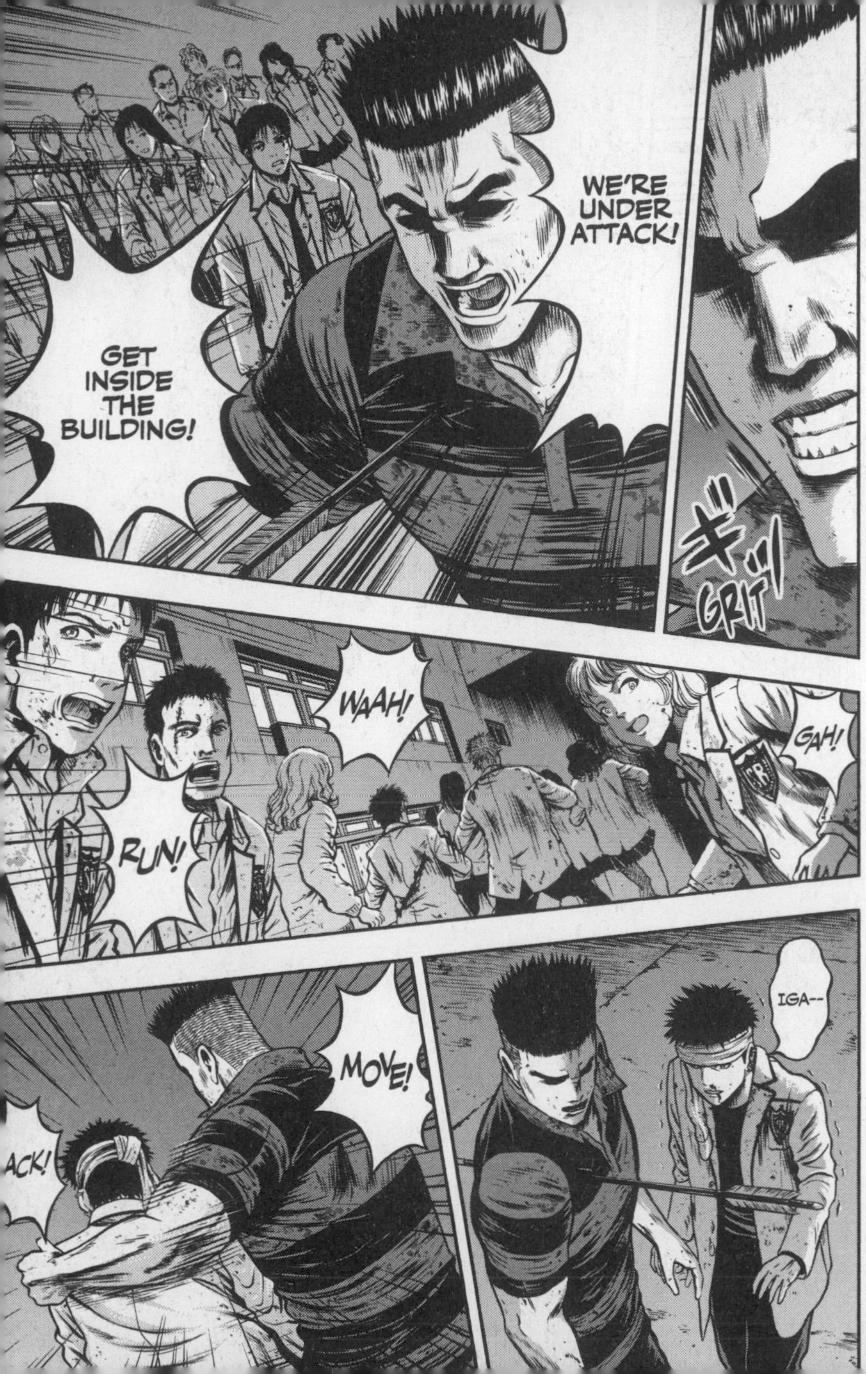
ギ
GRIT
WE'RE UNDER ATTACK!
GET INSIDE THE BUILDING!
GAH!
WAAH!
RUN!
IGA--
MOVE!
ACK!

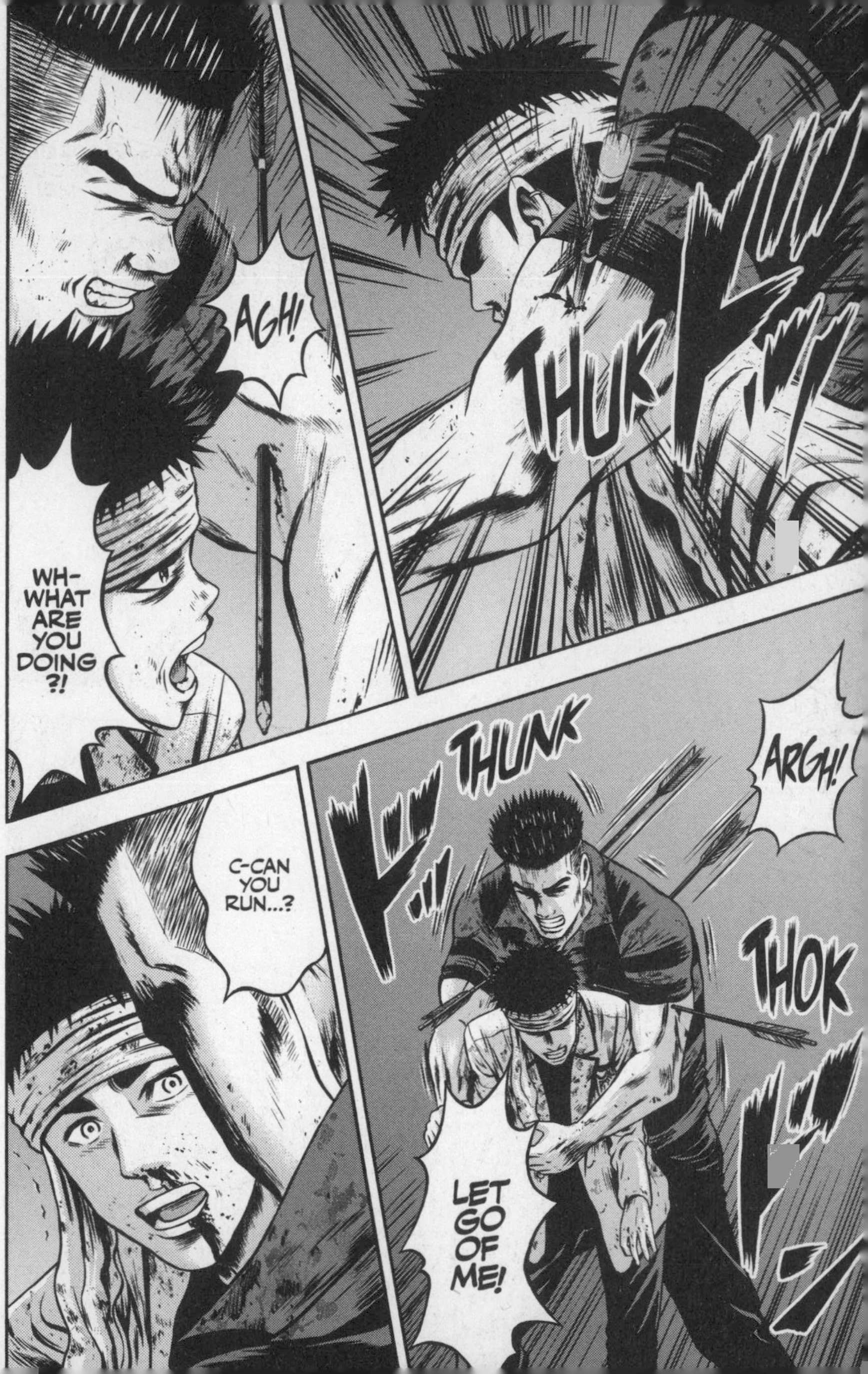
THUK
AGH!
WH-WHAT ARE YOU DOING?!
ARGH!
THUNK
THOK
LET GO OF ME!
C-CAN YOU RUN...?

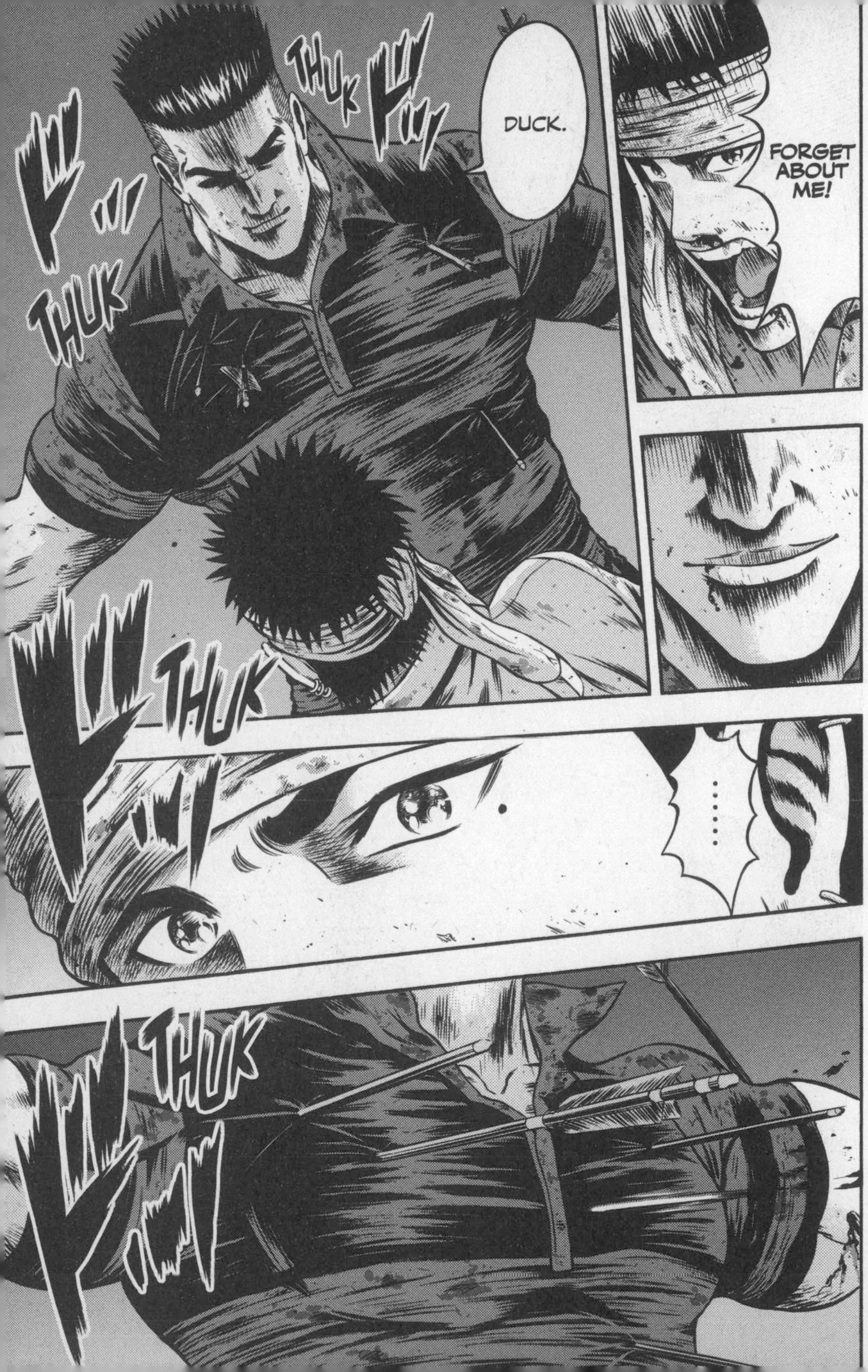
FORGET ABOUT ME!
DUCK.
THUK
THUK
THUK
......
THUK

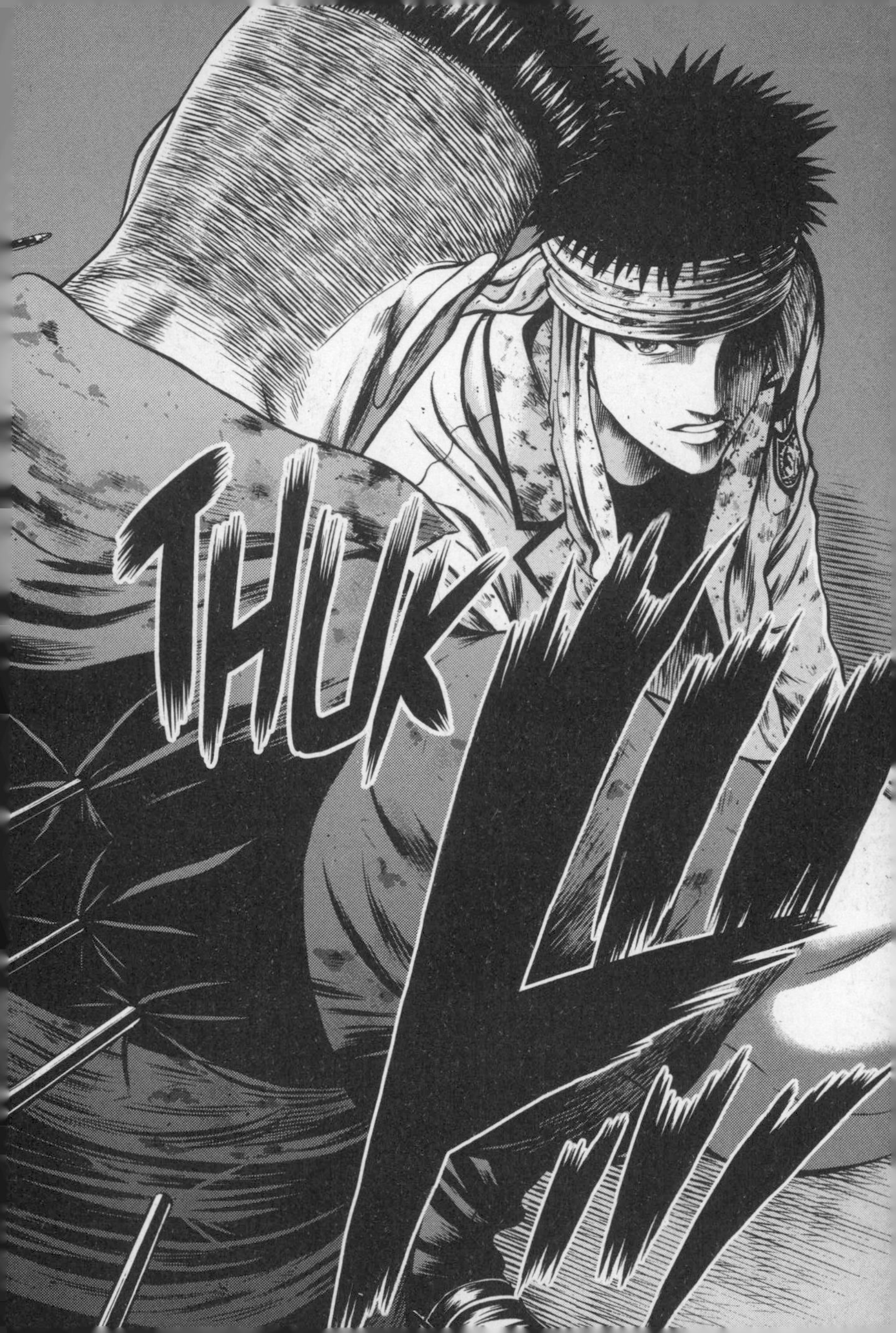
THUK

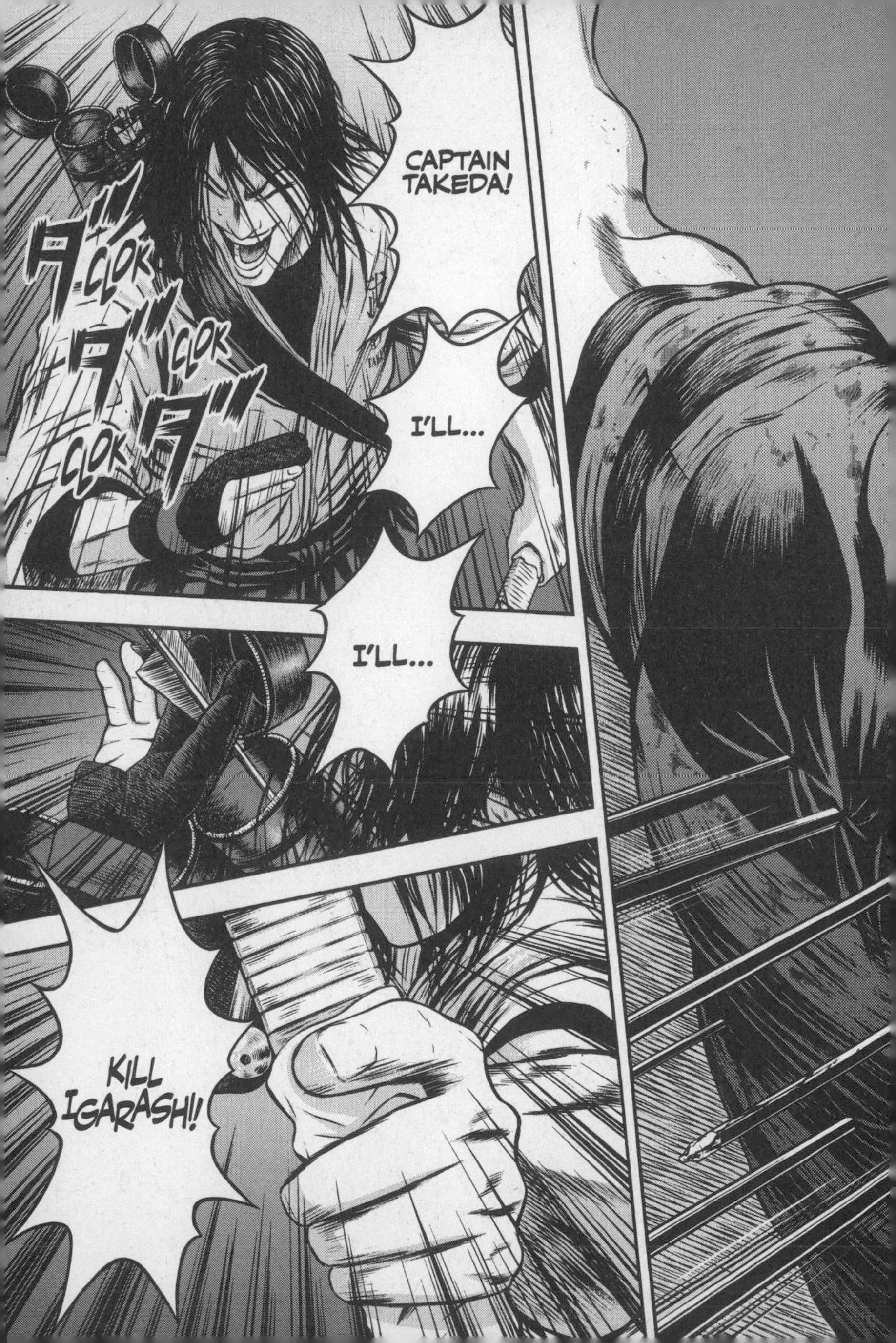
CAPTAIN TAKEDA!
CLOK
CLOK
CLOK
I'LL...
I'LL...
KILL IGARASHI!

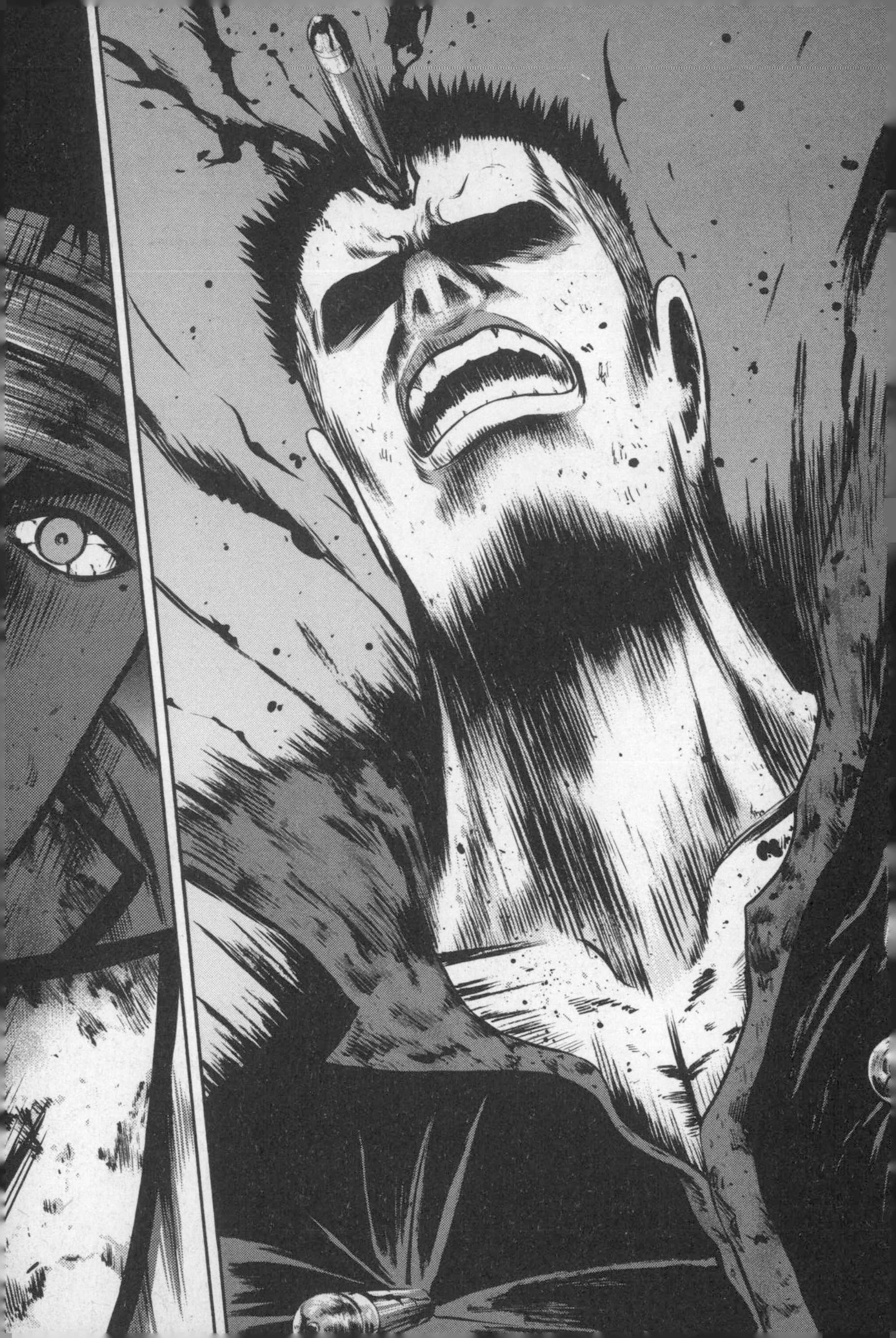

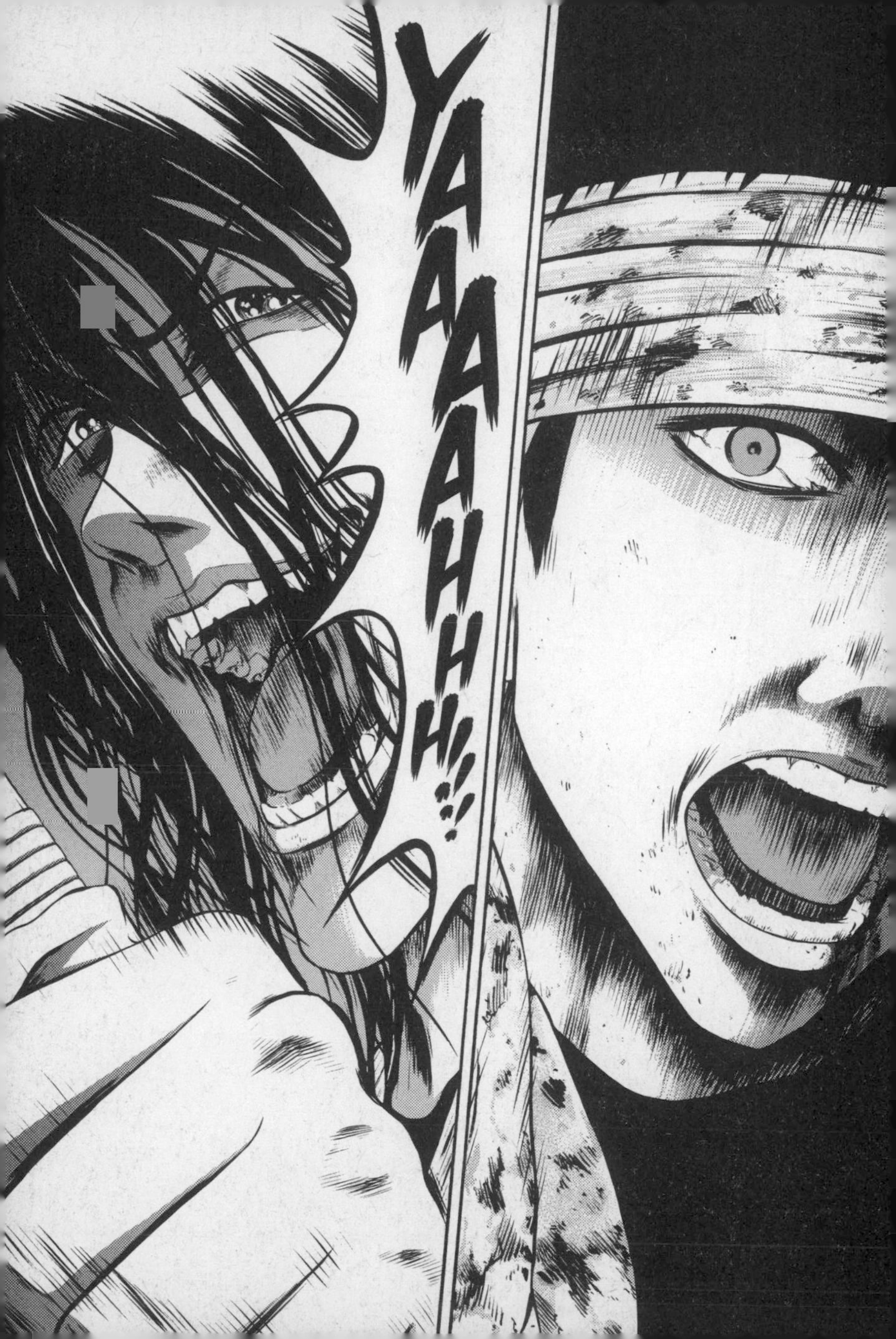
YAAAAHHH!!!

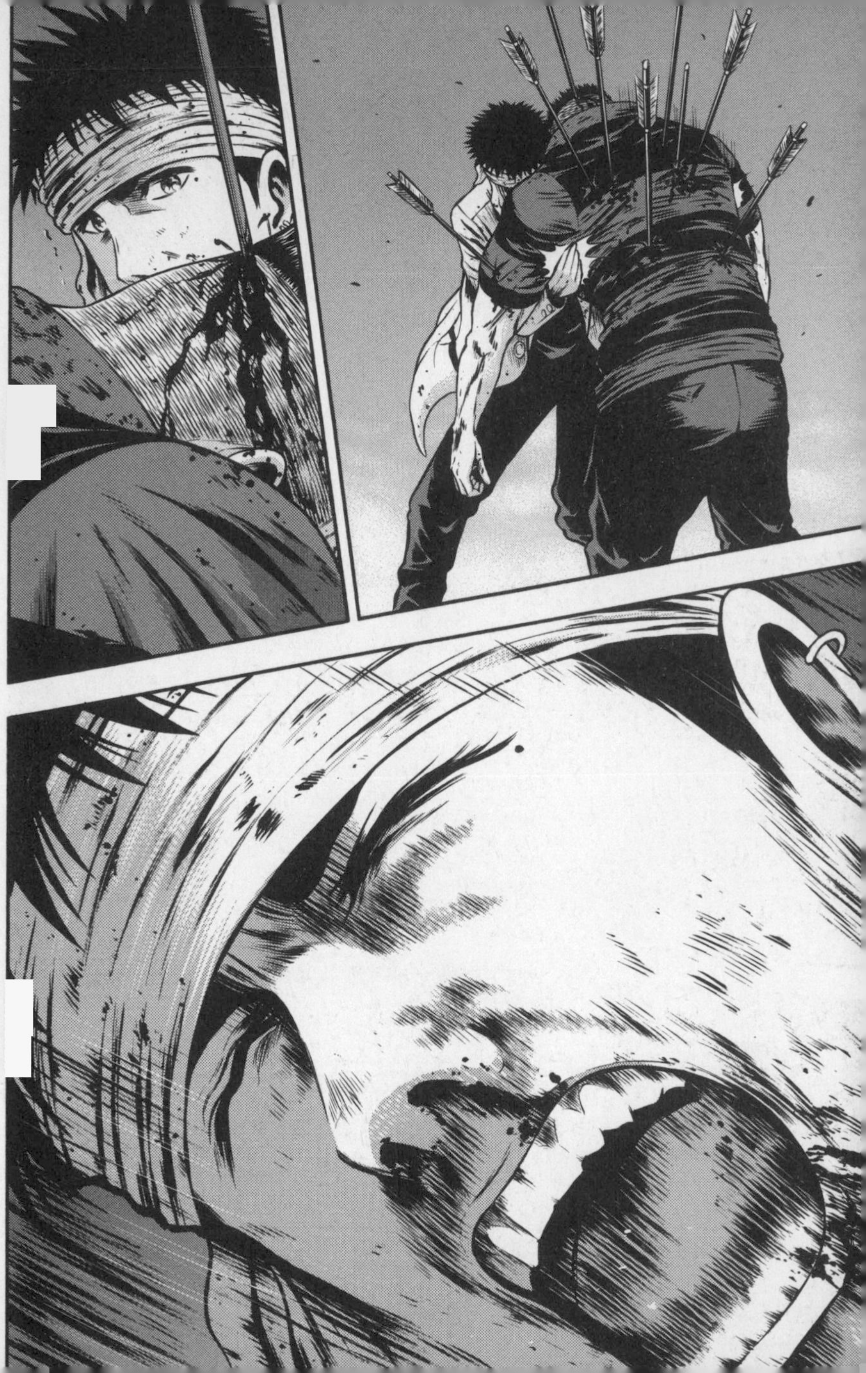

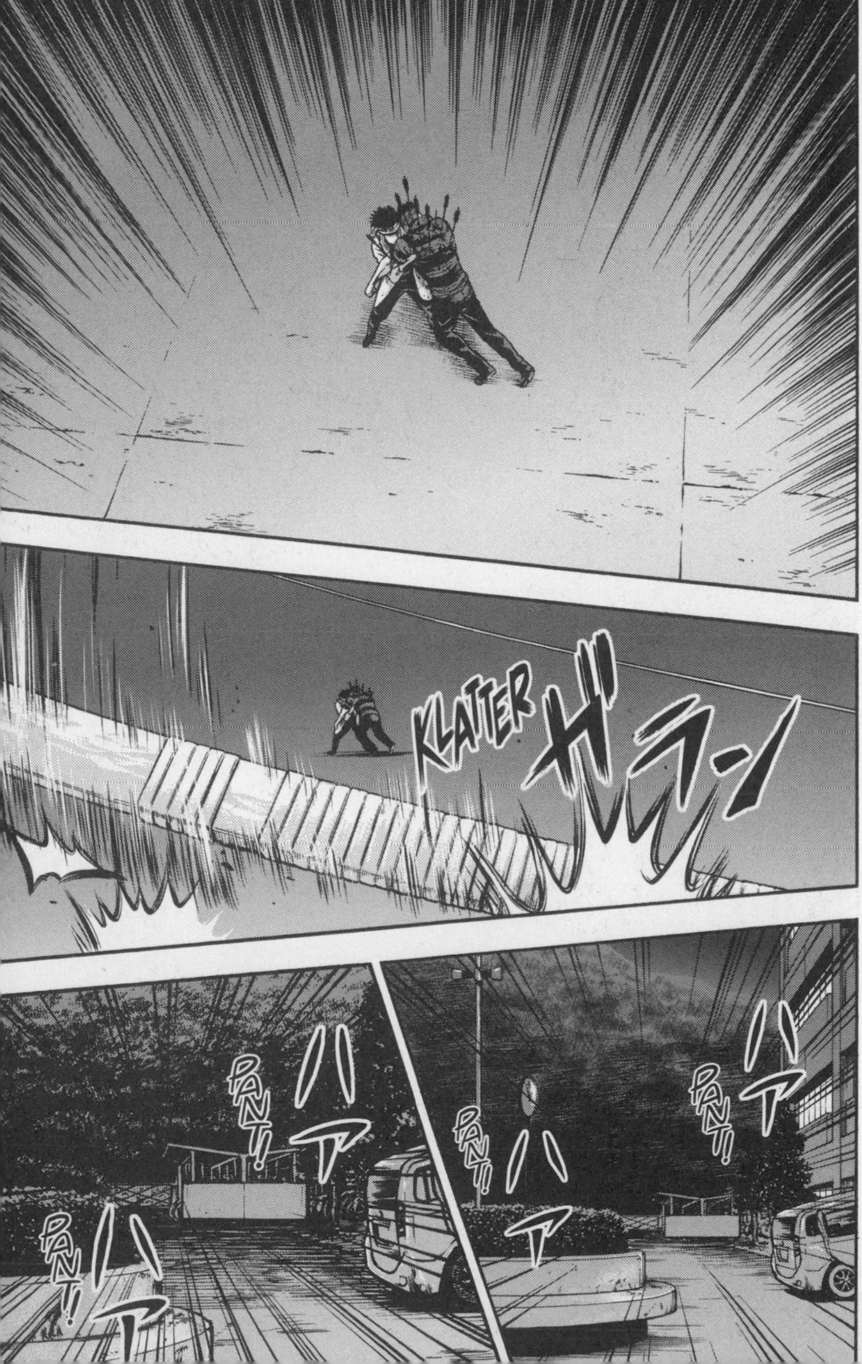
KLATTER
ガラーン
PANT!
ハァ
PANT!
ハァ
PANT!
ハァ
PANT!
ハァ

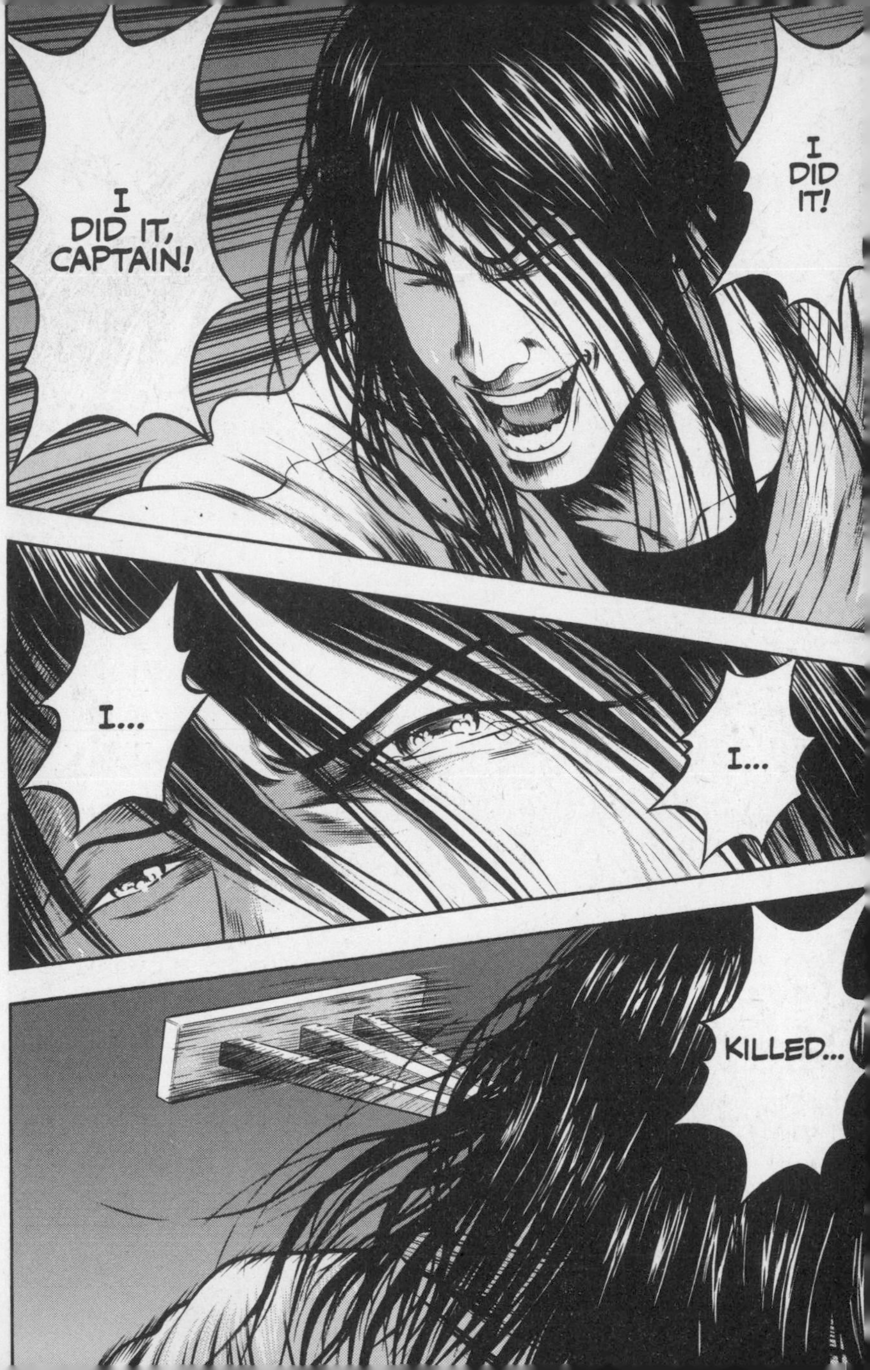
I DID IT!
I DID IT, CAPTAIN!
I...
I...
KILLED...

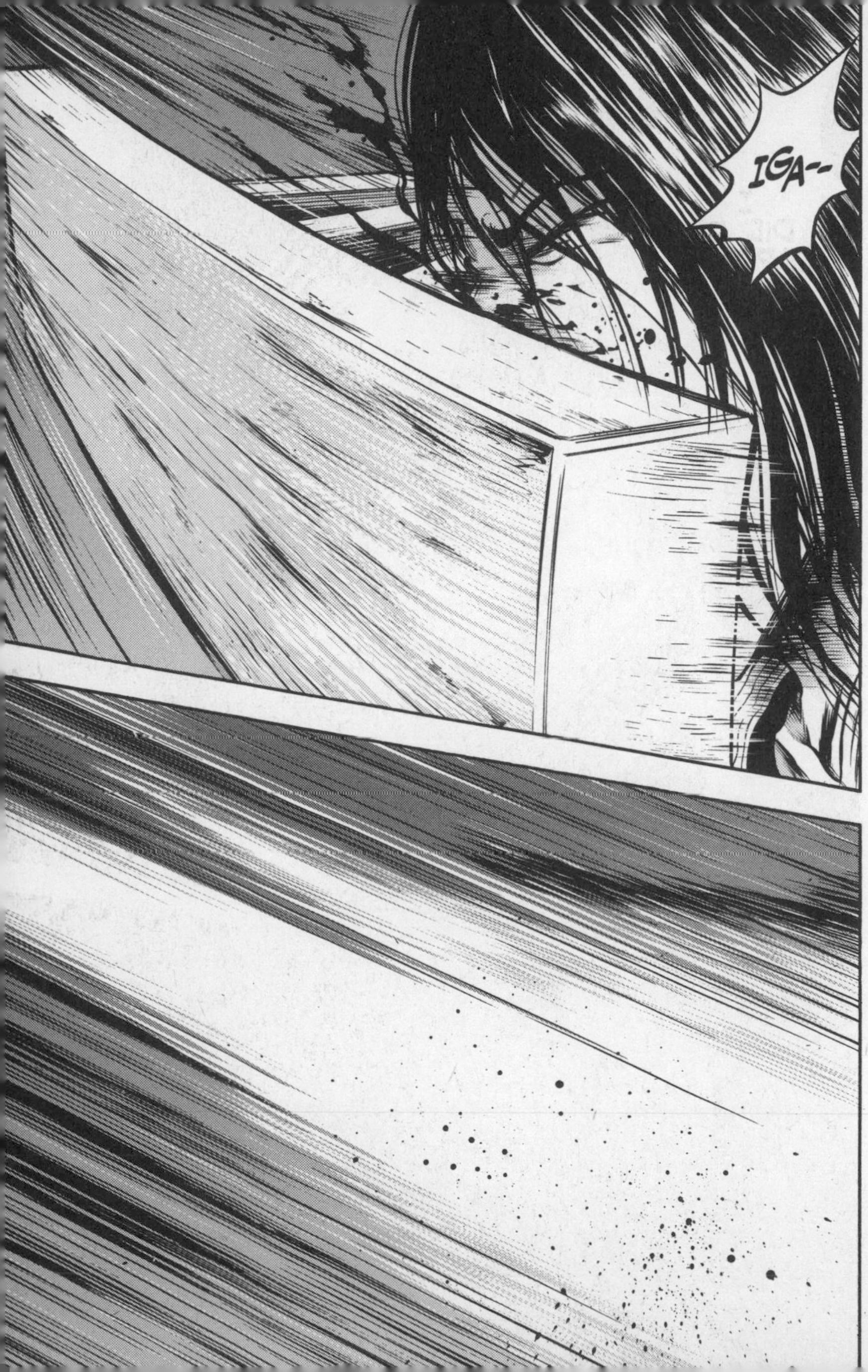
IGA--

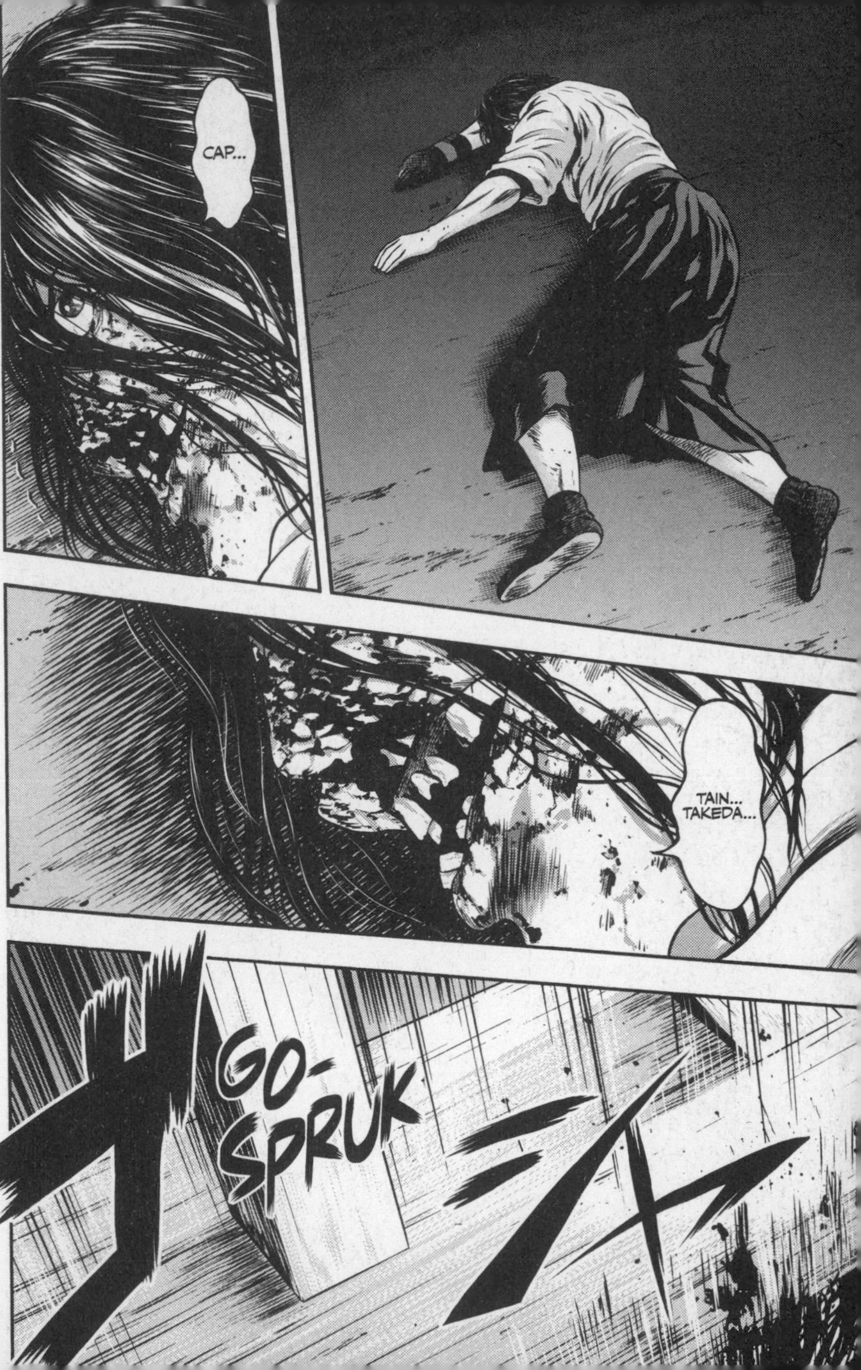
CAP...
TAIN... TAKEDA...
GO-SPRUK

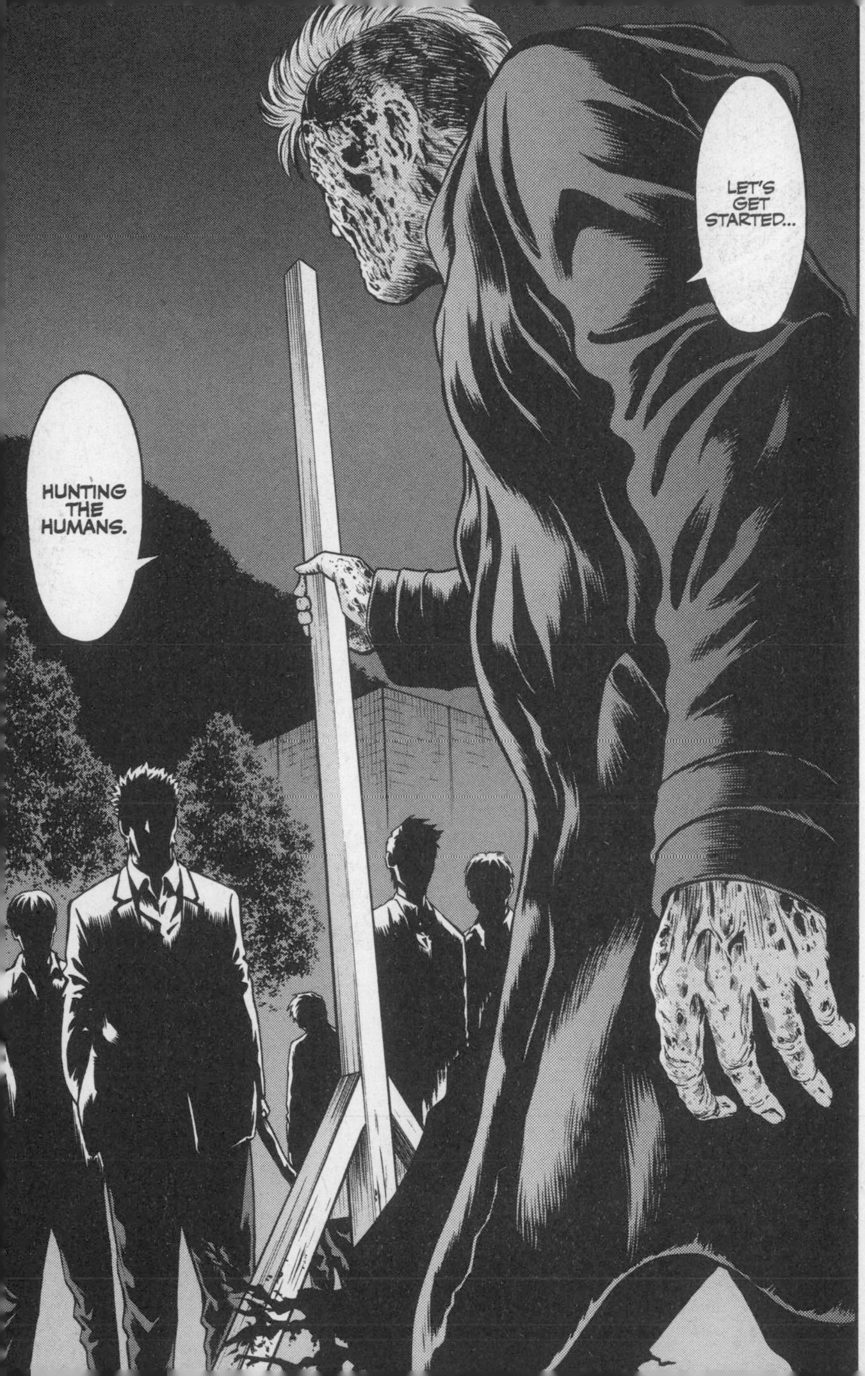
LET'S GET STARTED...
HUNTING THE HUMANS.

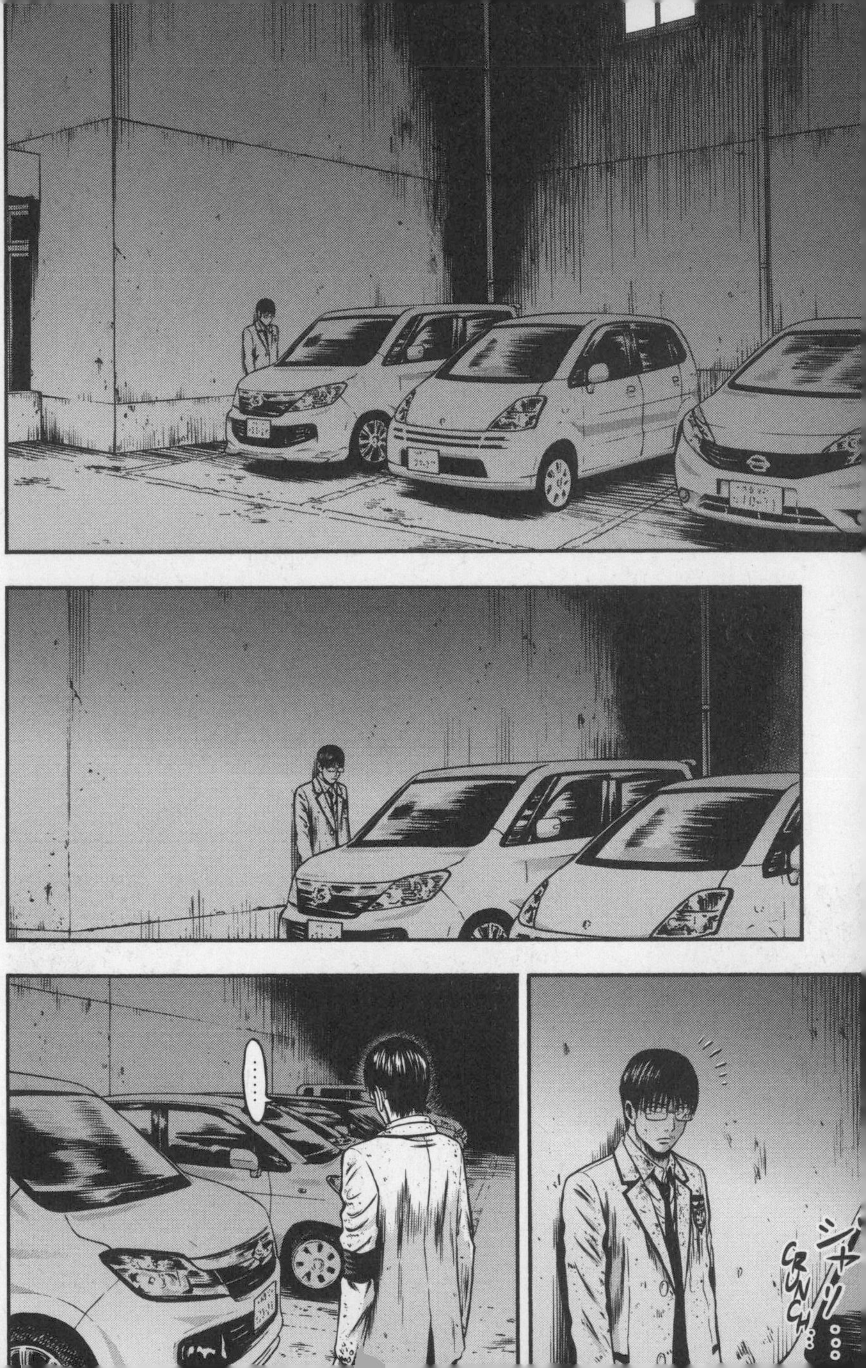
....
ジャリ
CRUNCH...

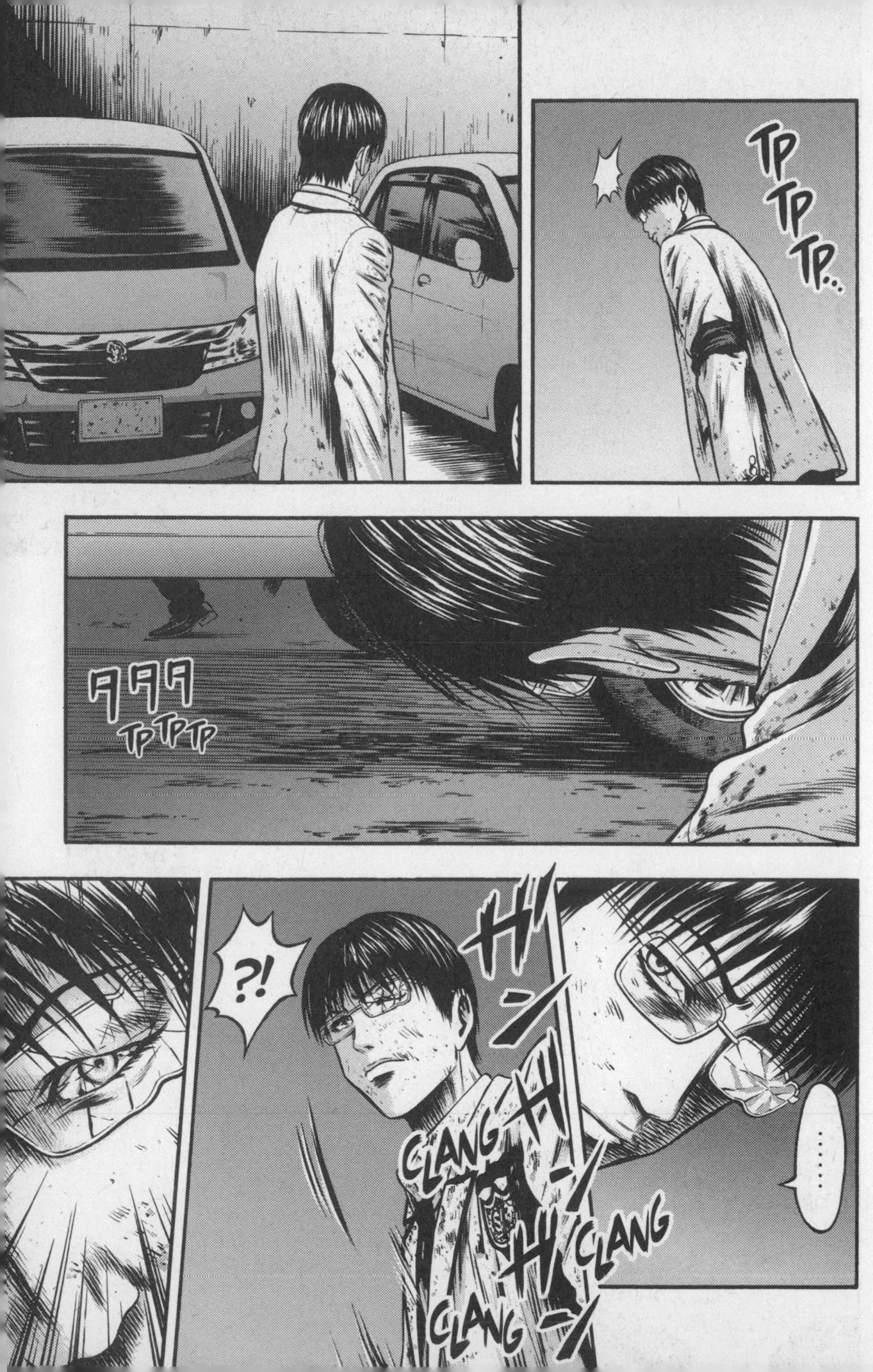
TP TP TP...
タタタ
TP TP TP
......
CLANG
CLANG
CLANG
?!

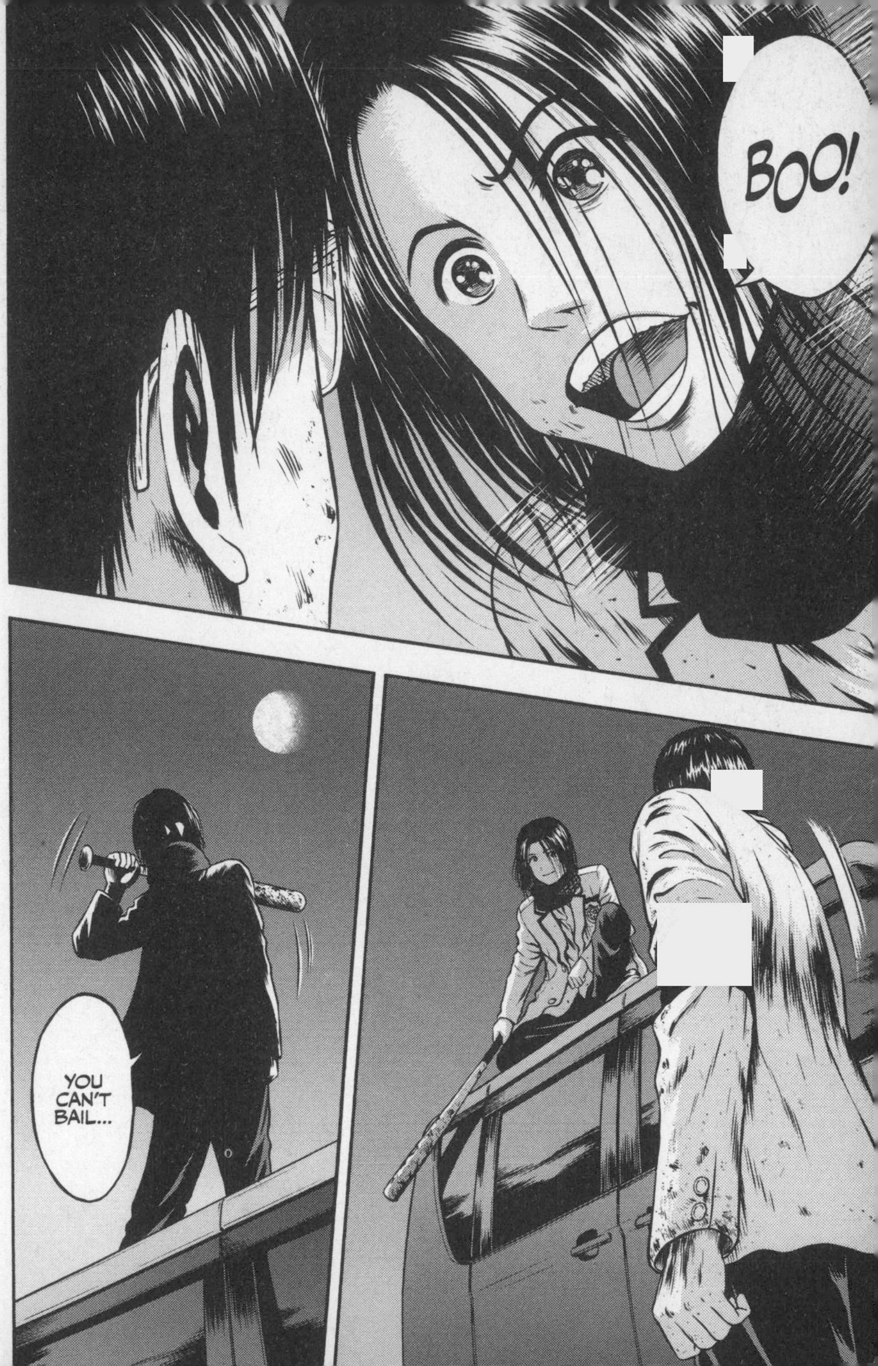
BOO!
YOU CAN'T BAIL...

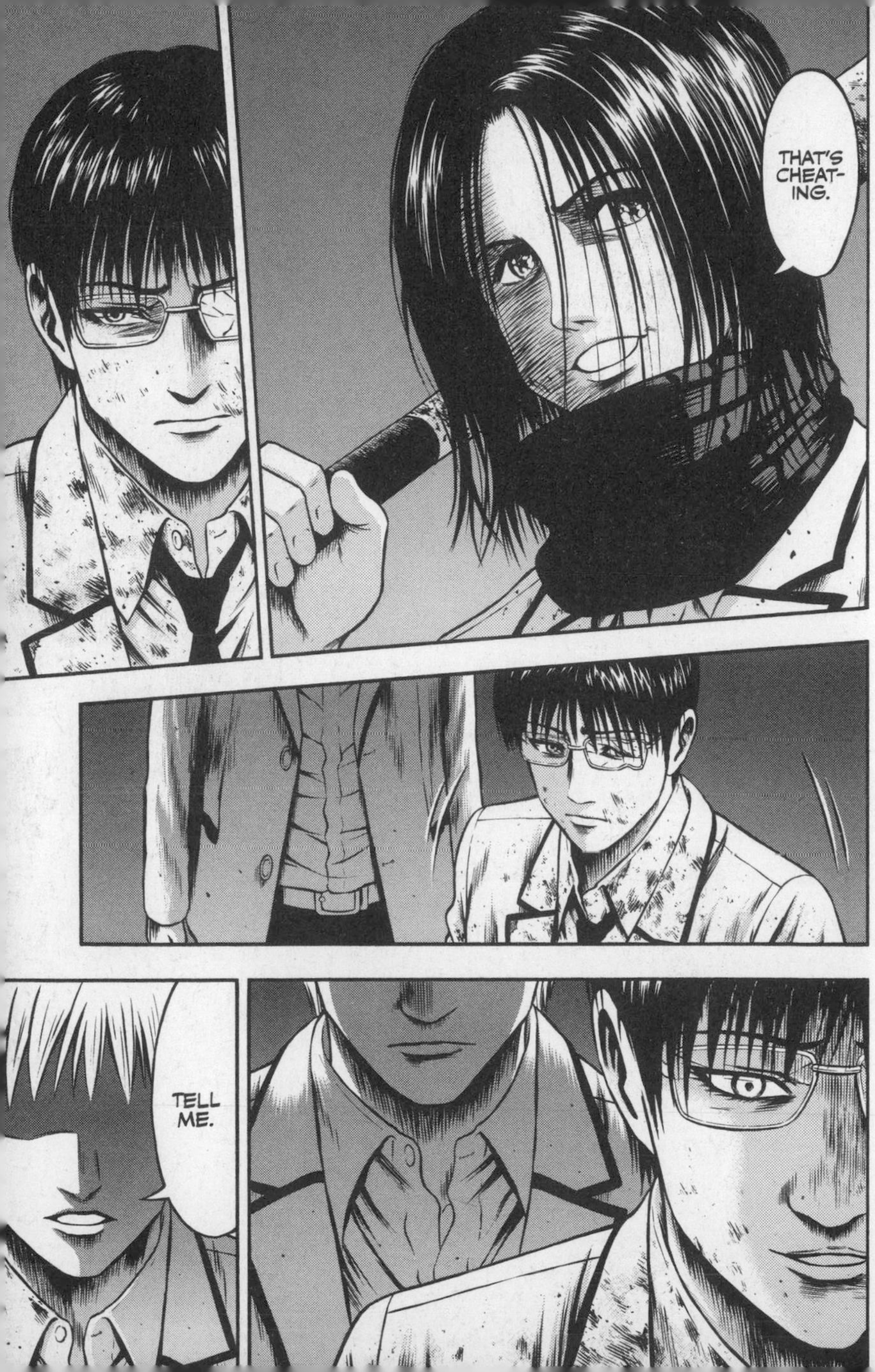
THAT'S CHEAT-ING.
TELL ME.

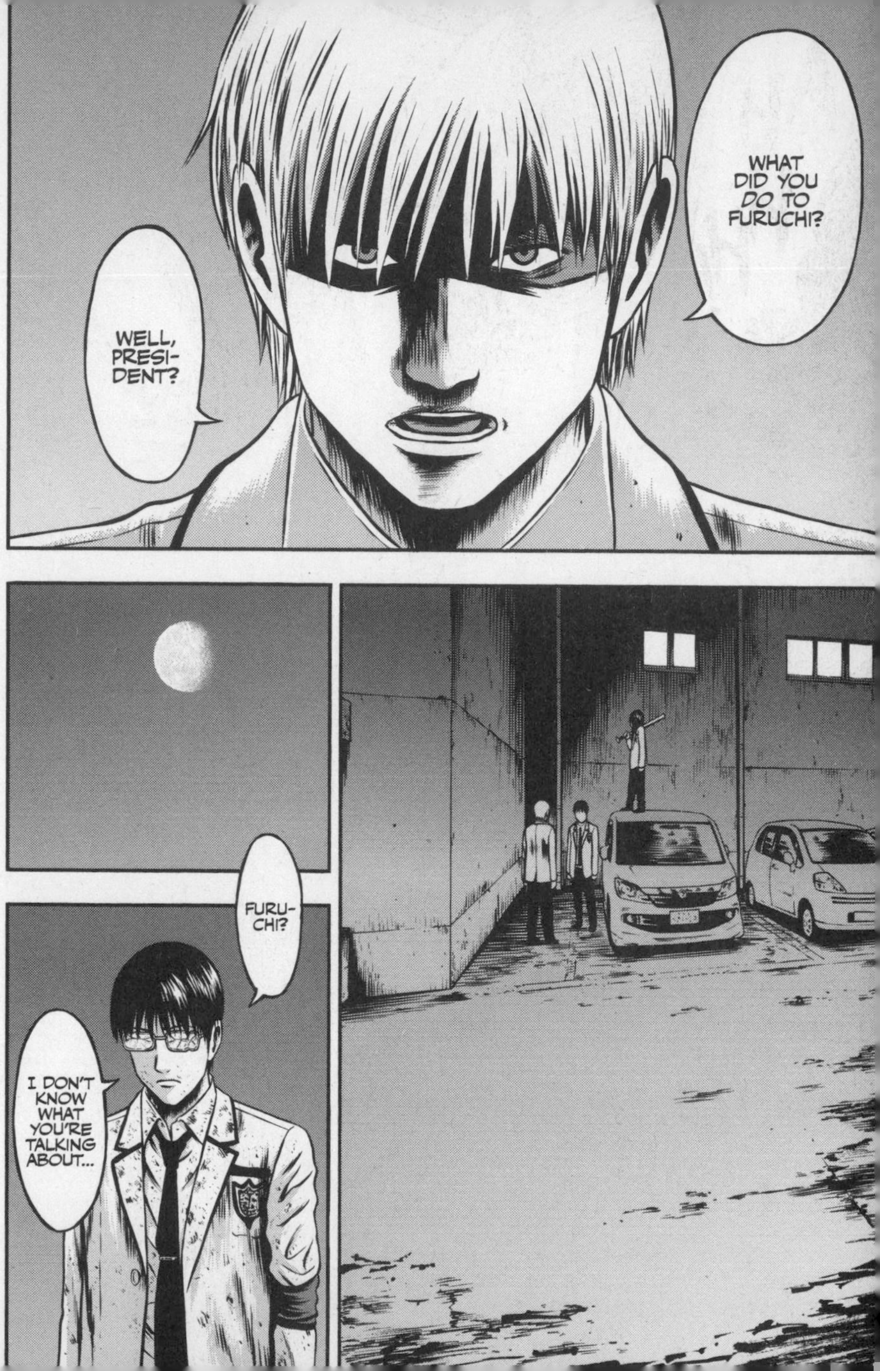
WHAT DID YOU *DO* TO FURUCHI!?
WELL, PRESI-DENT?
FURU-CHI!?
I DON'T KNOW WHAT YOU'RE TALKING ABOUT...

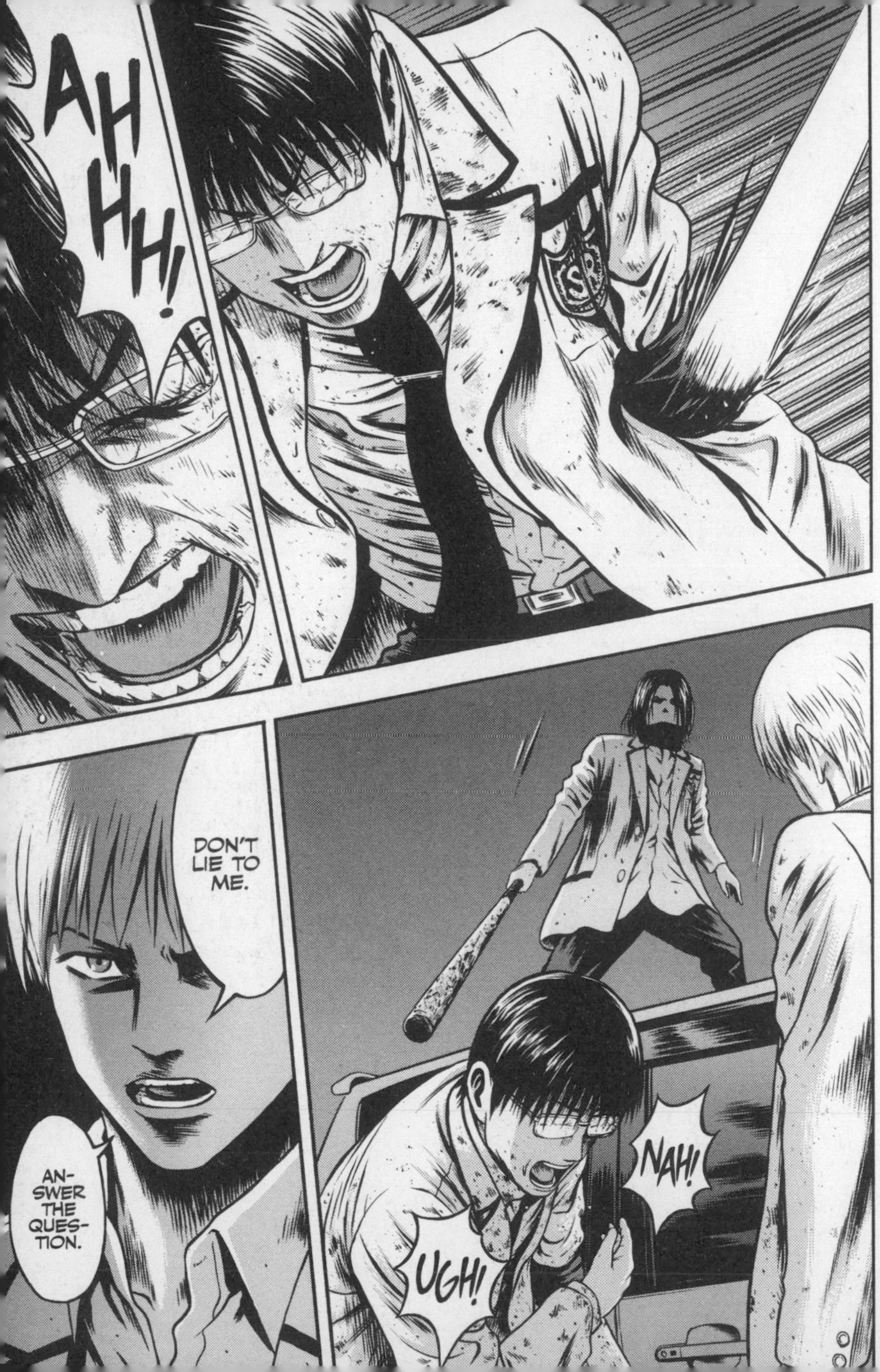
AHHHH!
NAH!
UGH!
DON'T LIE TO ME.
ANSWER THE QUESTION.

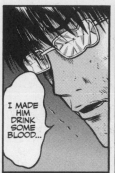

I MADE HIM DRINK SOME BLOOD...

HUFF!

HUFF!

HUFF!

WHOSE BLOOD?

I DON'T KNOW!

スタッ
TUP

AAH!

AH!

WHOK

GAH!

PRESI-DENT...

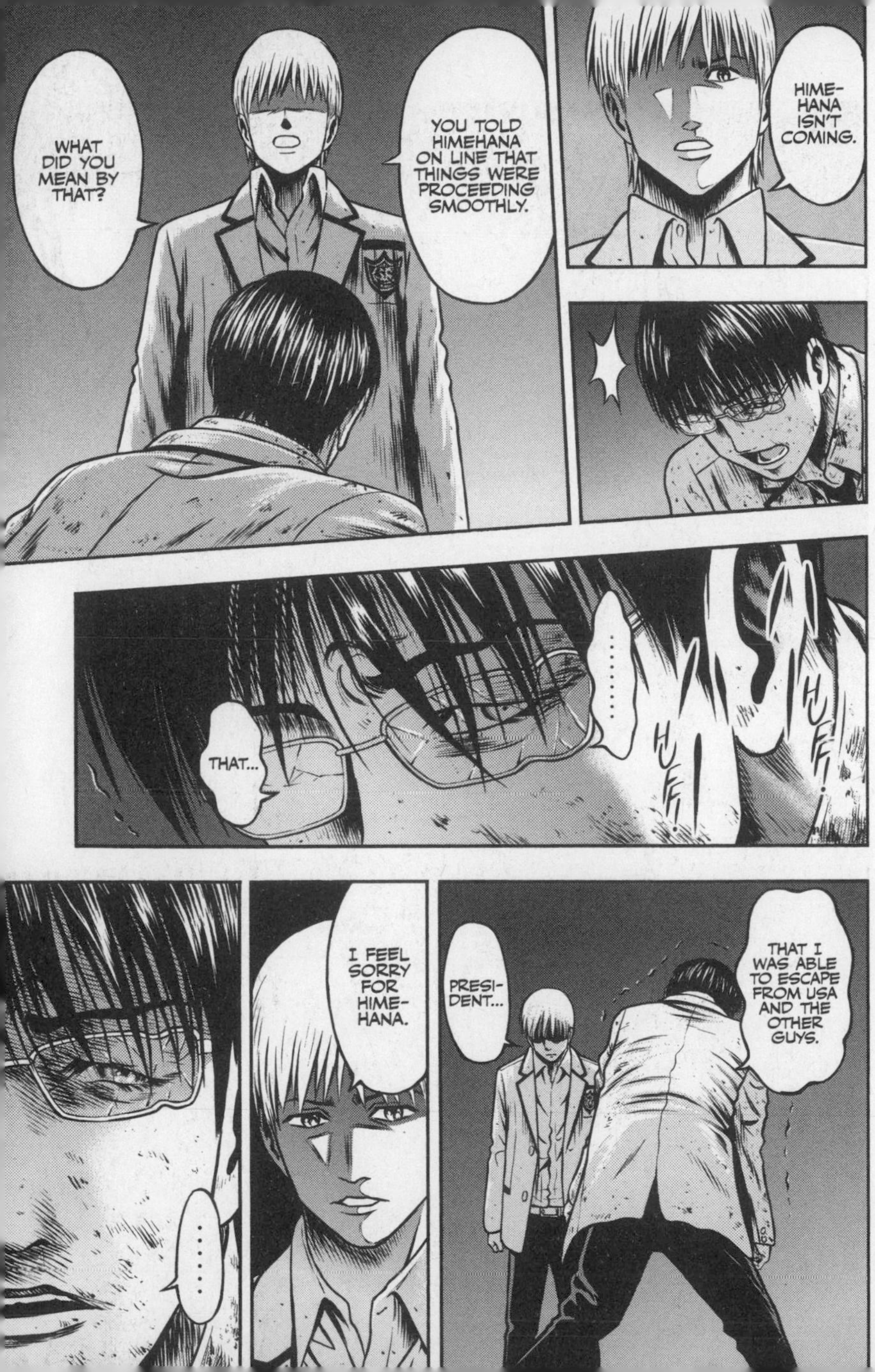
HIME-HANA ISN'T COMING.
YOU TOLD HIMEHANA ON LINE THAT THINGS WERE PROCEEDING SMOOTHLY.
WHAT DID YOU MEAN BY THAT?
HUFF! HUFF!
......
THAT...
THAT I WAS ABLE TO ESCAPE FROM USA AND THE OTHER GUYS.
PRESI-DENT...
I FEEL SORRY FOR HIME-HANA.
......

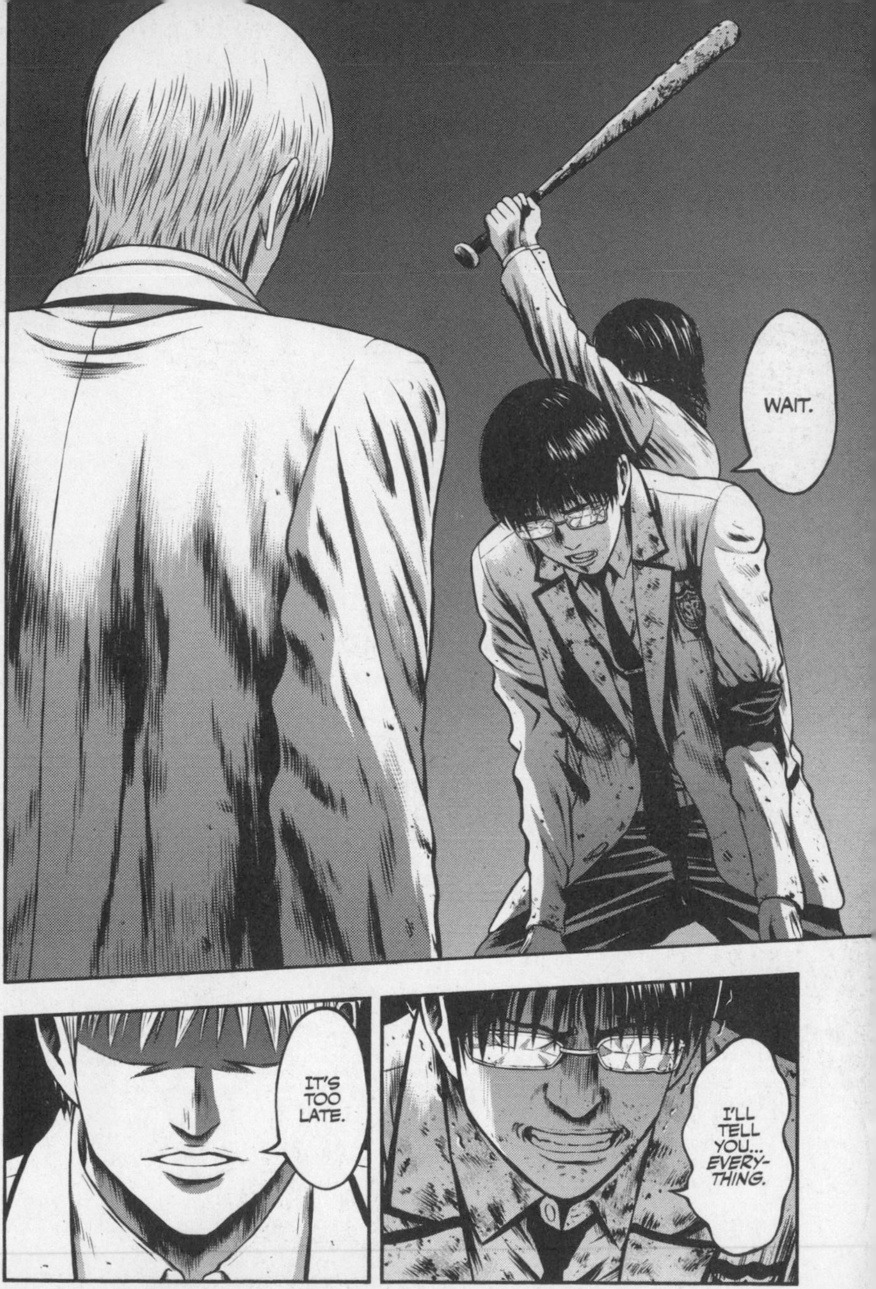
WAIT.
I'LL TELL YOU... EVERYTHING.
IT'S TOO LATE.

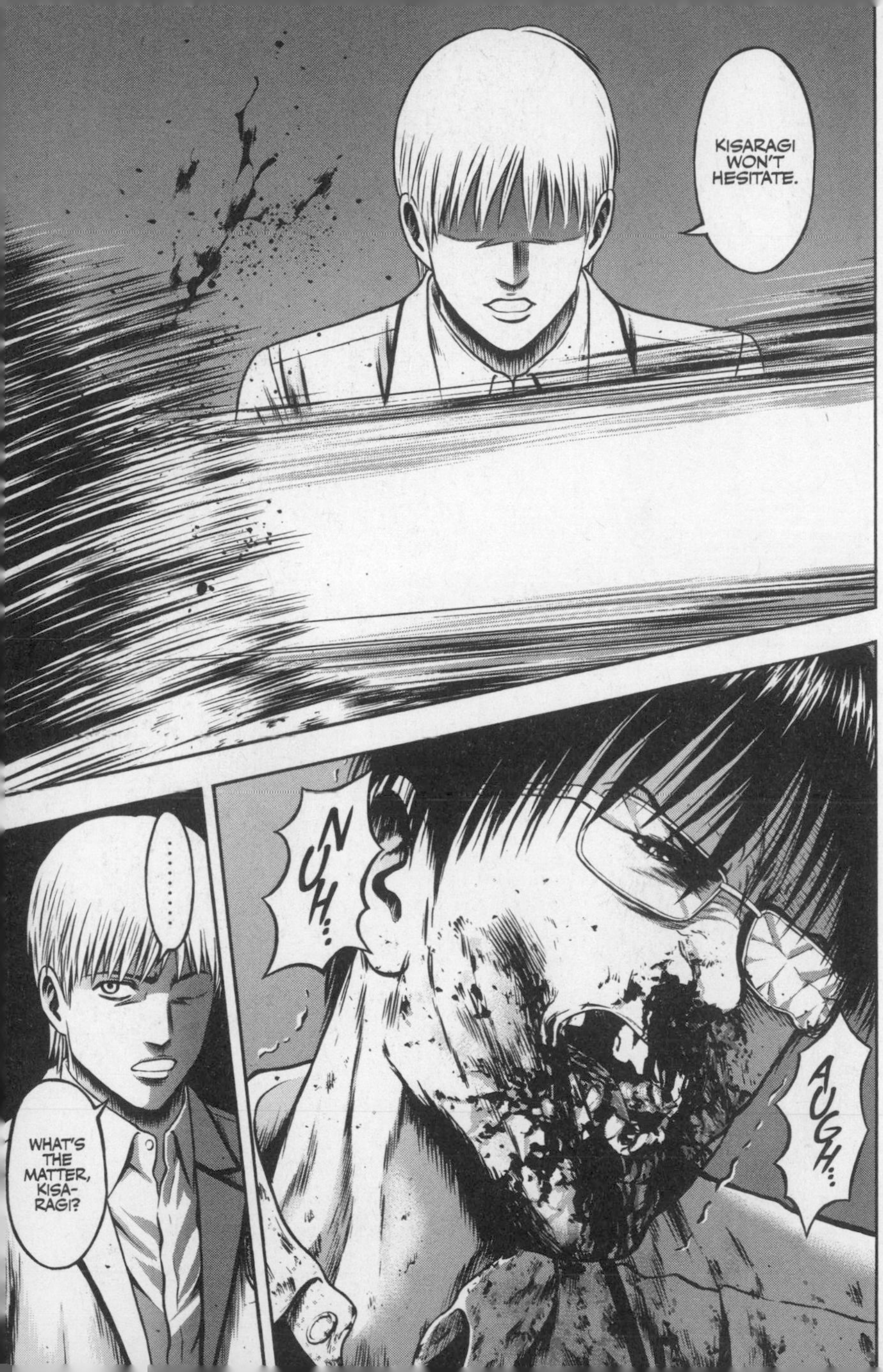
KISARAGI WON'T HESITATE.
NUH...!!
AUGH...
......
WHAT'S THE MATTER, KISA-RAGI?

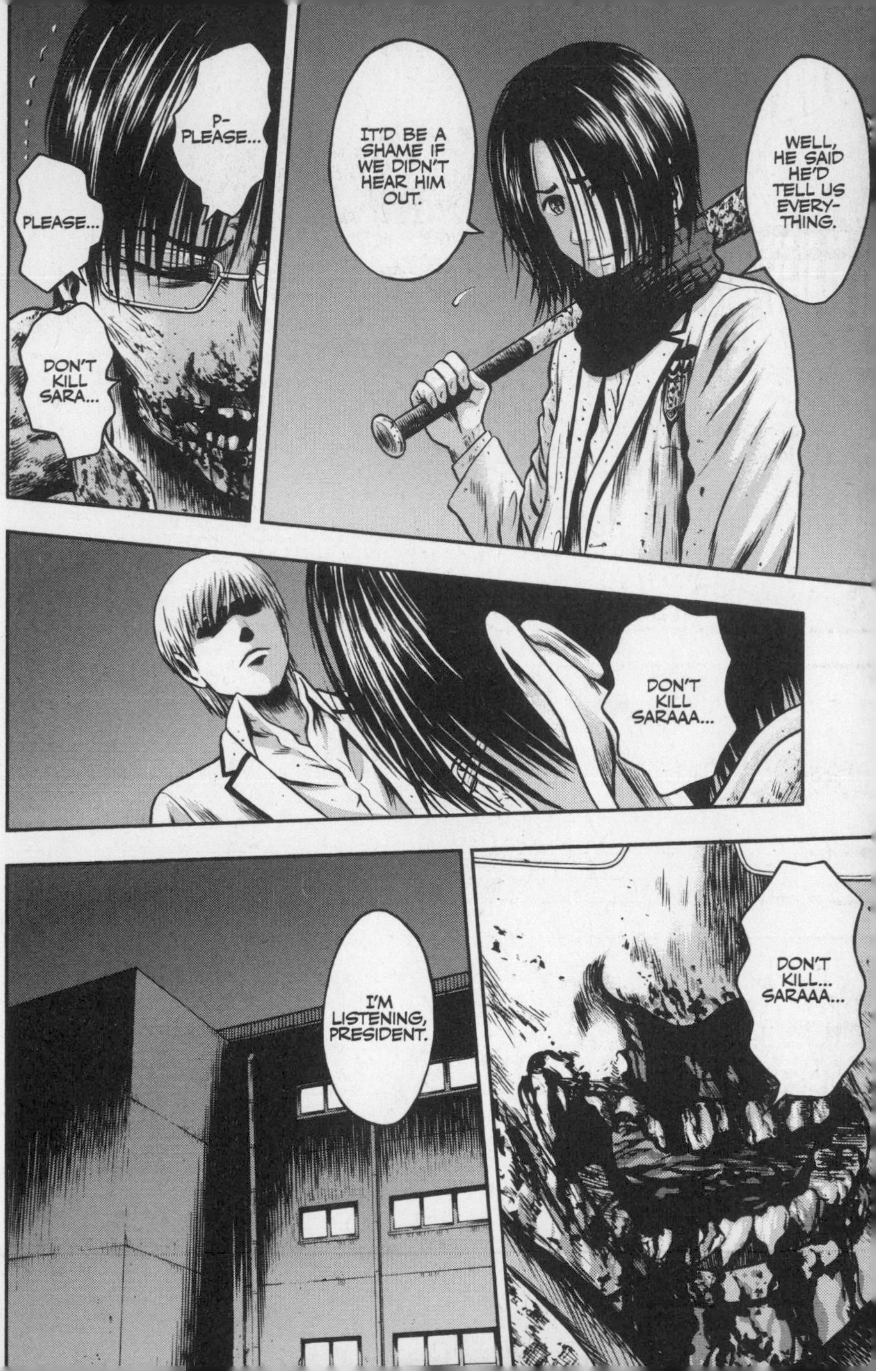
WELL, HE SAID HE'D TELL US EVERY-THING.
IT'D BE A SHAME IF WE DIDN'T HEAR HIM OUT.
P-PLEASE...
PLEASE...
DON'T KILL SARA...
DON'T KILL SARAAA...
DON'T KILL... SARAAA...
I'M LISTENING, PRESIDENT.

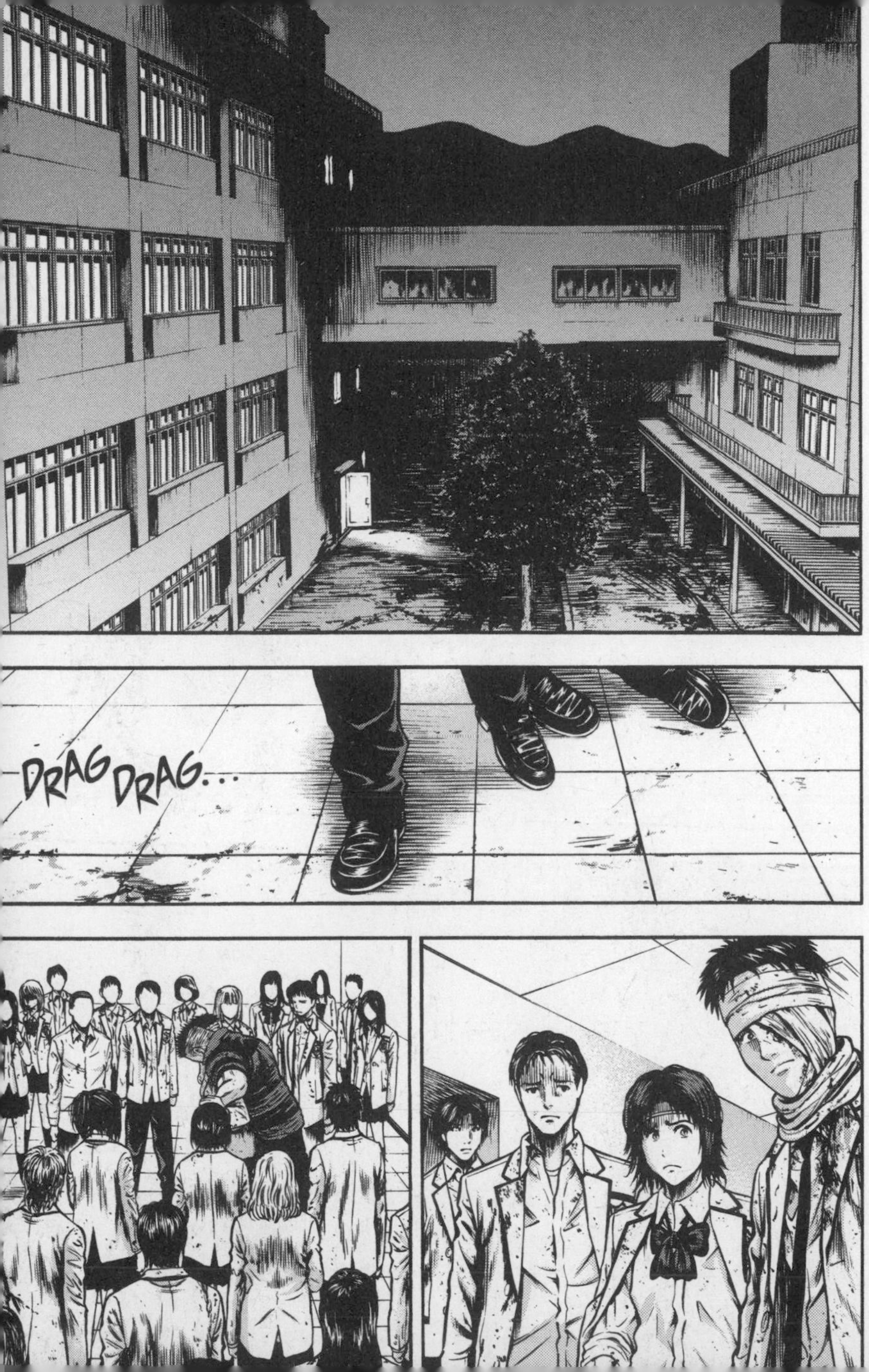
DRAG DRAG...

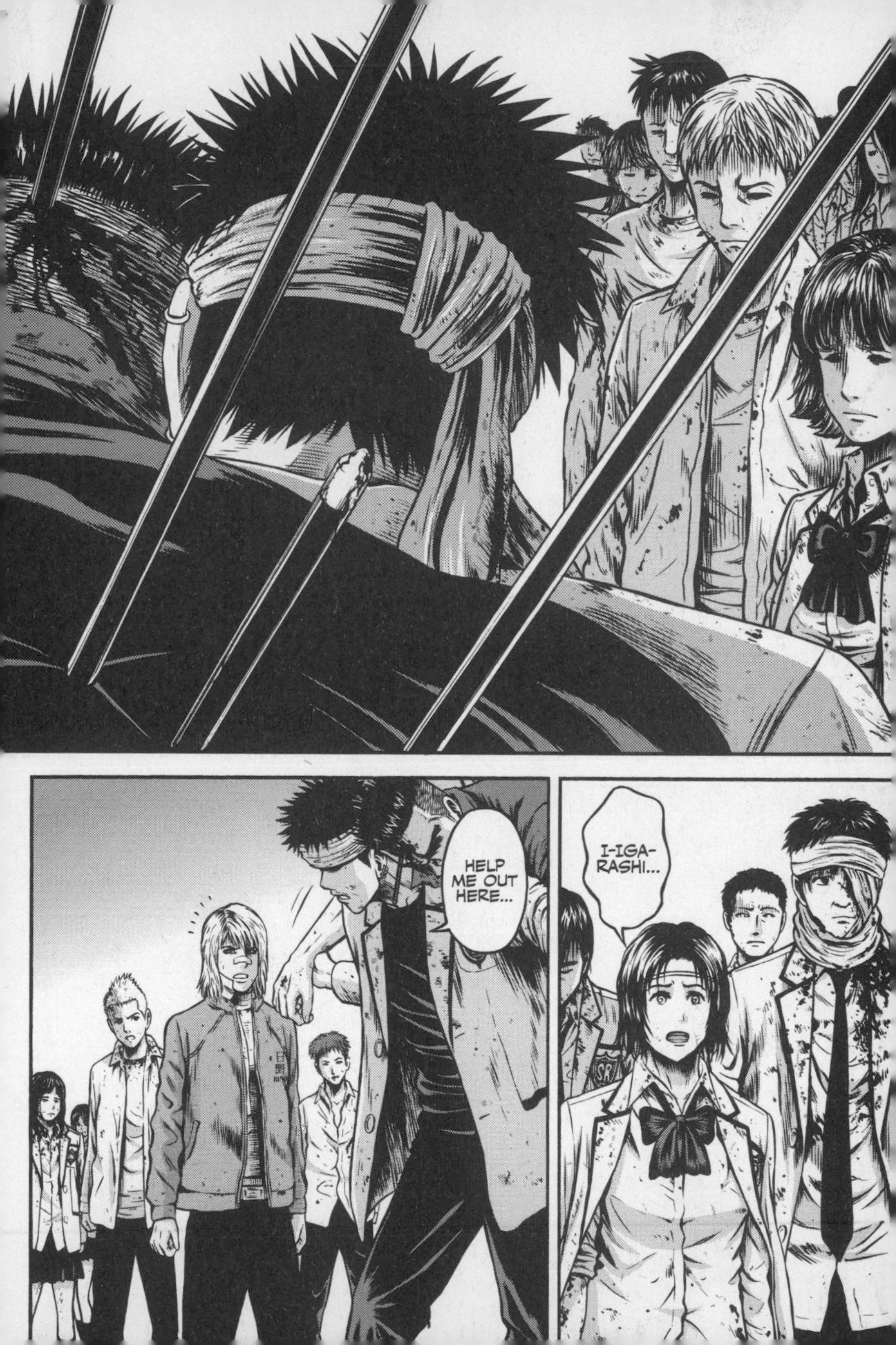
I-IGA-RASHI...
HELP ME OUT HERE...

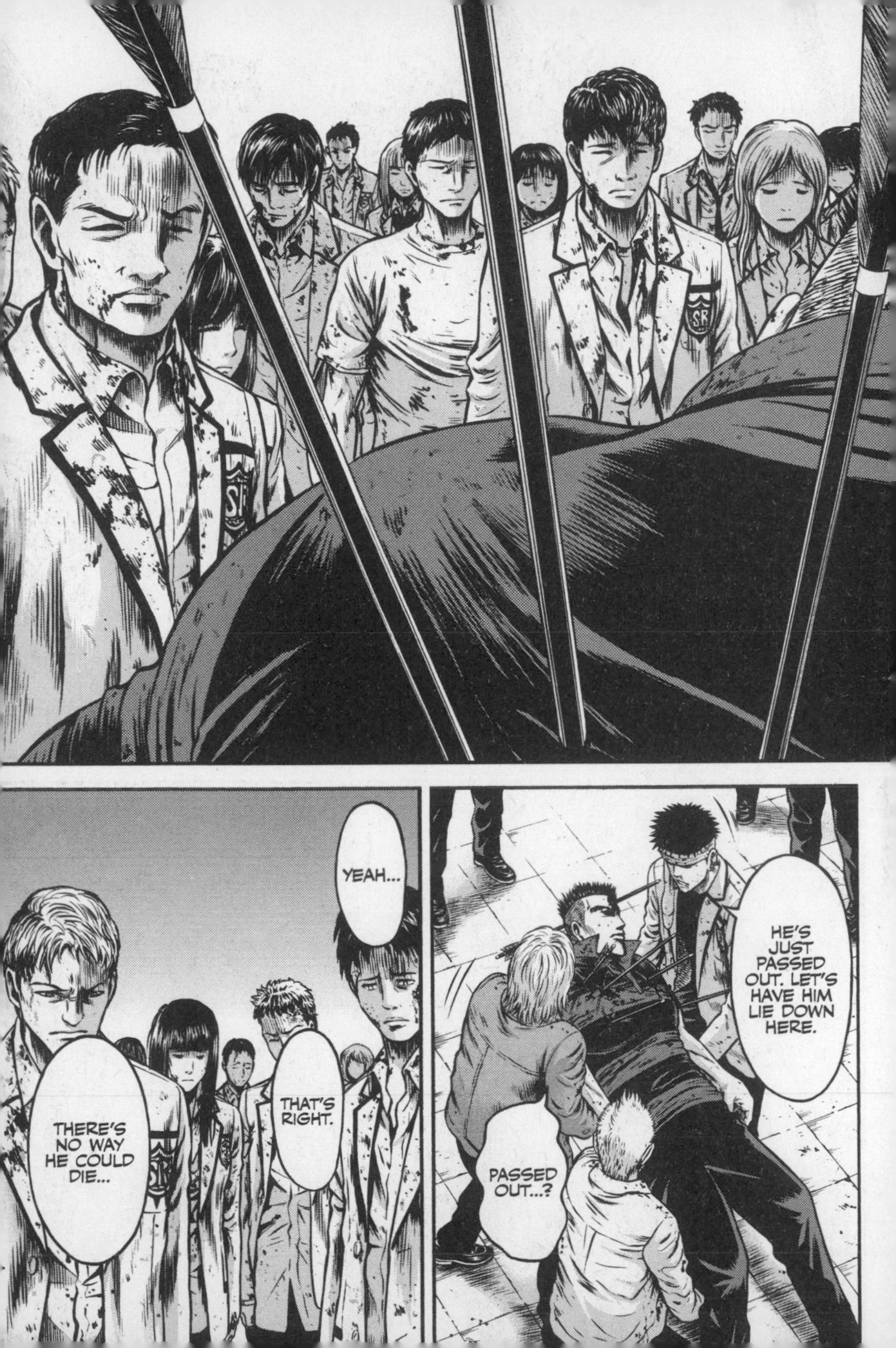
HE'S JUST PASSED OUT. LET'S HAVE HIM LIE DOWN HERE.
PASSED OUT...?
YEAH...
THAT'S RIGHT.
THERE'S NO WAY HE COULD DIE...

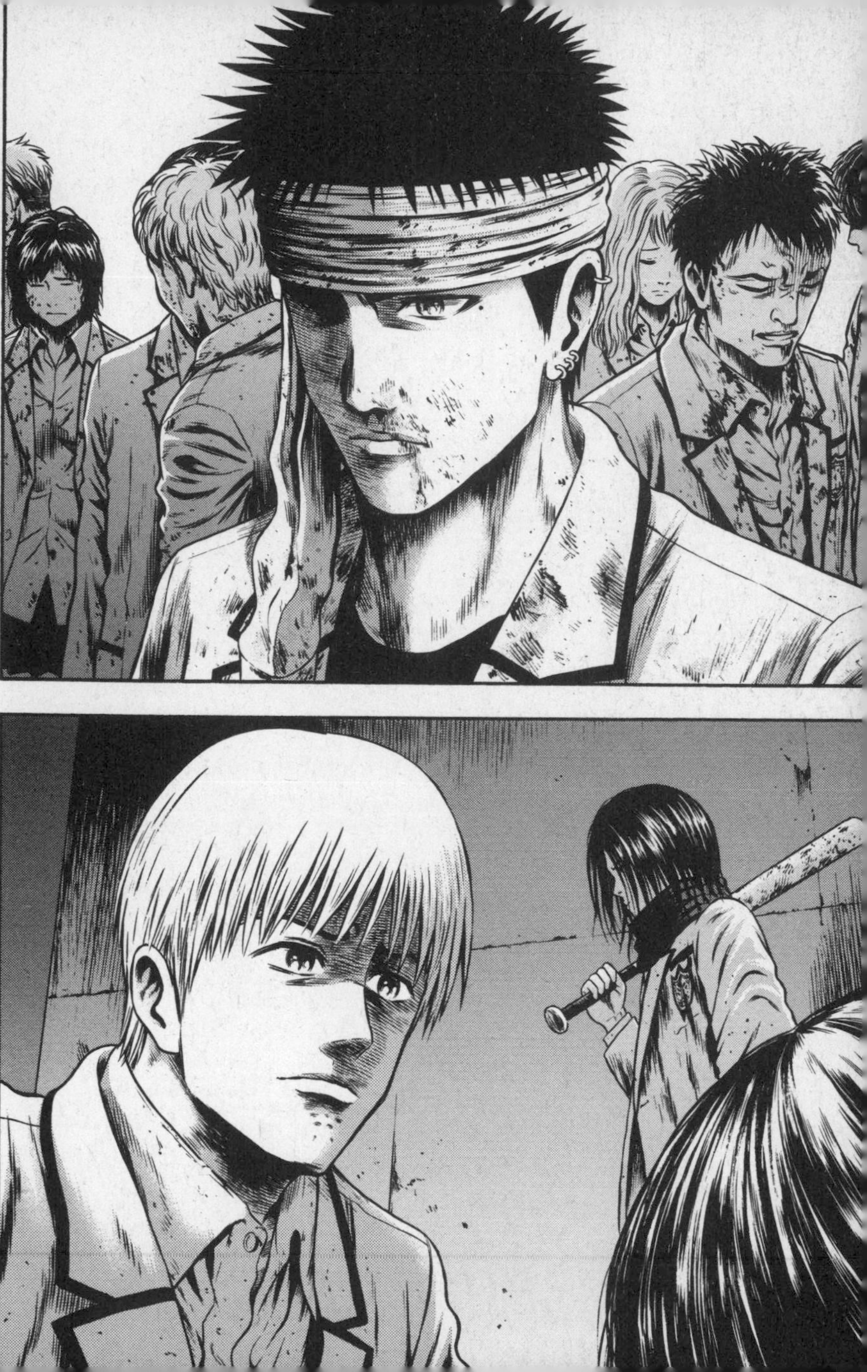

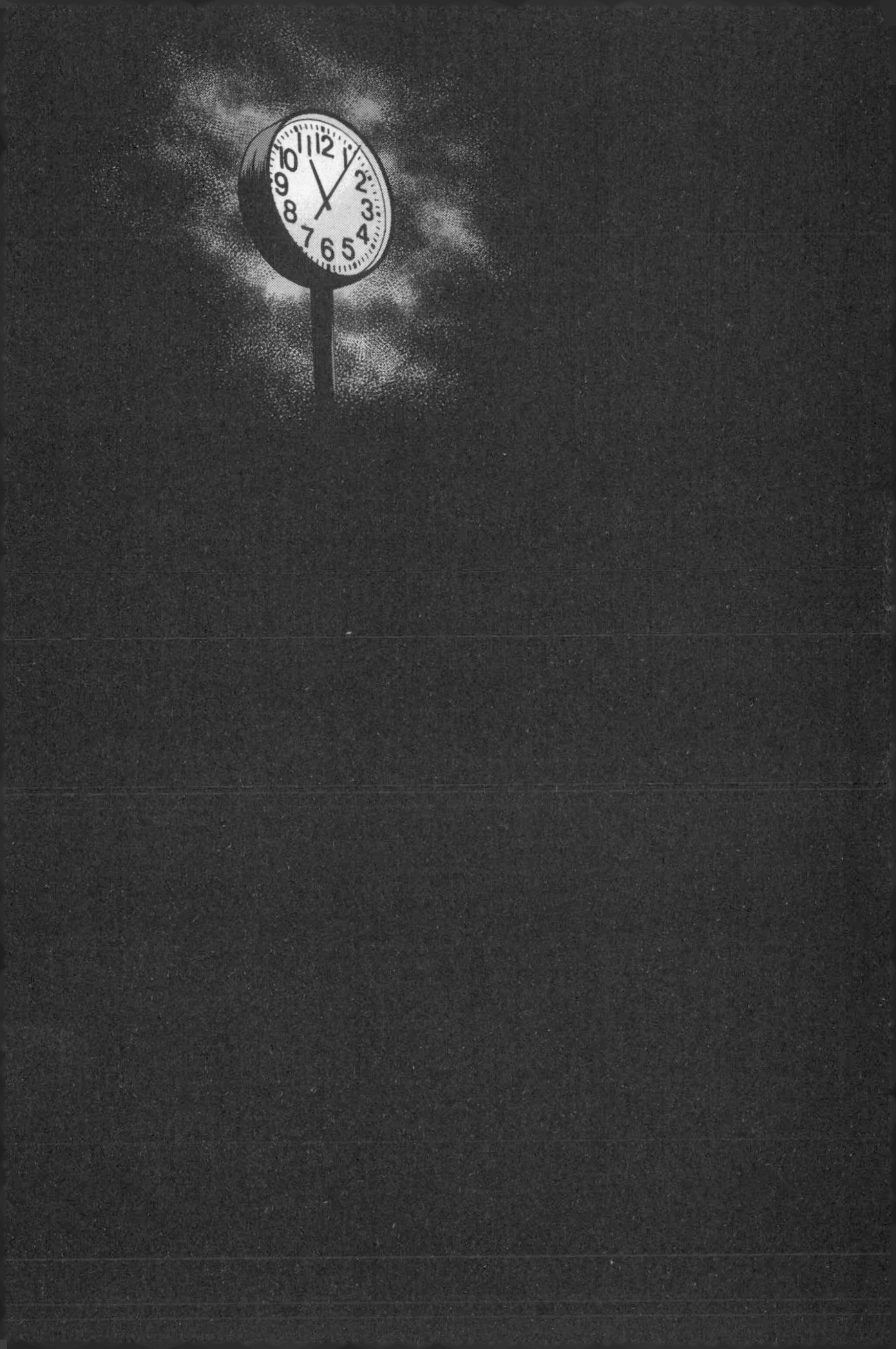

HOUR OF THE ZOMBIE

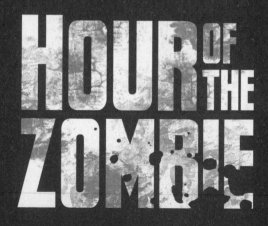

PHASE 35: Line of the Dead

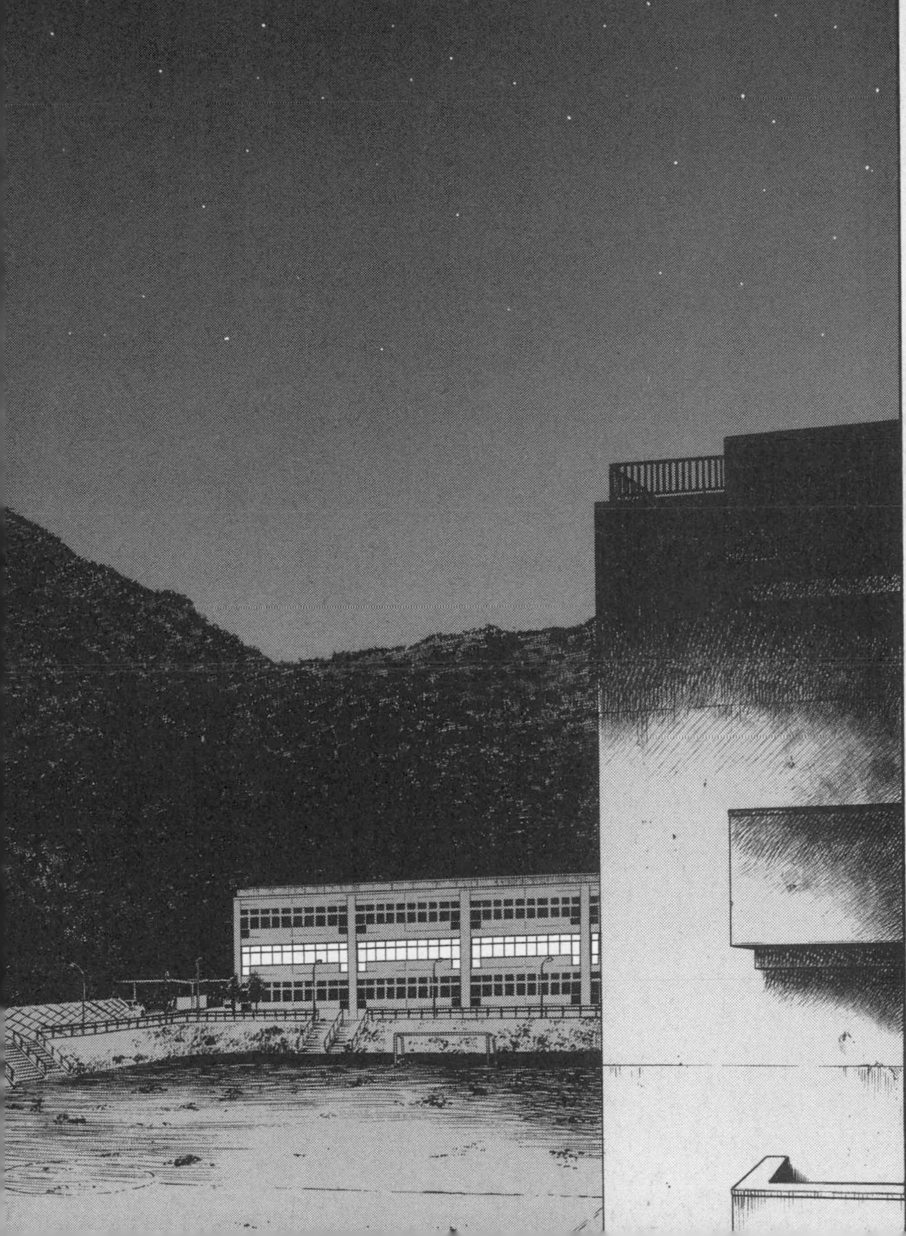

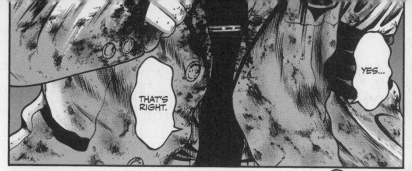

YES...

THAT'S RIGHT.

I MEAN IT...

ONLY USA, HIS GUYS, AND I KNEW ABOUT IT...

BELIEVE ME...

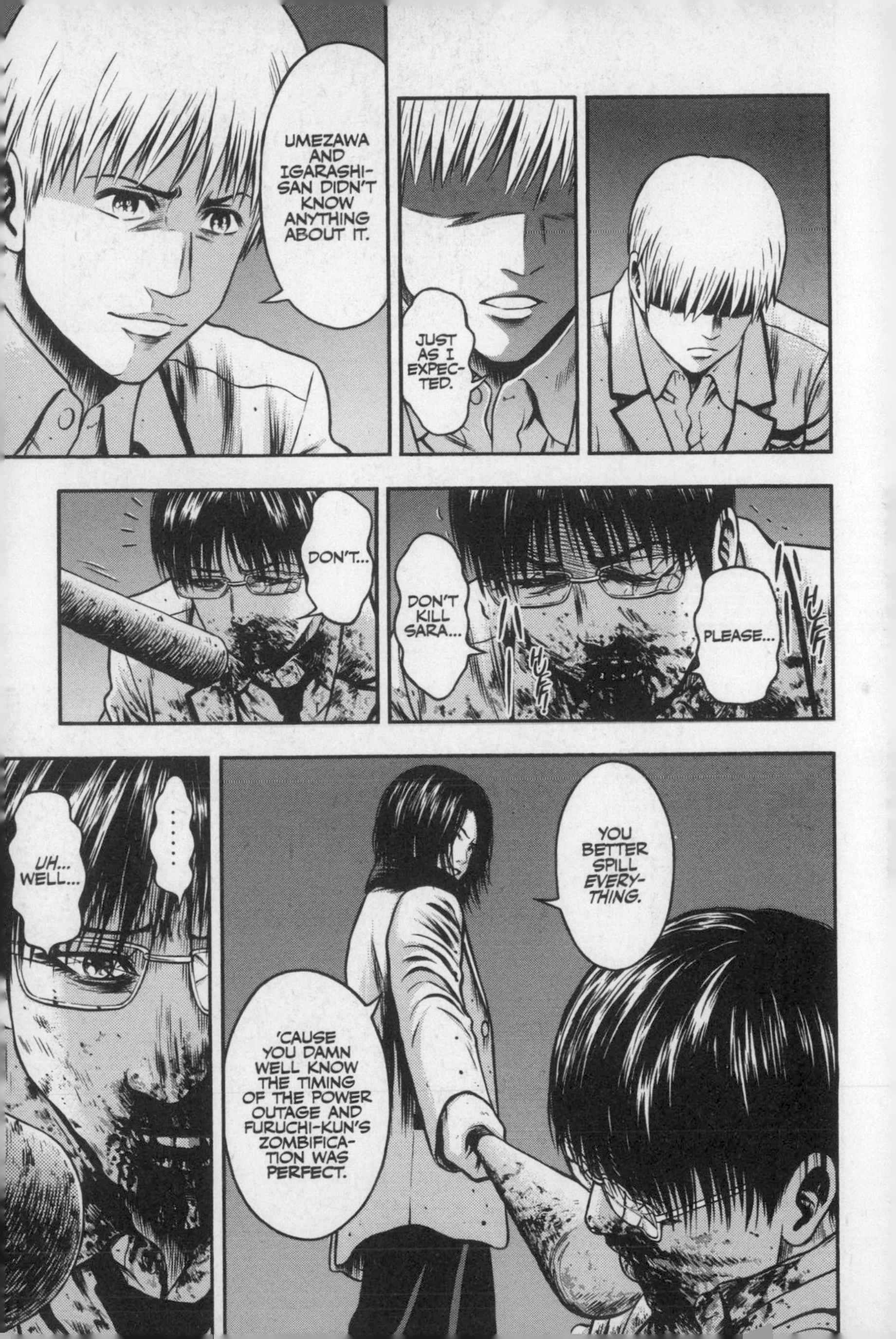

JUST AS I EXPECTED.
UMEZAWA AND IGARASHI-SAN DIDN'T KNOW ANYTHING ABOUT IT.
HUFF!
PLEASE...
DON'T KILL SARA...
HUFF!
DON'T...
YOU BETTER SPILL EVERYTHING.
'CAUSE YOU DAMN WELL KNOW THE TIMING OF THE POWER OUTAGE AND FURUCHI-KUN'S ZOMBIFICATION WAS PERFECT.
......
UH... WELL...

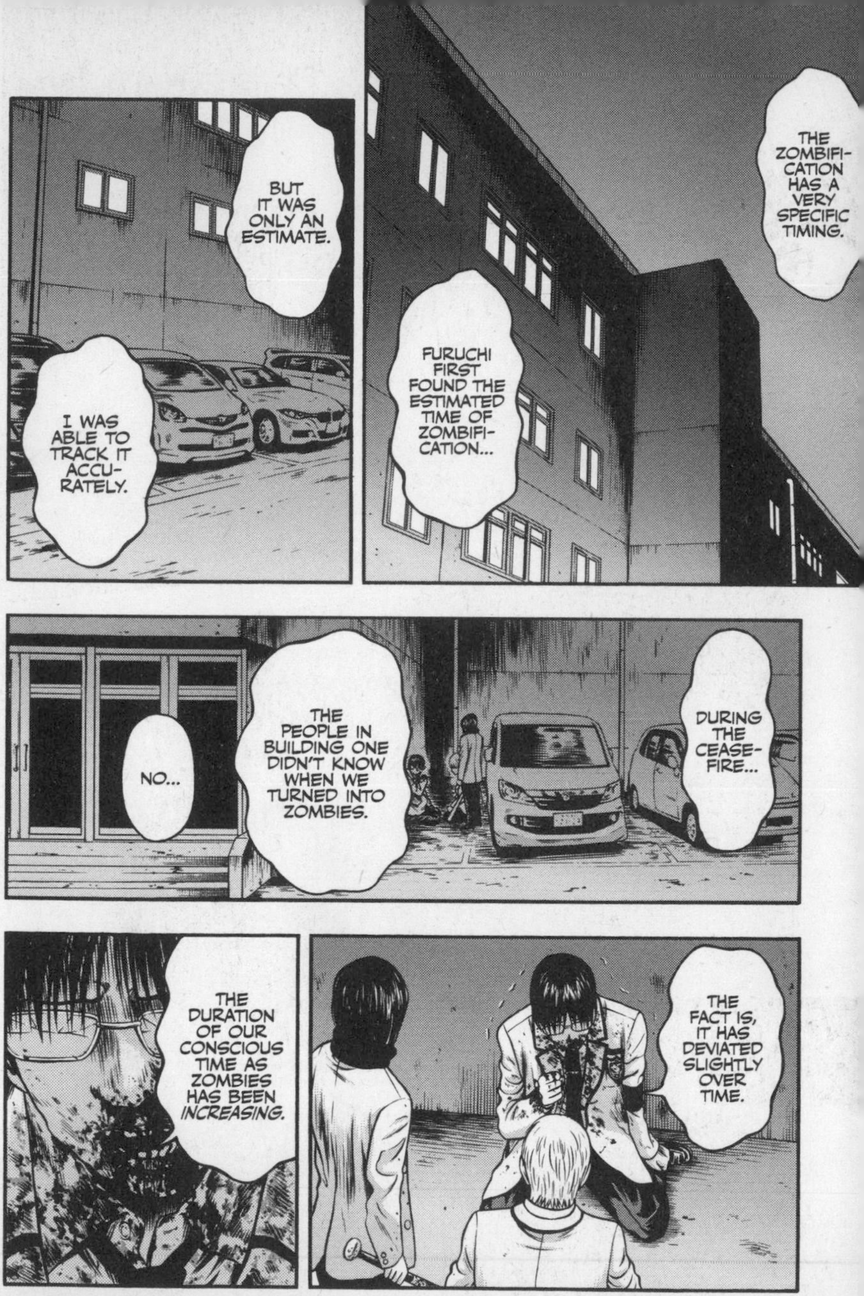
THE ZOMBIFICATION HAS A VERY SPECIFIC TIMING.
FURUCHI FIRST FOUND THE ESTIMATED TIME OF ZOMBIFICATION...
BUT IT WAS ONLY AN ESTIMATE.
I WAS ABLE TO TRACK IT ACCURATELY.
DURING THE CEASE-FIRE...
THE PEOPLE IN BUILDING ONE DIDN'T KNOW WHEN WE TURNED INTO ZOMBIES.
NO...
THE FACT IS, IT HAS DEVIATED SLIGHTLY OVER TIME.
THE DURATION OF OUR CONSCIOUS TIME AS ZOMBIES HAS BEEN *INCREASING.*

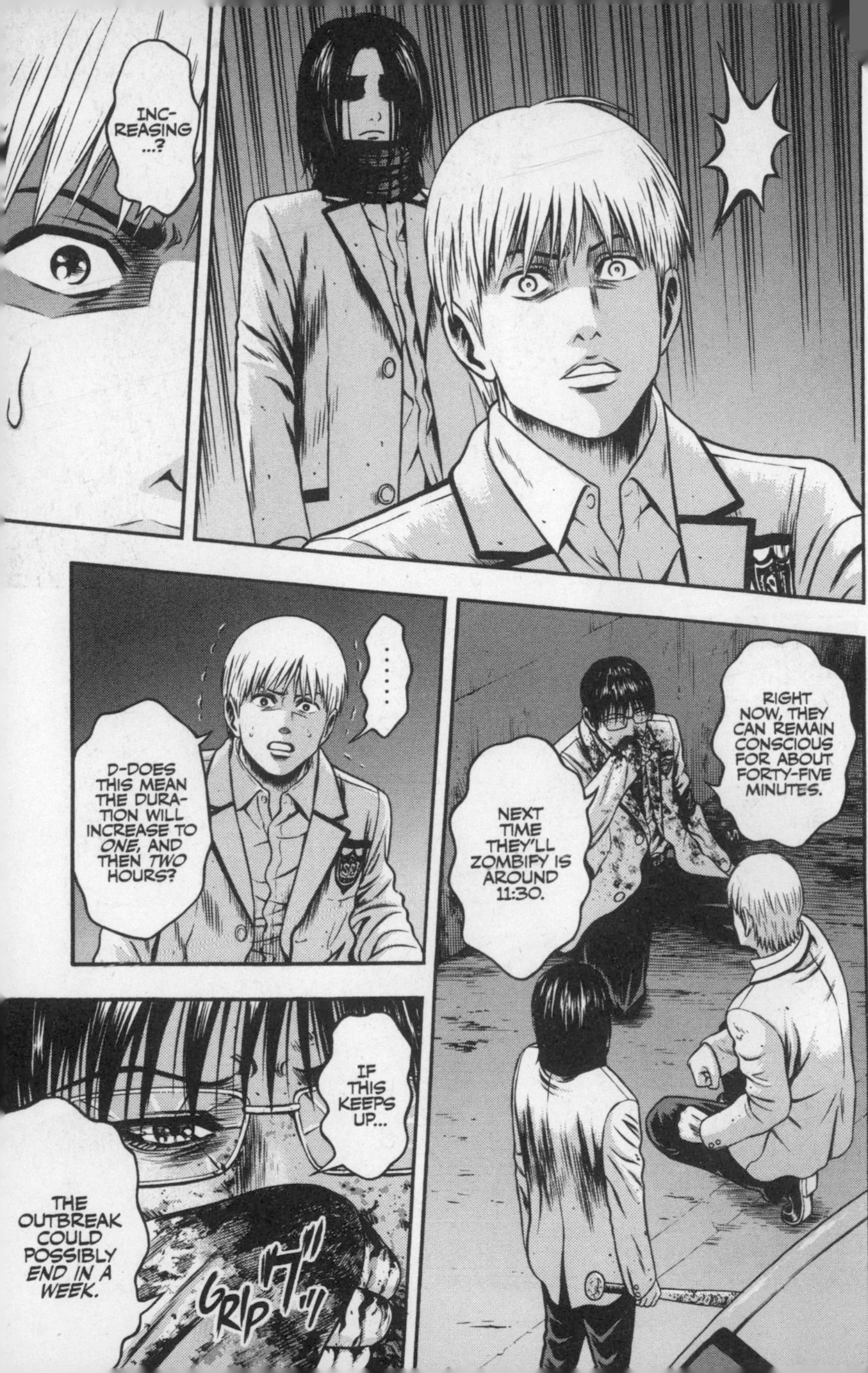
INC-
REASING
...?
RIGHT NOW, THEY CAN REMAIN CONSCIOUS FOR ABOUT FORTY-FIVE MINUTES.
NEXT TIME THEY'LL ZOMBIFY IS AROUND 11:30.
......
D-DOES THIS MEAN THE DURATION WILL INCREASE TO *ONE*, AND THEN *TWO* HOURS?
IF THIS KEEPS UP...
THE OUTBREAK COULD POSSIBLY *END IN A WEEK.*
GRIP

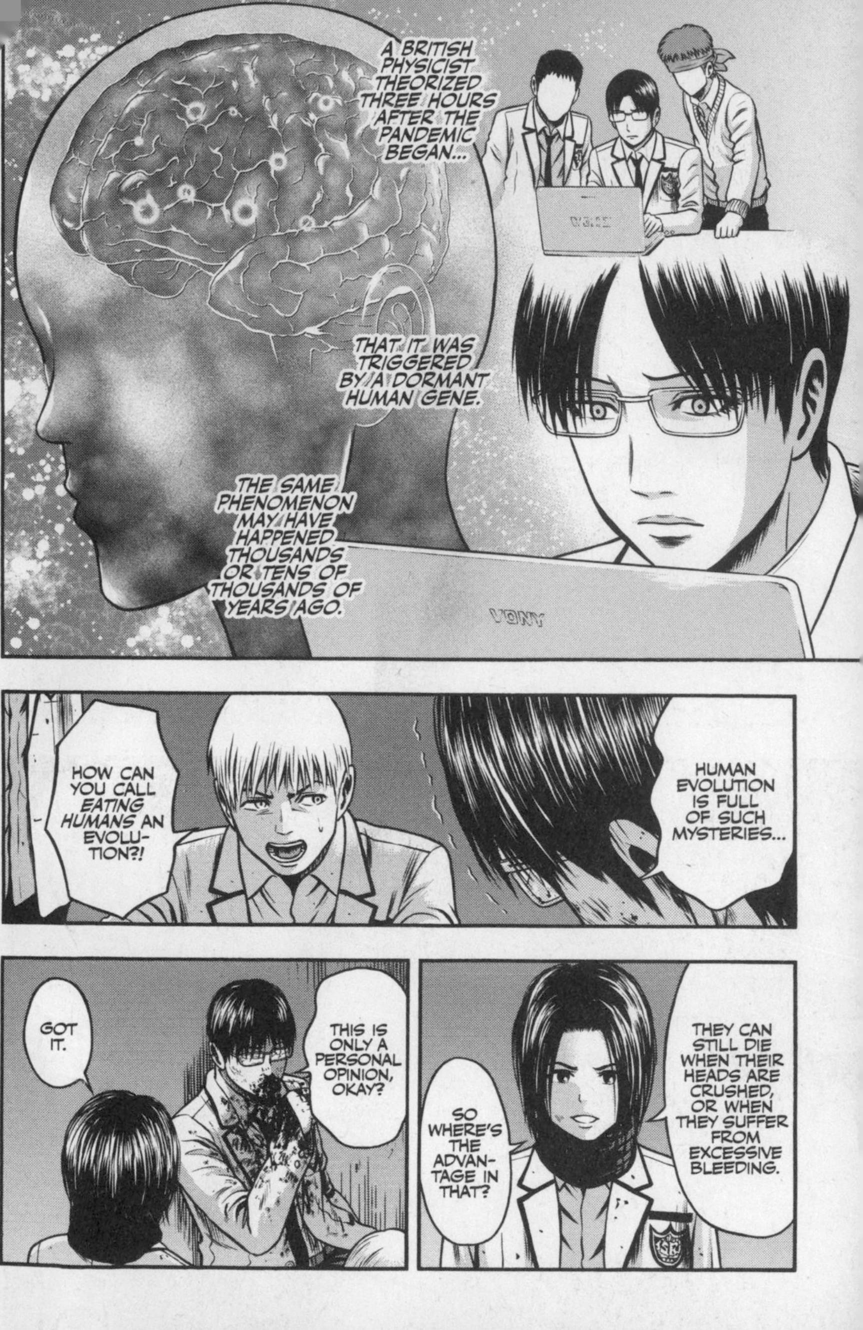
A BRITISH PHYSICIST THEORIZED THREE HOURS AFTER THE PANDEMIC BEGAN...
THAT IT WAS TRIGGERED BY A DORMANT HUMAN GENE.
THE SAME PHENOMENON MAY HAVE HAPPENED THOUSANDS OR TENS OF THOUSANDS OF YEARS AGO.
HUMAN EVOLUTION IS FULL OF SUCH MYSTERIES...
HOW CAN YOU CALL EATING HUMANS AN EVOLUTION?!
THEY CAN STILL DIE WHEN THEIR HEADS ARE CRUSHED, OR WHEN THEY SUFFER FROM EXCESSIVE BLEEDING.
SO WHERE'S THE ADVANTAGE IN THAT?
THIS IS ONLY A PERSONAL OPINION, OKAY?
GOT IT.

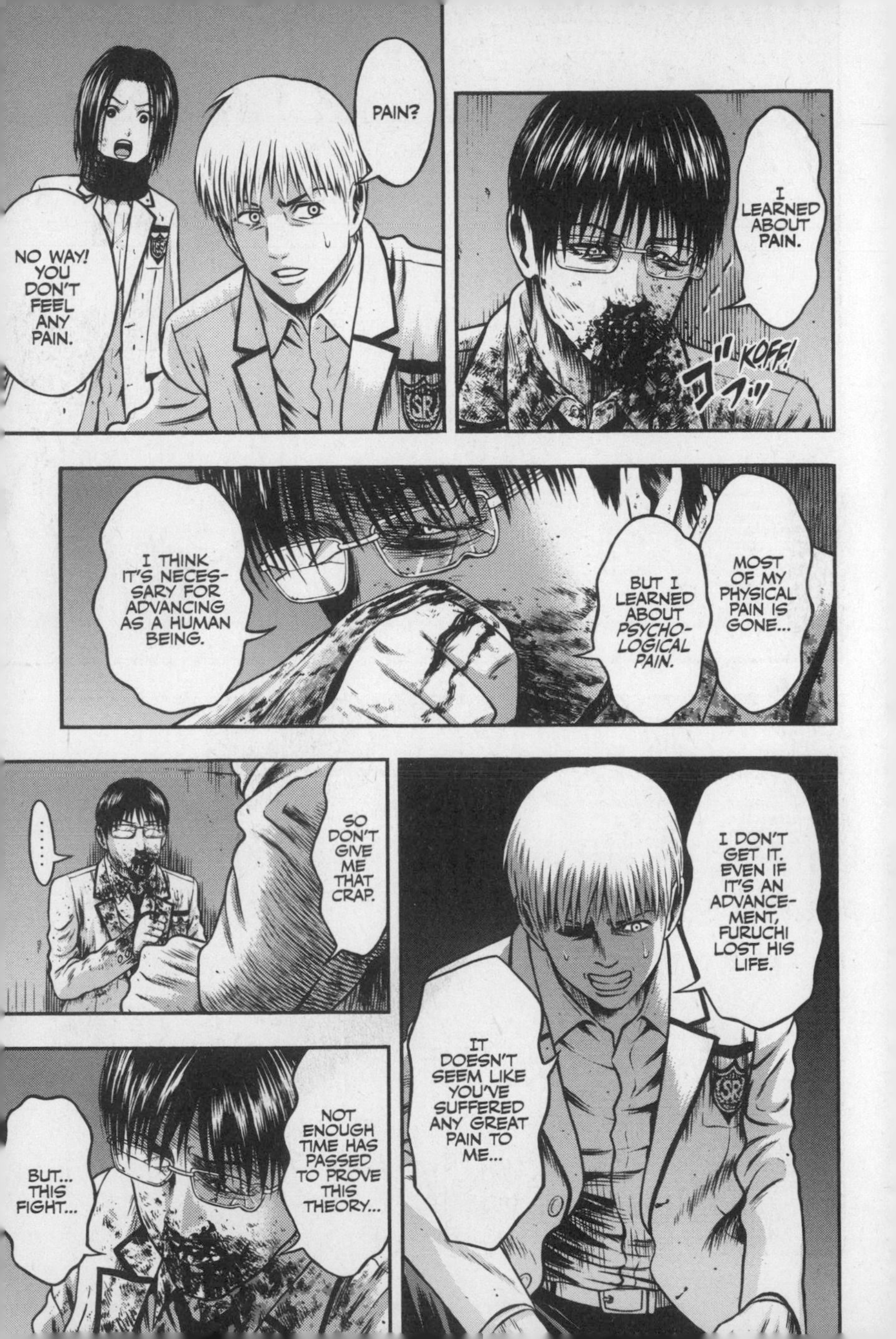
I LEARNED ABOUT PAIN.
KOFF!
ゴフッ
PAIN?
NO WAY! YOU DON'T FEEL ANY PAIN.
MOST OF MY PHYSICAL PAIN IS GONE...
BUT I LEARNED ABOUT PSYCHOLOGICAL PAIN.
I THINK IT'S NECESSARY FOR ADVANCING AS A HUMAN BEING.
I DON'T GET IT. EVEN IF IT'S AN ADVANCEMENT, FURUCHI LOST HIS LIFE.
IT DOESN'T SEEM LIKE YOU'VE SUFFERED ANY GREAT PAIN TO ME...
SO DON'T GIVE ME THAT CRAP.
......
NOT ENOUGH TIME HAS PASSED TO PROVE THIS THEORY...
BUT... THIS FIGHT...

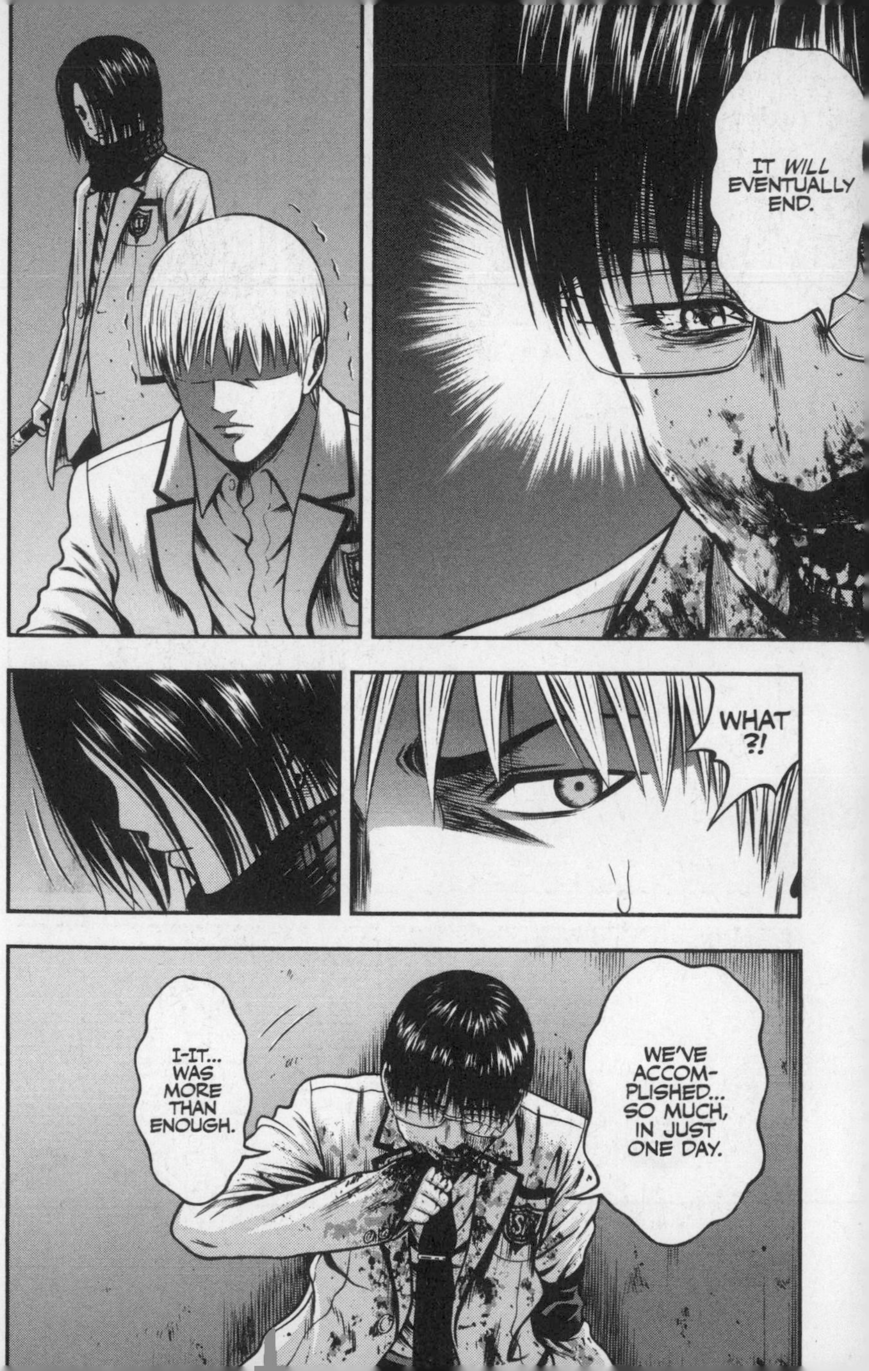
IT WILL EVENTUALLY END.
WHAT ?!
WE'VE ACCOMPLISHED... SO MUCH, IN JUST ONE DAY.
I-IT... WAS MORE THAN ENOUGH.

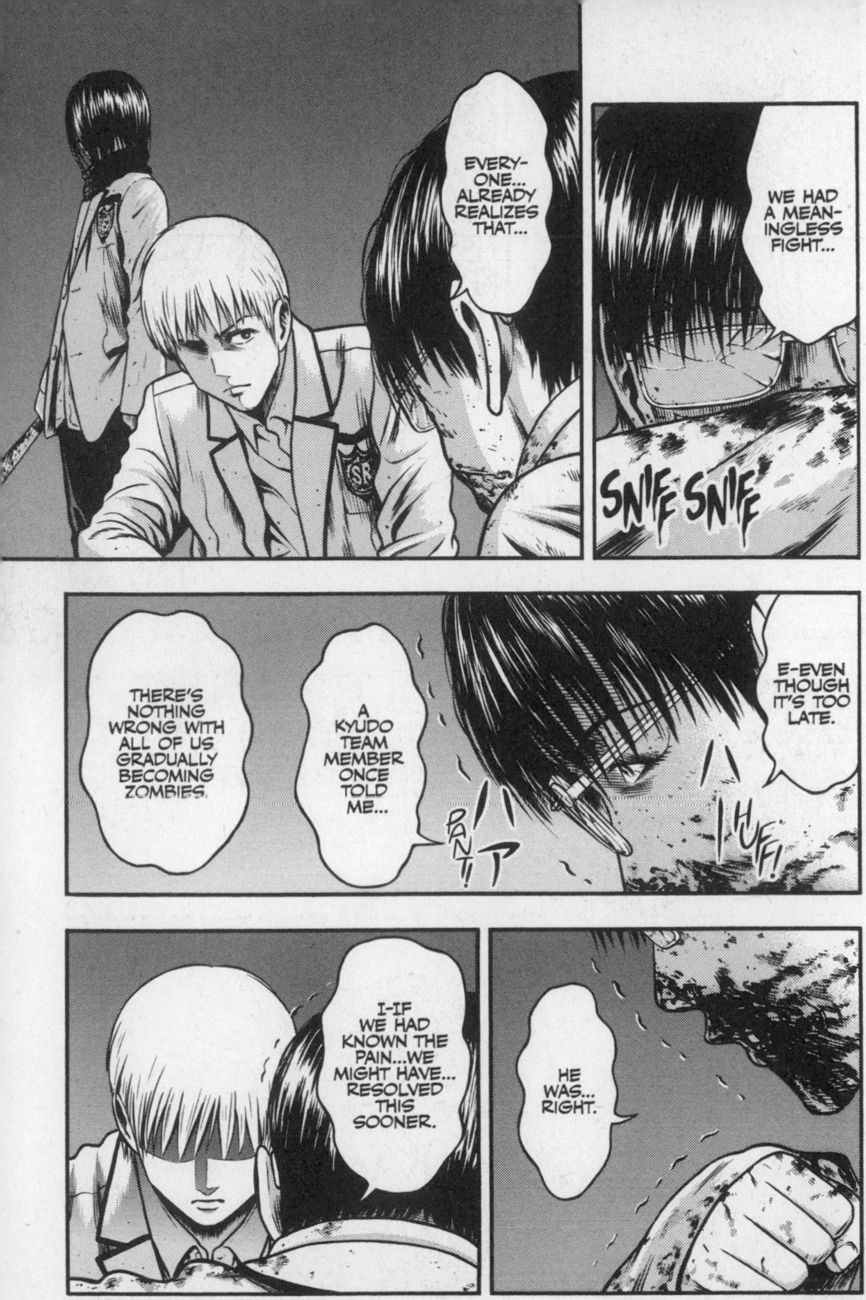
WE HAD A MEANINGLESS FIGHT...
SNIFF SNIFF
EVERYONE... ALREADY REALIZES THAT...
E-EVEN THOUGH IT'S TOO LATE.
HUFF!
PANT!
A KYUDO TEAM MEMBER ONCE TOLD ME...
THERE'S NOTHING WRONG WITH ALL OF US GRADUALLY BECOMING ZOMBIES.
HE WAS... RIGHT.
I-IF WE HAD KNOWN THE PAIN...WE MIGHT HAVE... RESOLVED THIS SOONER.

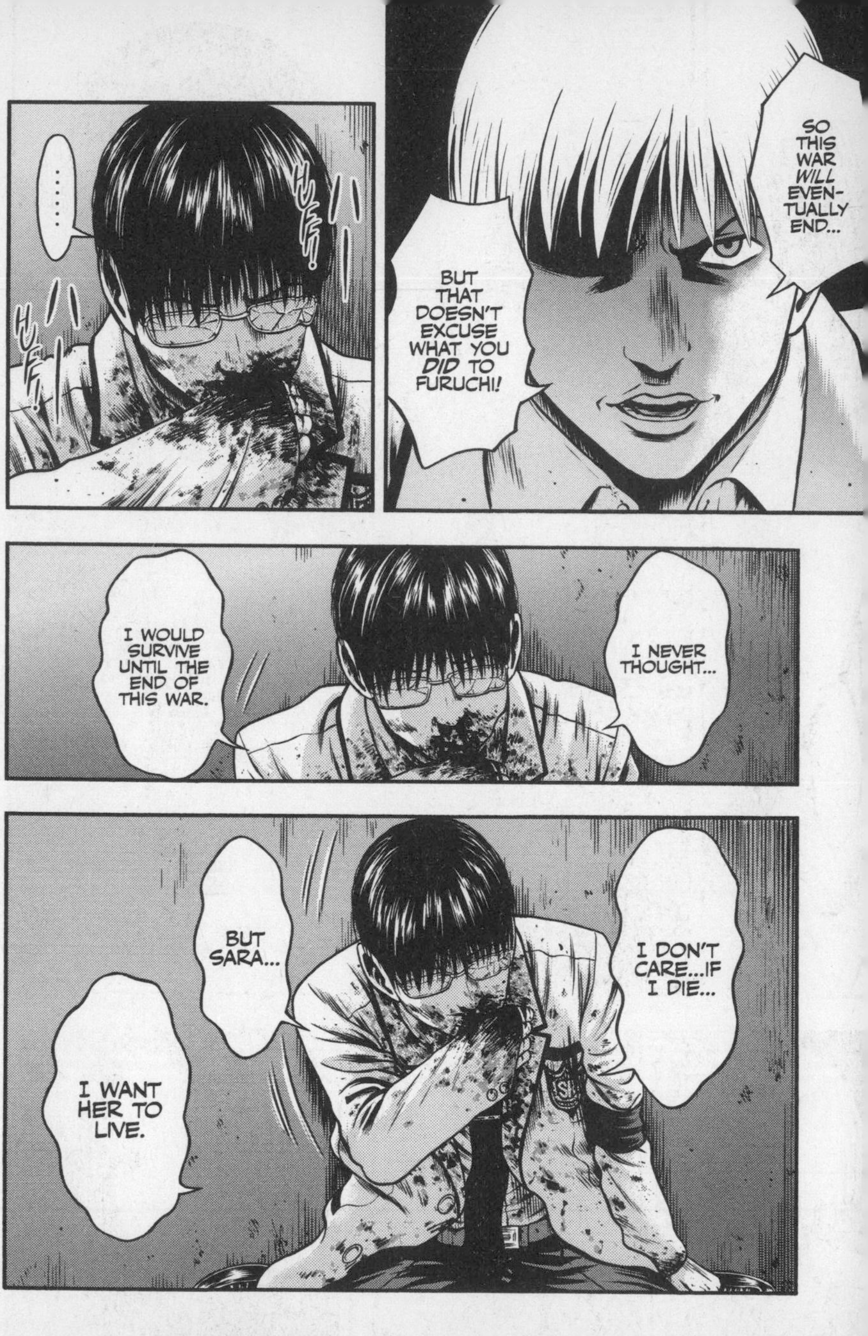
SO THIS WAR WILL EVENTUALLY END...
BUT THAT DOESN'T EXCUSE WHAT YOU DID TO FURUCHI!
......
HUFF!
HUFF!
I NEVER THOUGHT...
I WOULD SURVIVE UNTIL THE END OF THIS WAR.
I DON'T CARE...IF I DIE...
BUT SARA...
I WANT HER TO LIVE.

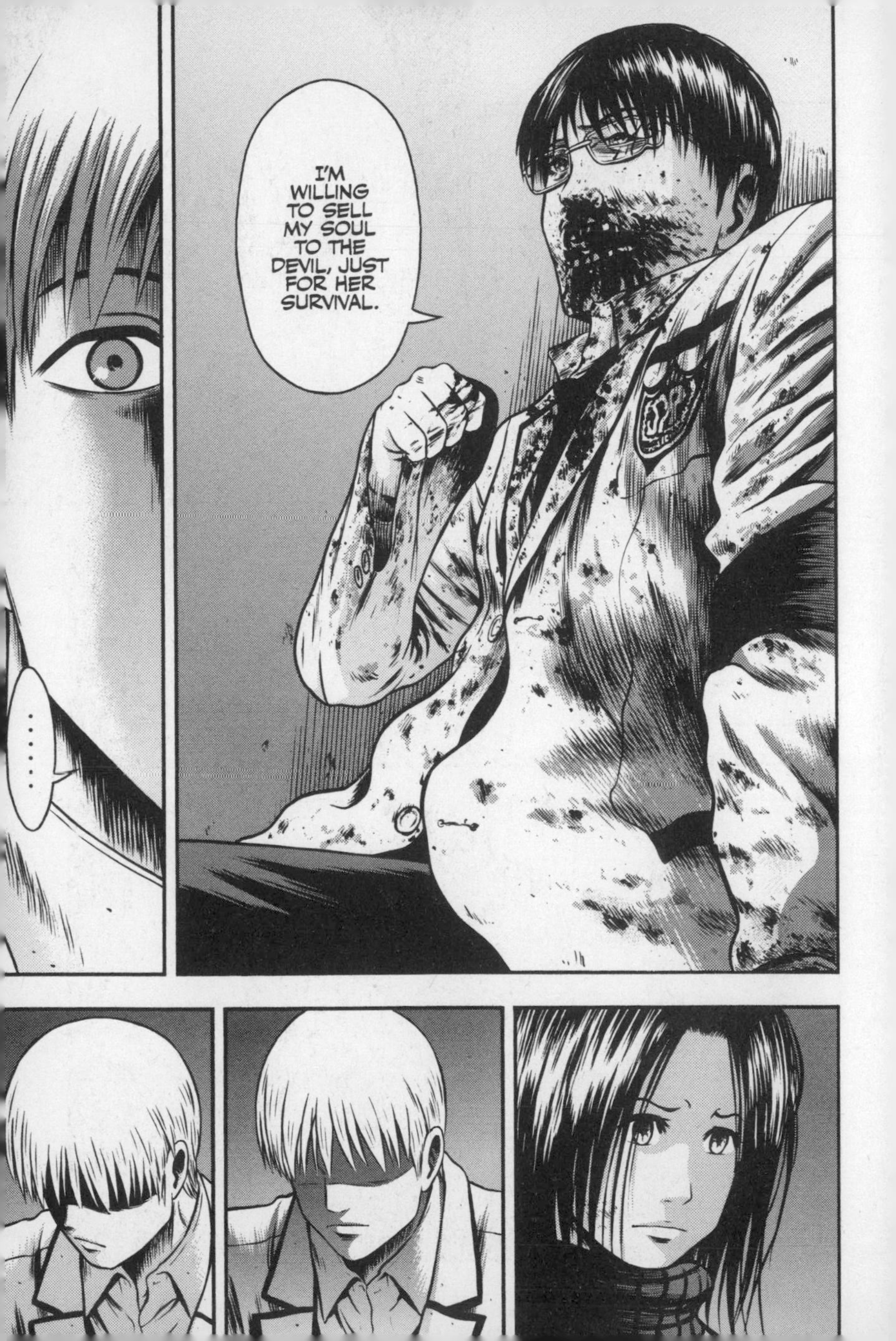
I'M WILLING TO SELL MY SOUL TO THE DEVIL, JUST FOR HER SURVIVAL.
......

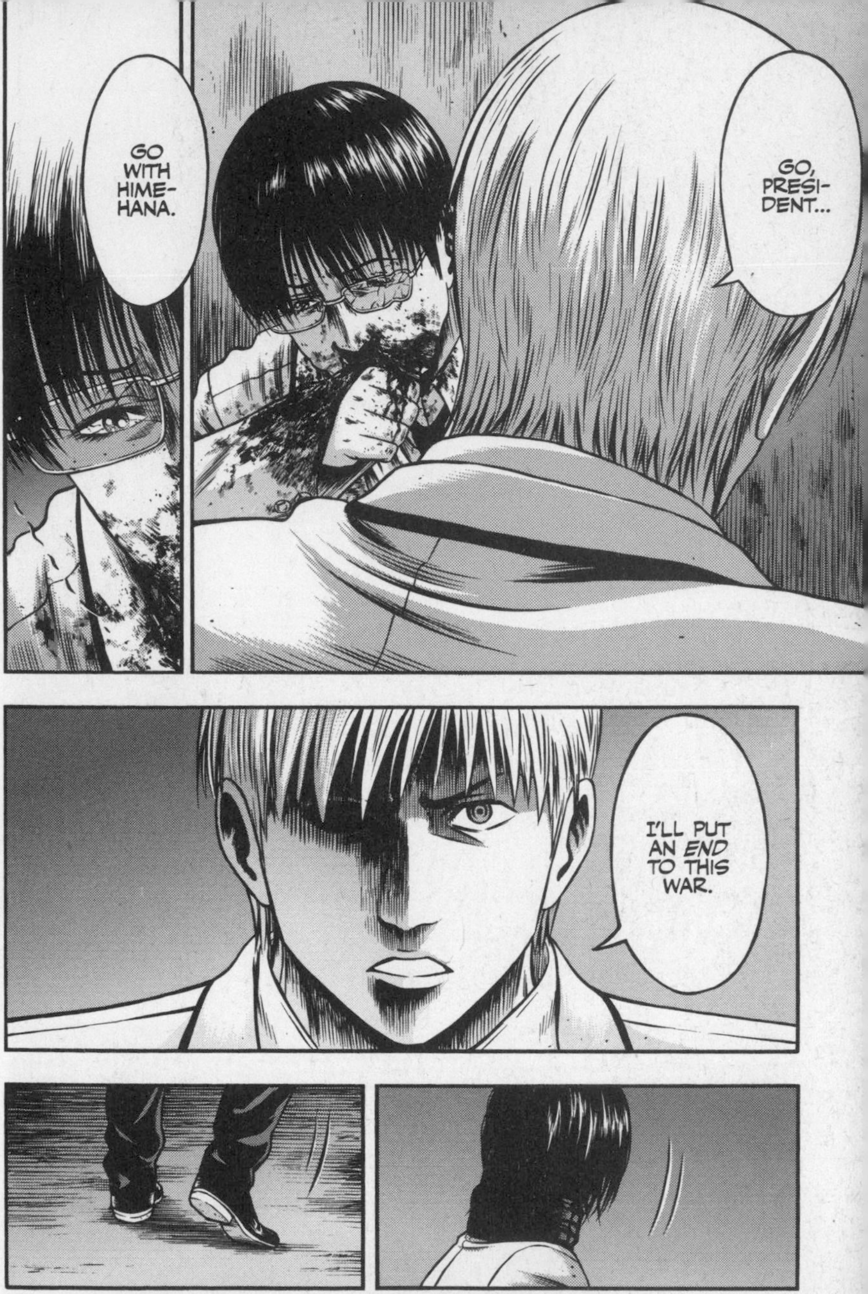
GO, PRESIDENT...
GO WITH HIMEHANA.
I'LL PUT AN *END* TO THIS WAR.

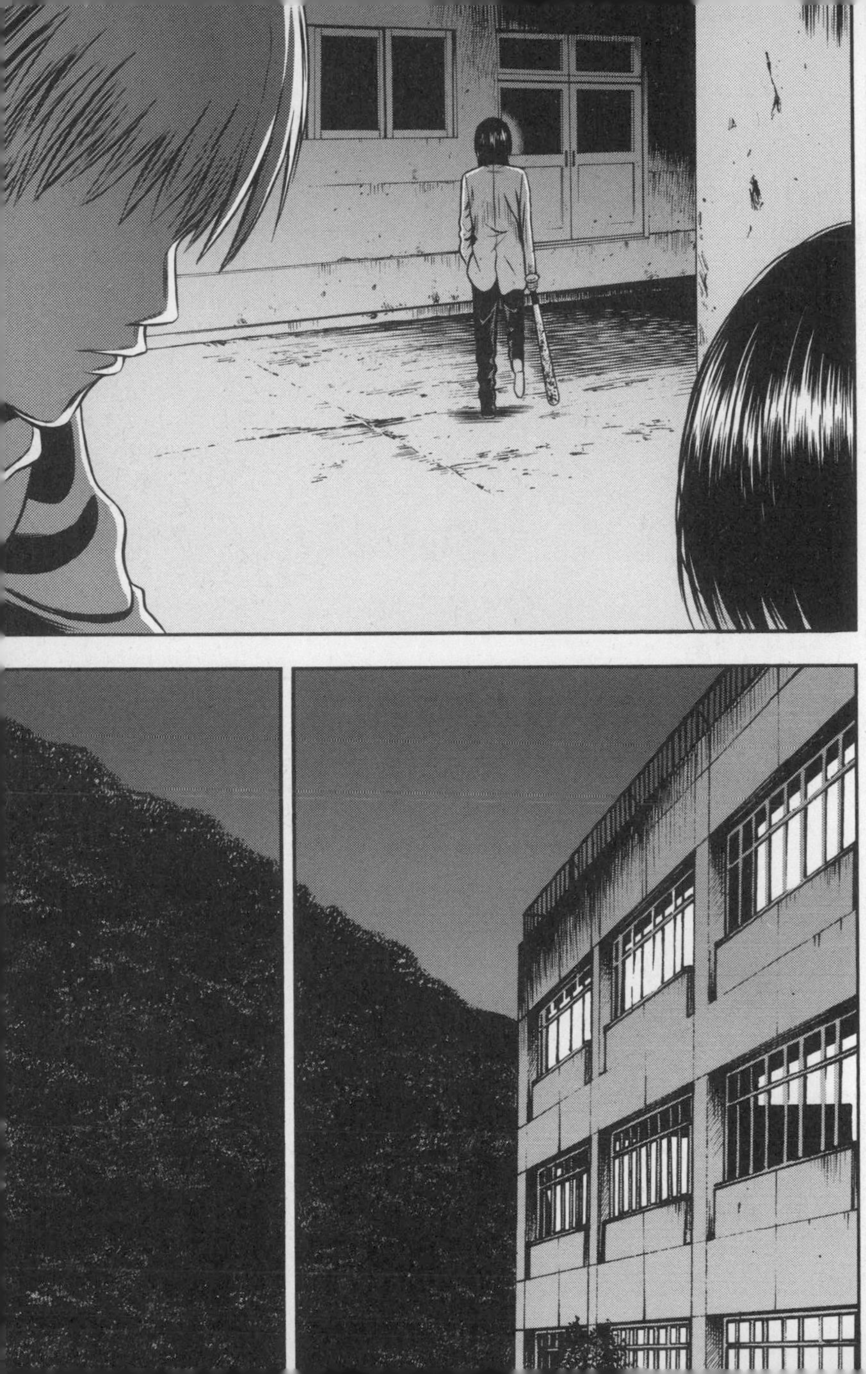

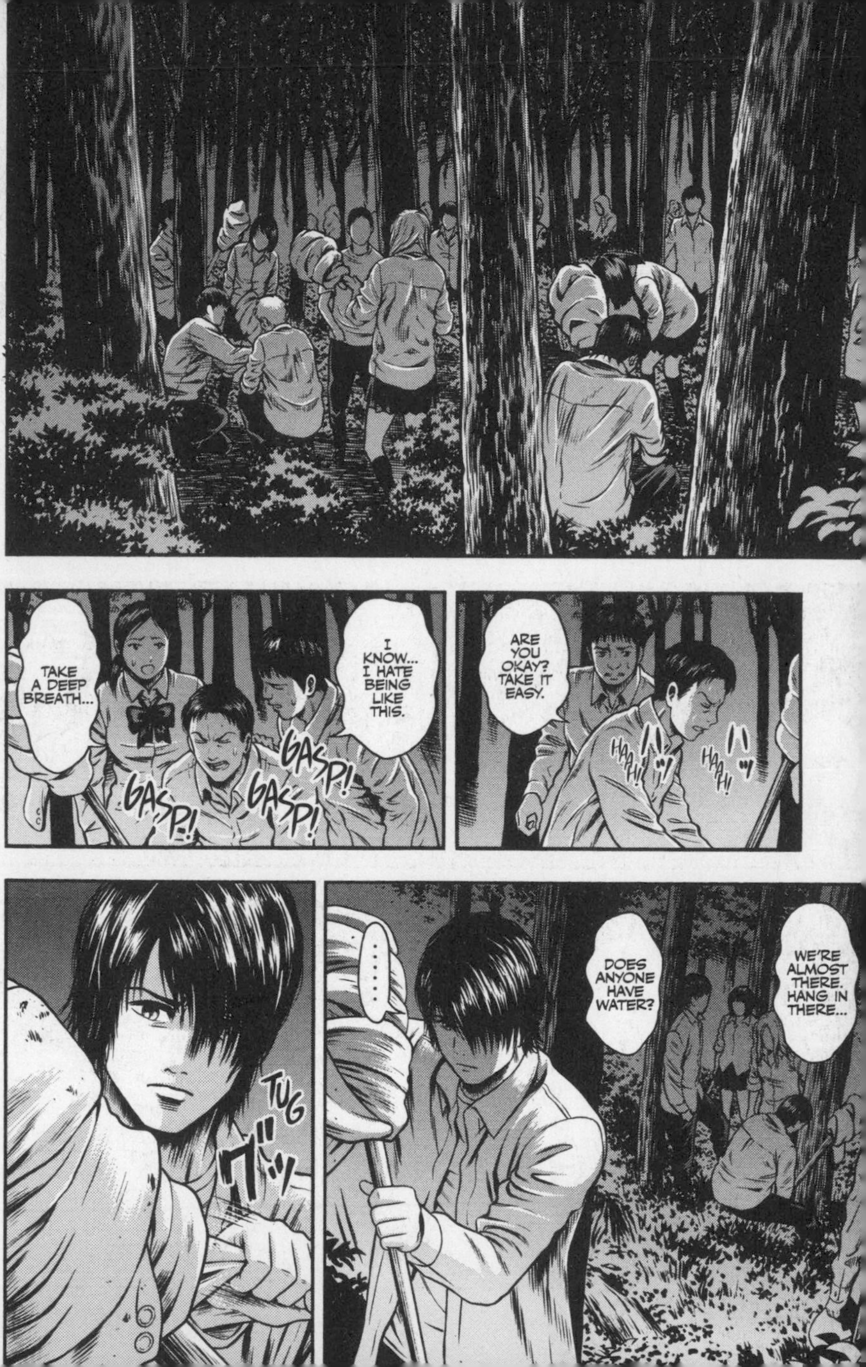
ARE YOU OKAY? TAKE IT EASY.
HAAH!
HAAH!
I KNOW... I HATE BEING LIKE THIS.
GASP!
GASP!
GASP!
TAKE A DEEP BREATH...
WE'RE ALMOST THERE. HANG IN THERE...
DOES ANYONE HAVE WATER?
......
TUG

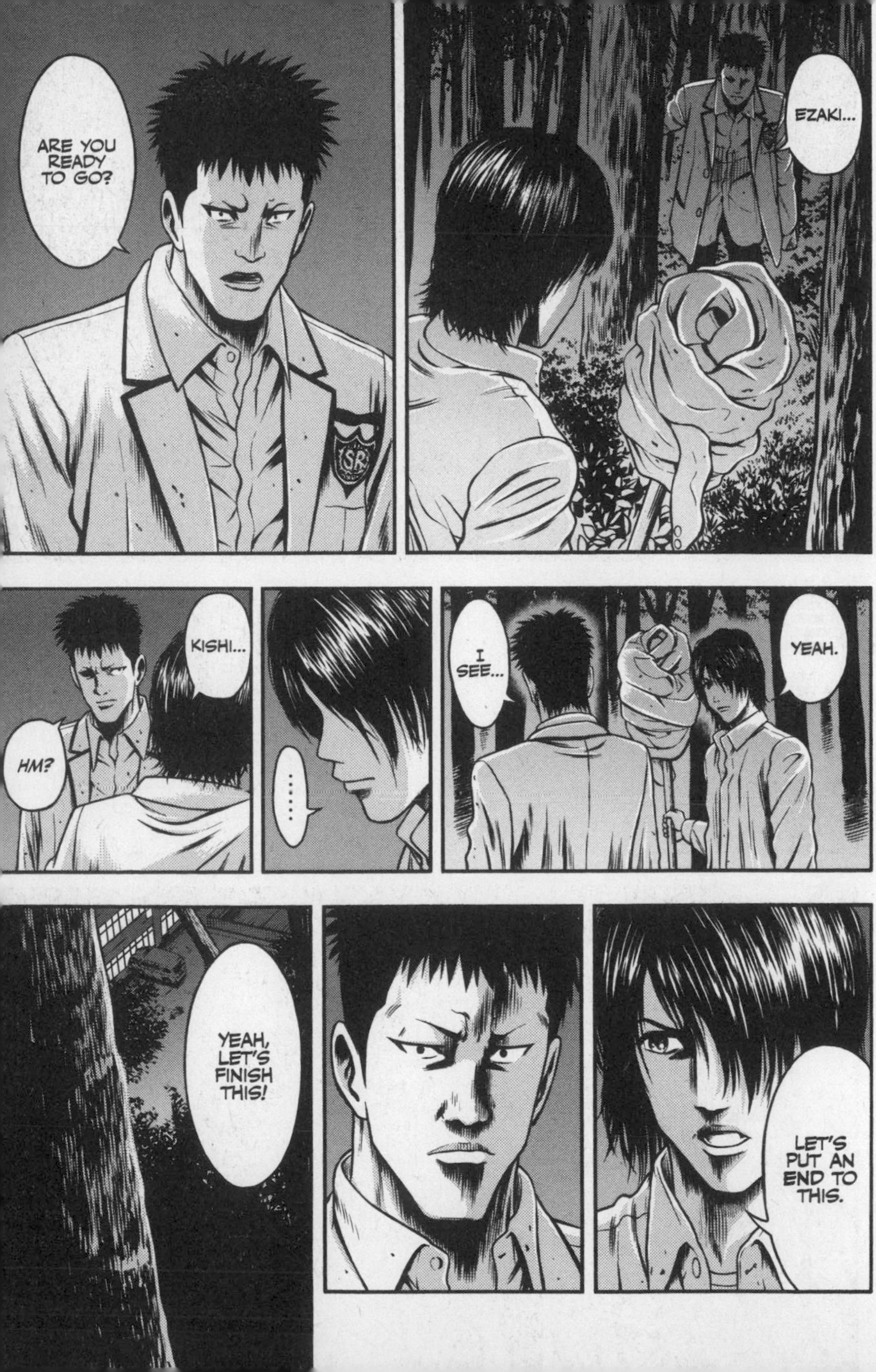
EZAKI...
ARE YOU READY TO GO?
YEAH.
I SEE...
......
KISHI...
HM?
LET'S PUT AN END TO THIS.
YEAH, LET'S FINISH THIS!

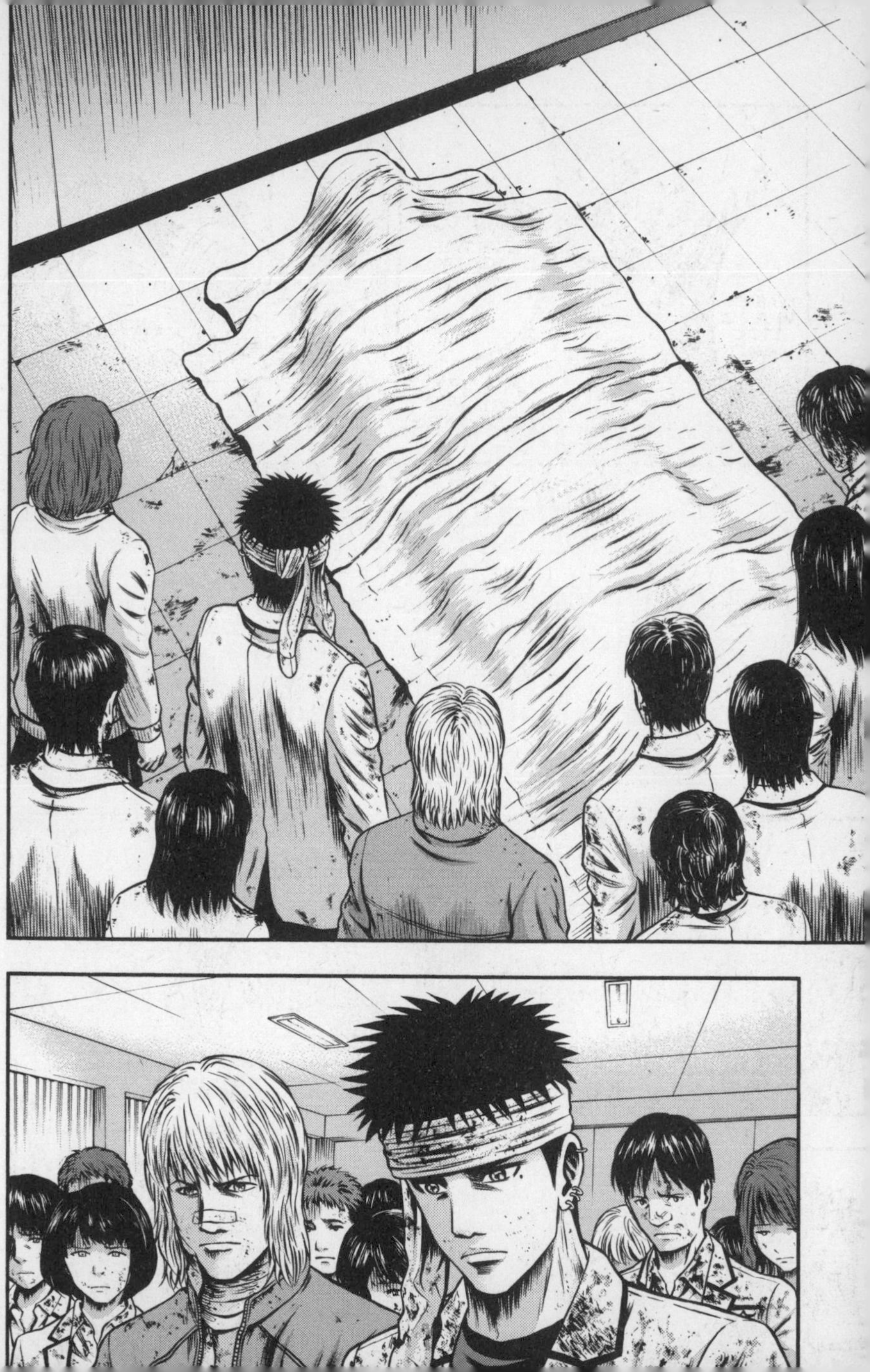

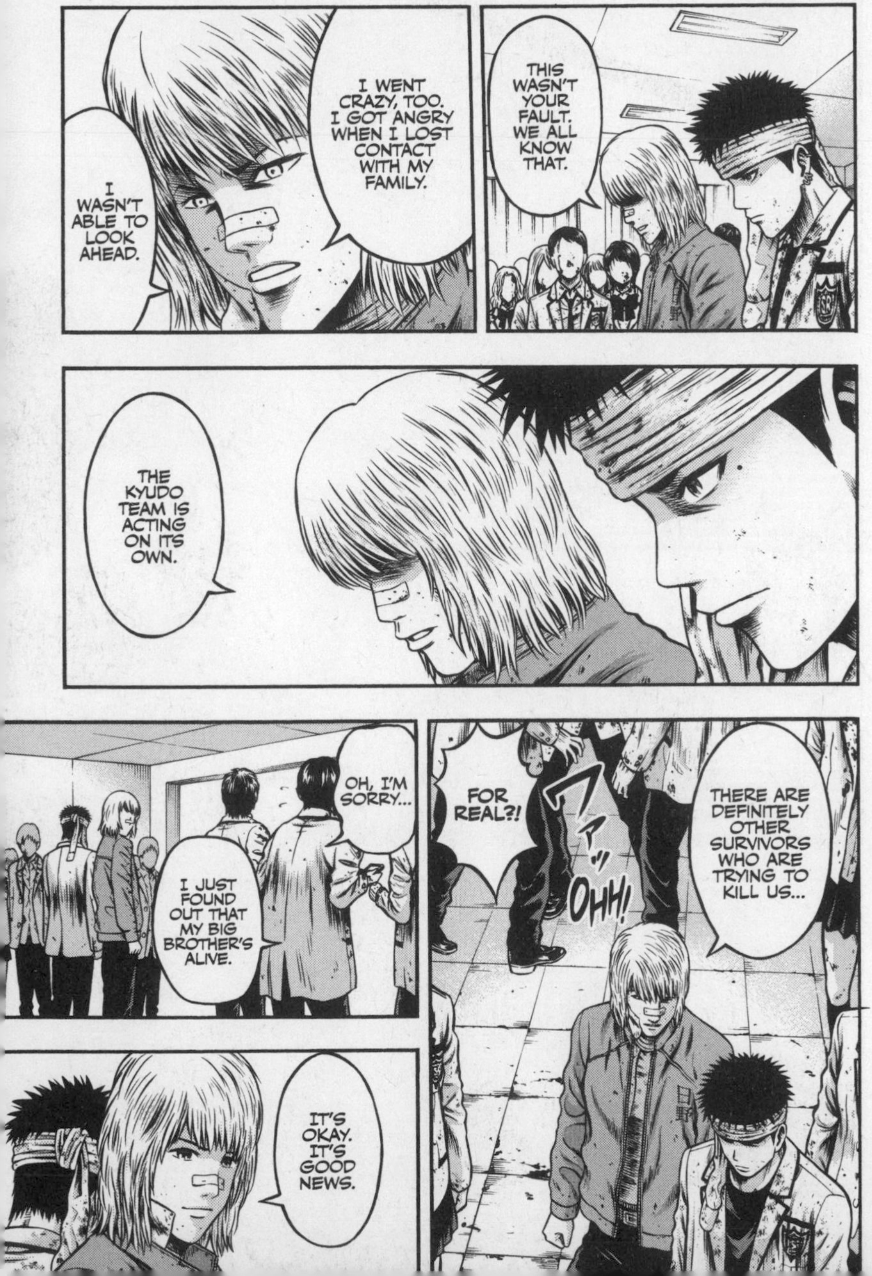
THIS WASN'T YOUR FAULT. WE ALL KNOW THAT.
I WENT CRAZY, TOO. I GOT ANGRY WHEN I LOST CONTACT WITH MY FAMILY.
I WASN'T ABLE TO LOOK AHEAD.
THE KYUDO TEAM IS ACTING ON ITS OWN.
THERE ARE DEFINITELY OTHER SURVIVORS WHO ARE TRYING TO KILL US...
FOR REAL?!
アッ
OHH!
OH, I'M SORRY...
I JUST FOUND OUT THAT MY BIG BROTHER'S ALIVE.
IT'S OKAY. IT'S GOOD NEWS.

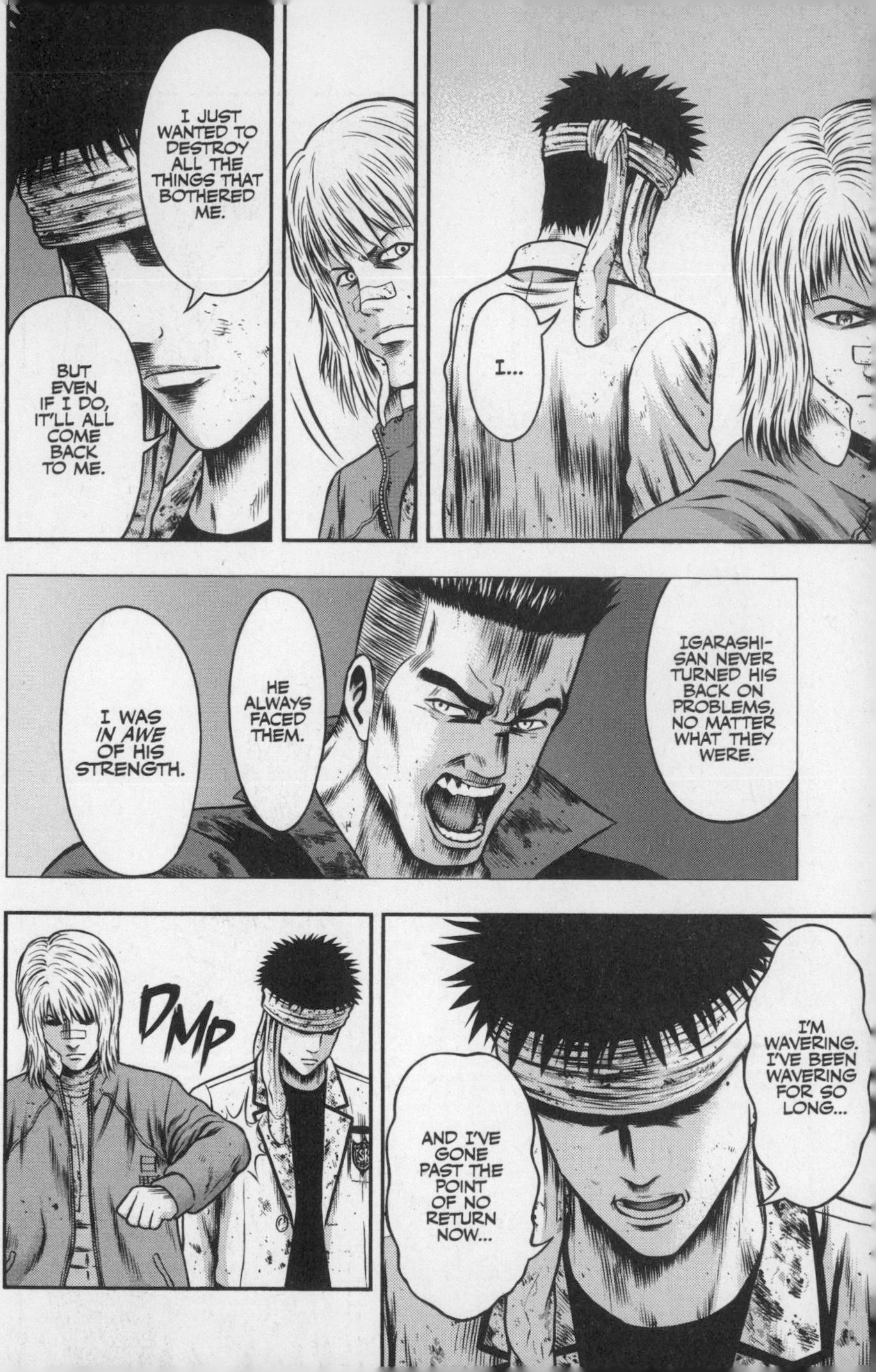
I...
I JUST WANTED TO DESTROY ALL THE THINGS THAT BOTHERED ME.
BUT EVEN IF I DO, IT'LL ALL COME BACK TO ME.
IGARASHI-SAN NEVER TURNED HIS BACK ON PROBLEMS, NO MATTER WHAT THEY WERE.
HE ALWAYS FACED THEM.
I WAS *IN AWE* OF HIS STRENGTH.
I'M WAVERING. I'VE BEEN WAVERING FOR SO LONG...
AND I'VE GONE PAST THE POINT OF NO RETURN NOW...
DMP

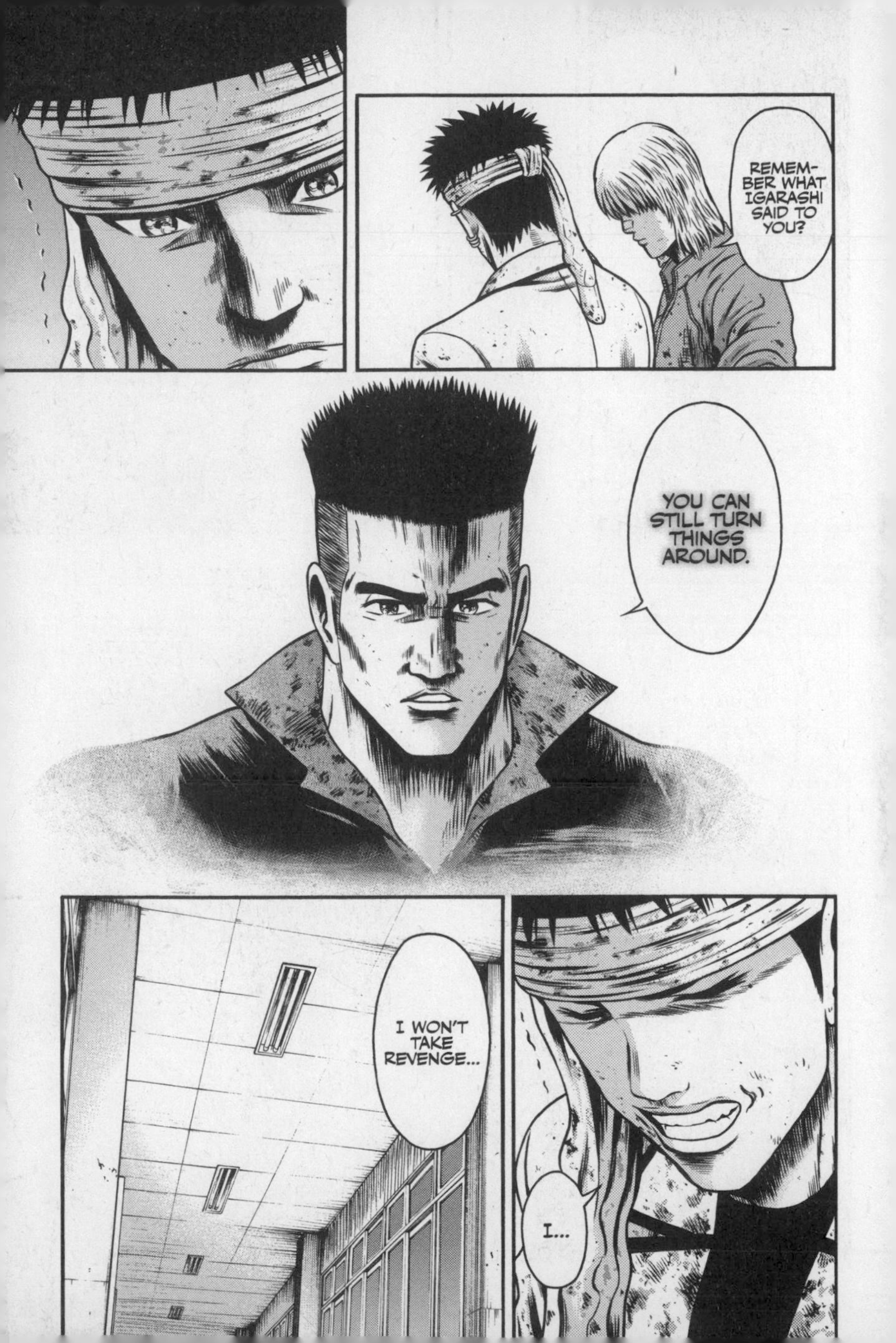
REMEMBER WHAT IGARASHI SAID TO YOU?
YOU CAN STILL TURN THINGS AROUND.
I...
I WON'T TAKE REVENGE...

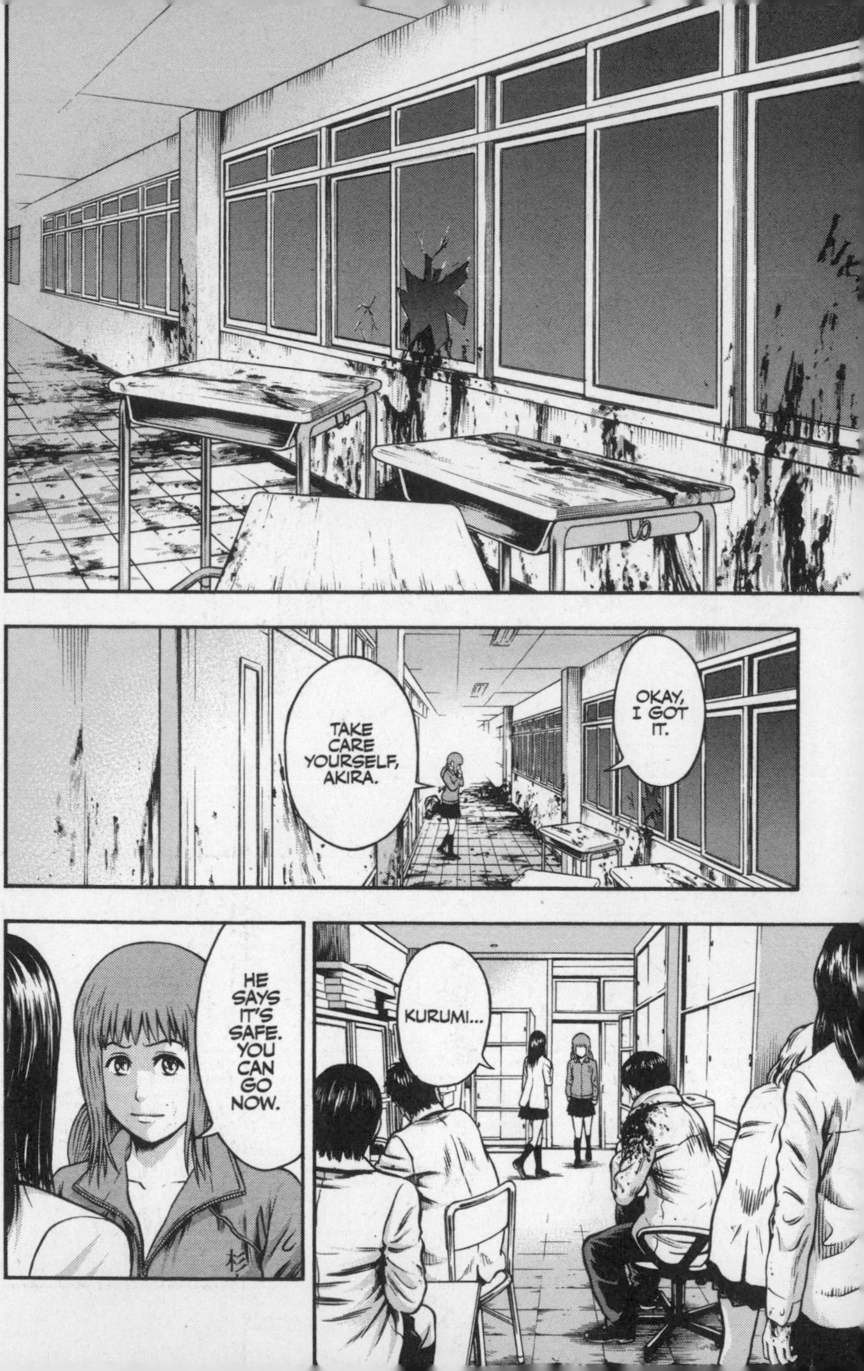
OKAY, I GOT IT.
TAKE CARE YOURSELF, AKIRA.
KURUMI...
HE SAYS IT'S SAFE. YOU CAN GO NOW.

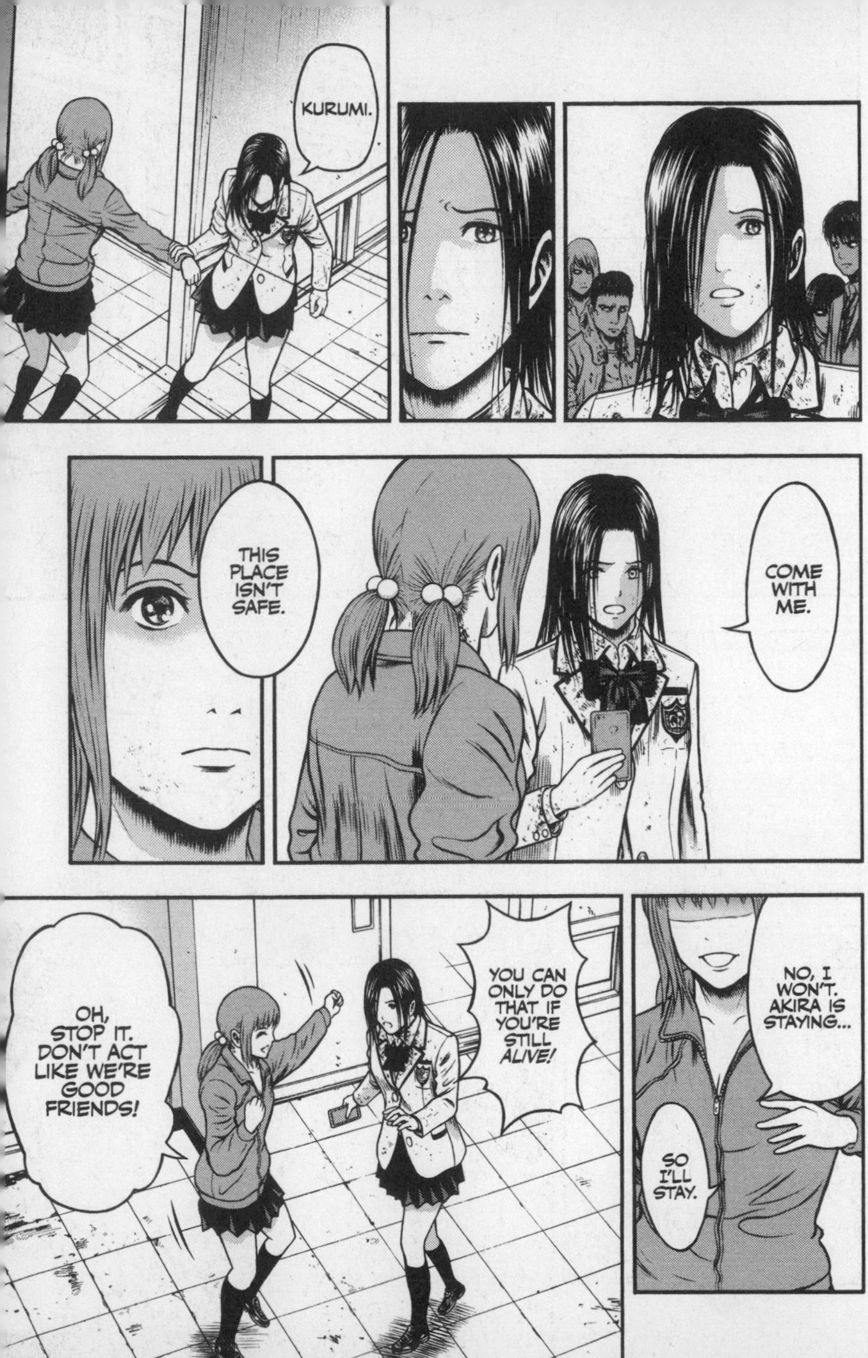
KURUMI.
COME WITH ME.
THIS PLACE ISN'T SAFE.
NO, I WON'T. AKIRA IS STAYING...
SO I'LL STAY.
YOU CAN ONLY DO THAT IF YOU'RE STILL *ALIVE!*
OH, STOP IT. DON'T ACT LIKE WE'RE GOOD FRIENDS!

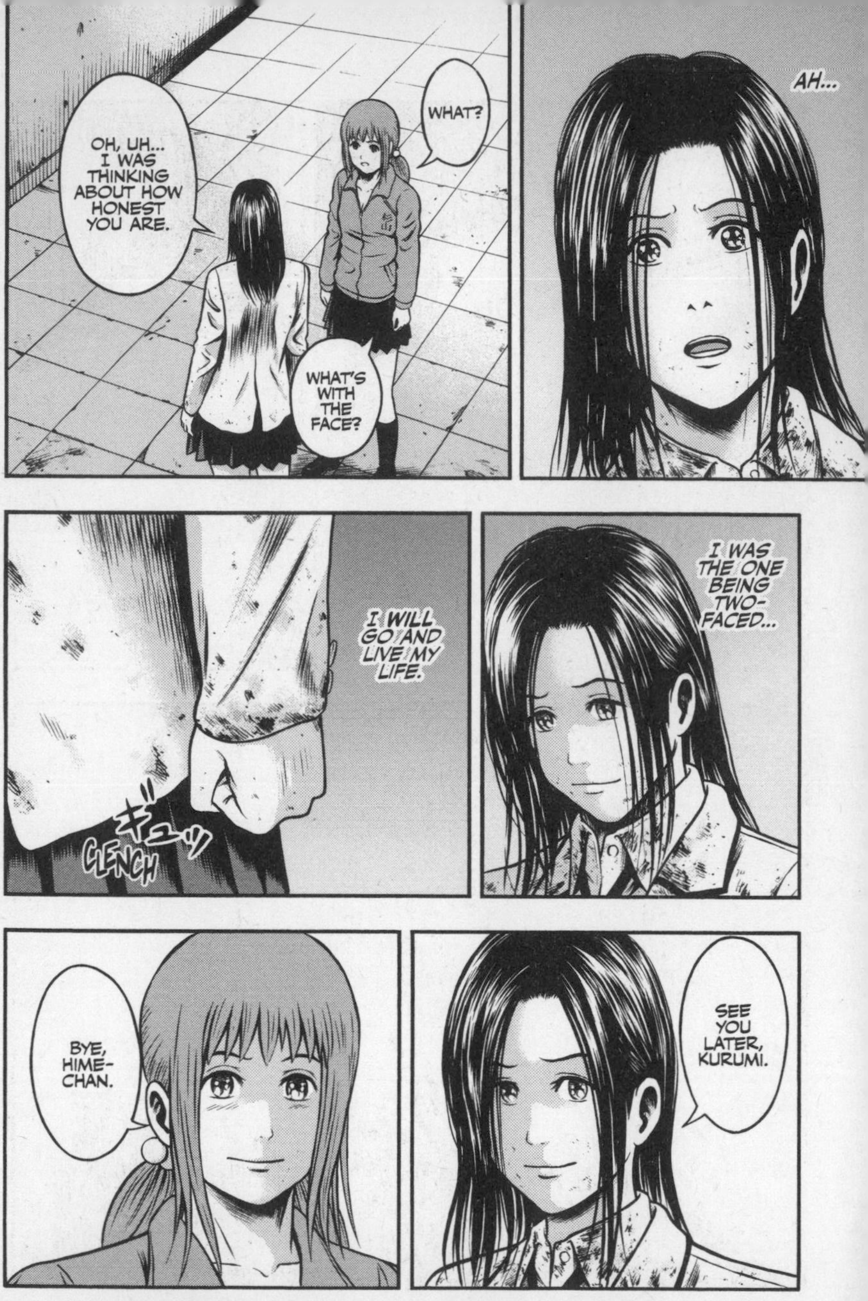
AH...
WHAT?
OH, UH... I WAS THINKING ABOUT HOW HONEST YOU ARE.
WHAT'S WITH THE FACE?
I WAS THE ONE BEING TWO-FACED...
I WILL GO AND LIVE MY LIFE.
ギュッ
CLENCH
SEE YOU LATER, KURUMI.
BYE, HIME-CHAN.

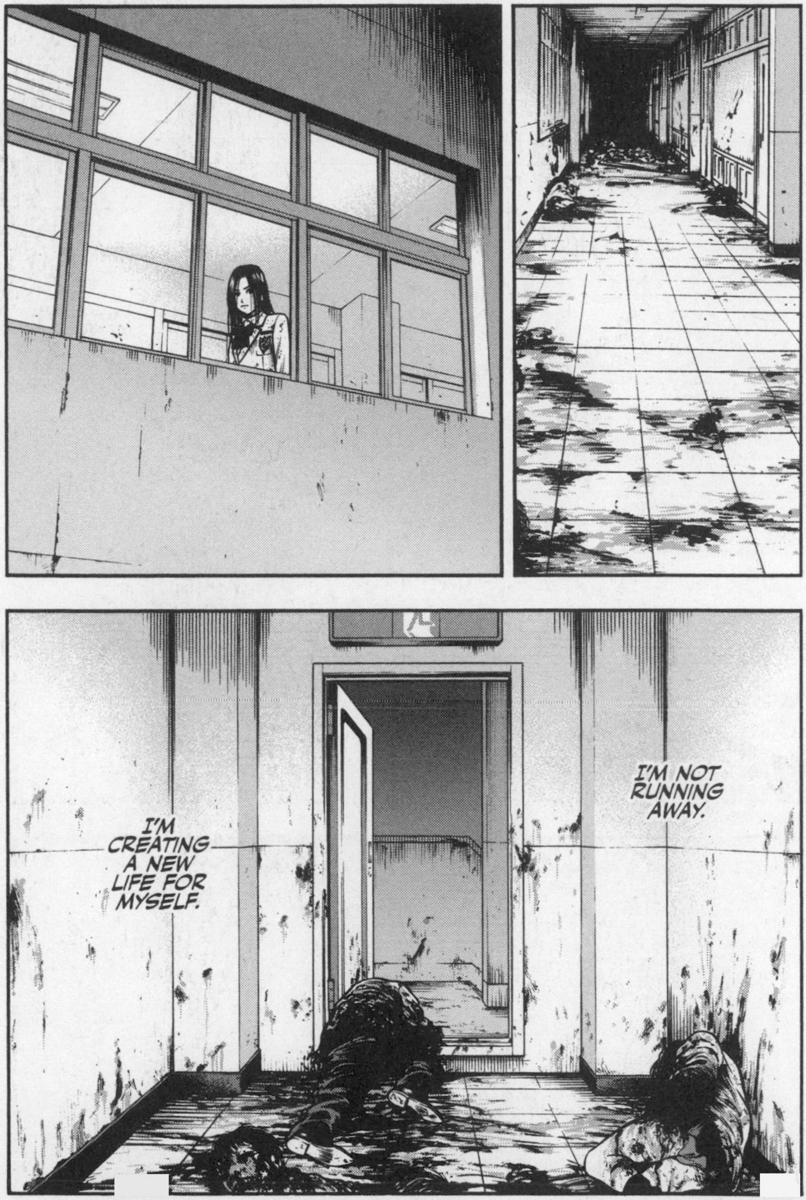
I'M NOT RUNNING AWAY.
I'M CREATING A NEW LIFE FOR MYSELF.

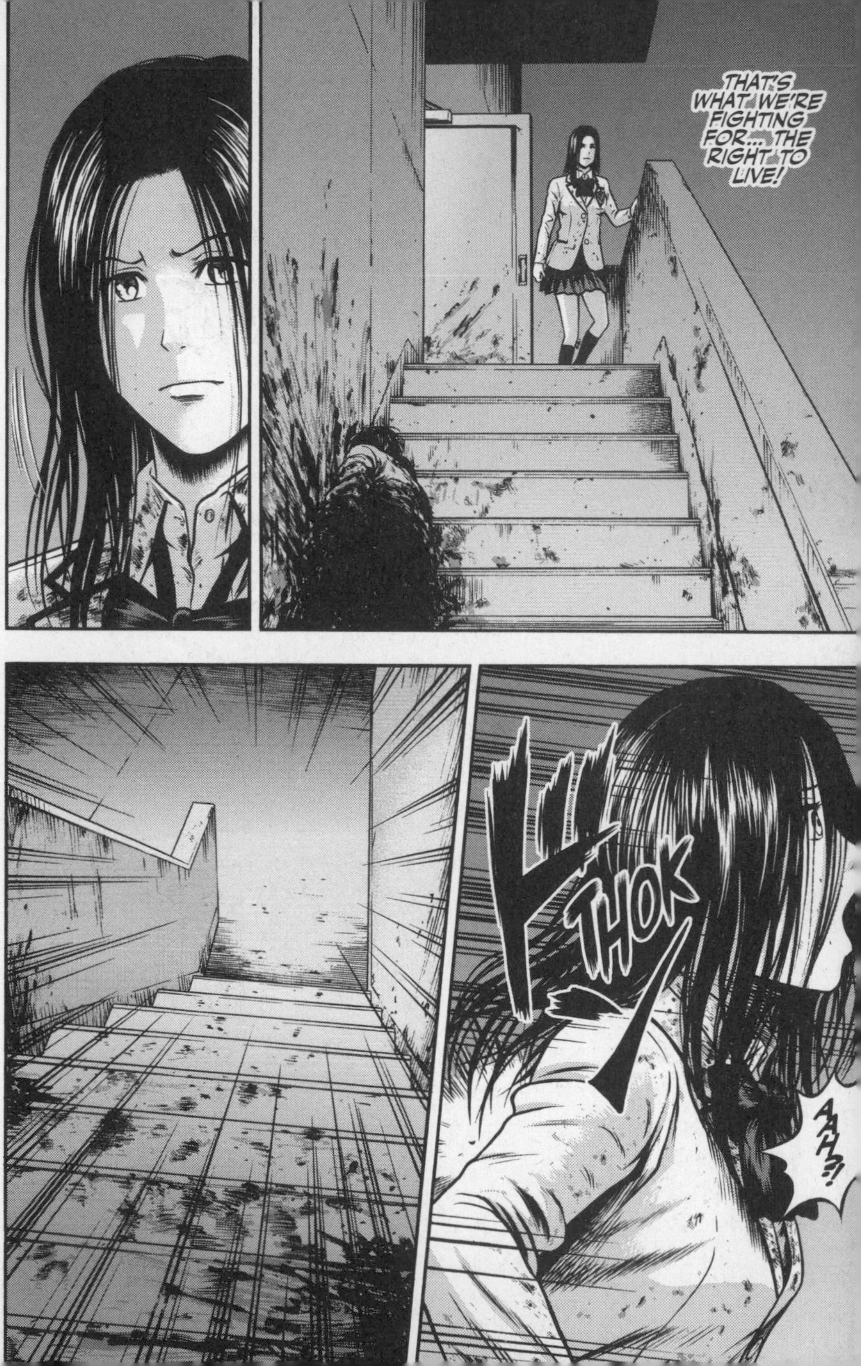
THAT'S WHAT WE'RE FIGHTING FOR... THE RIGHT TO LIVE!
THOK
AAAH?!

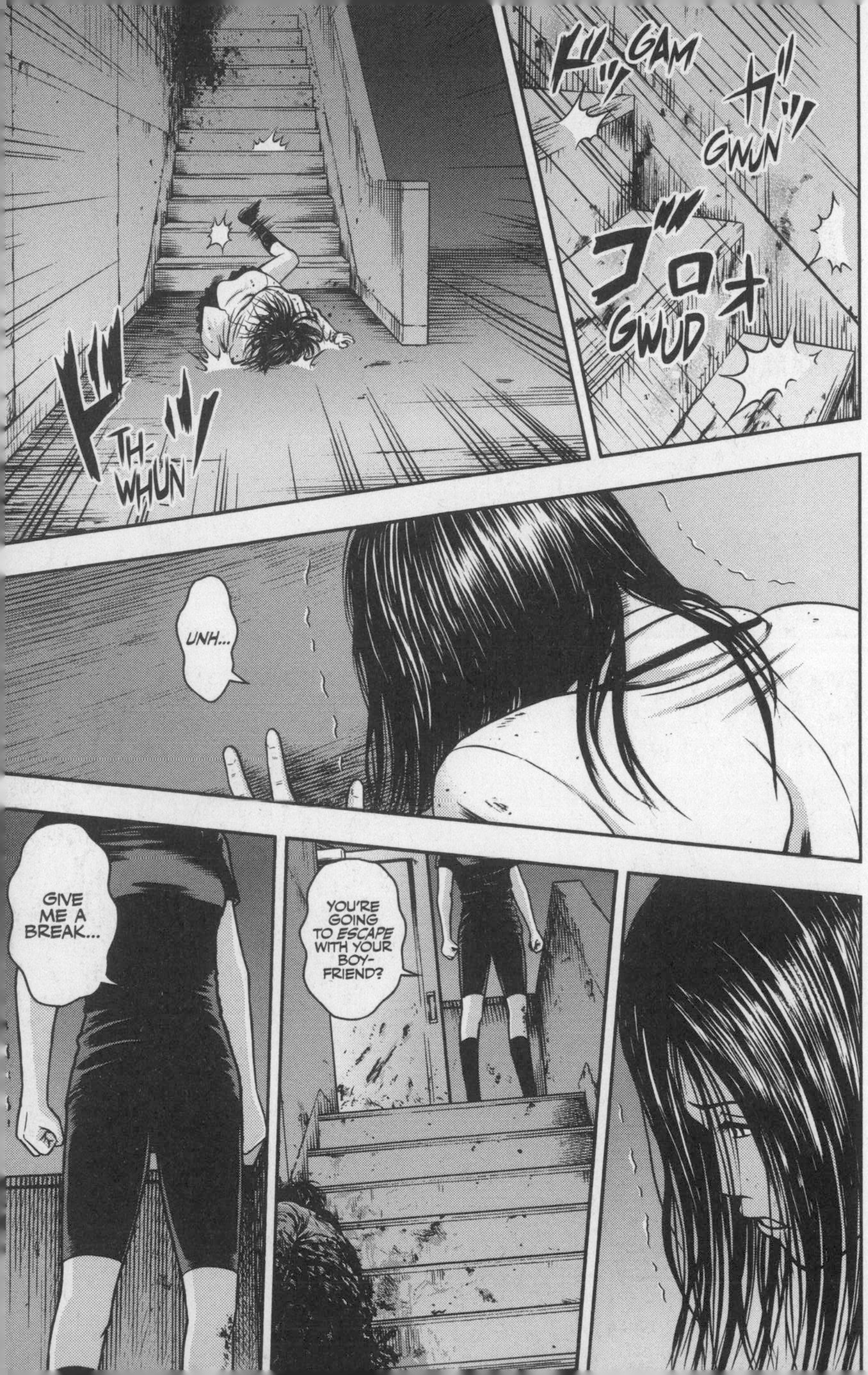
ドッ
GAM
ガッ
GWUN
ゴロオ
GWUD
ドッ
TH-WHUN
UNH...
YOU'RE GOING TO *ESCAPE* WITH YOUR BOY-FRIEND?
GIVE ME A BREAK...

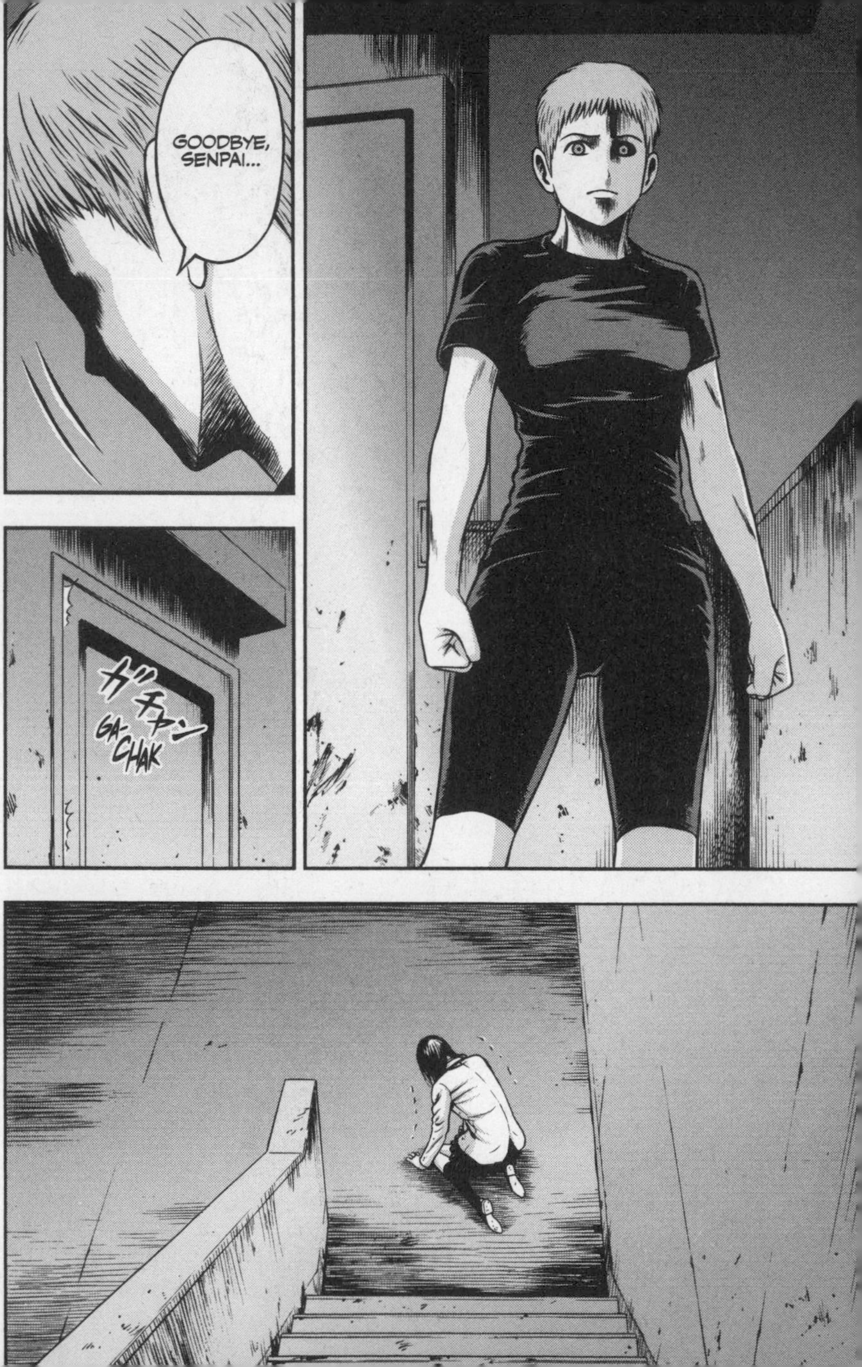
GOODBYE, SENPAI...
ガチャン
GA-CHAK

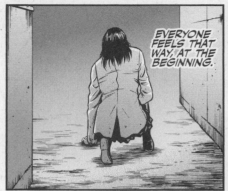

THAT GIRL...
EVERYONE FEELS THAT WAY, AT THE BEGINNING.
THEY'RE DESPERATE... TO HOLD ON TO THEMSELVES.
I...ALMOST LOST MY MIND, TOO.

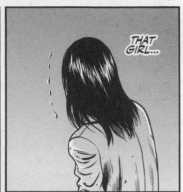

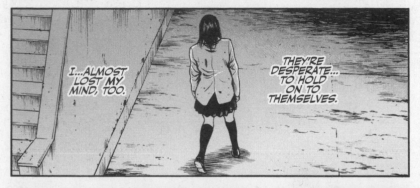

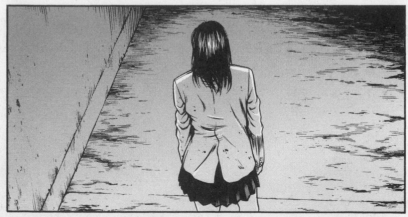

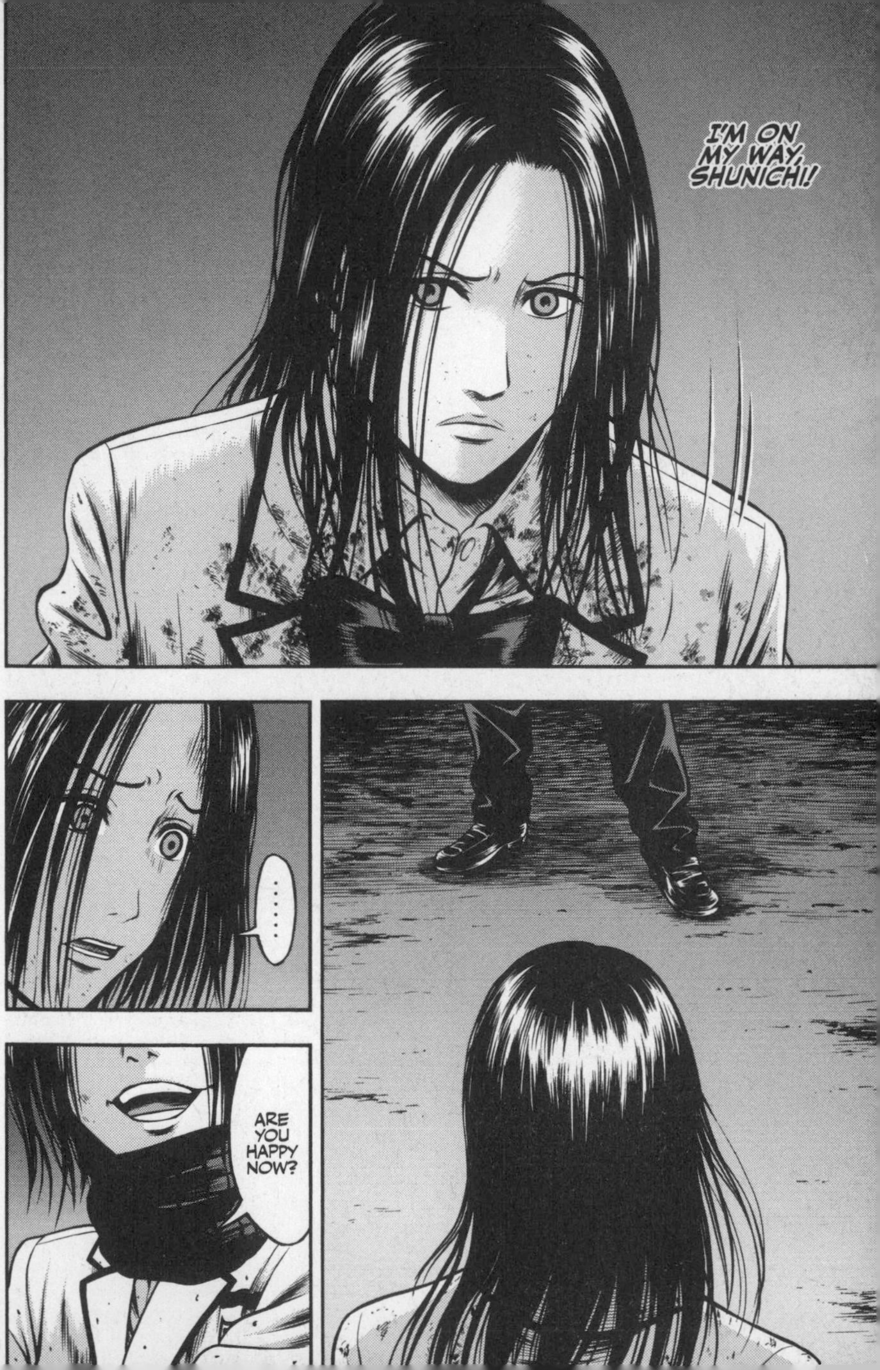
I'M ON MY WAY, SHUNICHI!
......
ARE YOU HAPPY NOW?

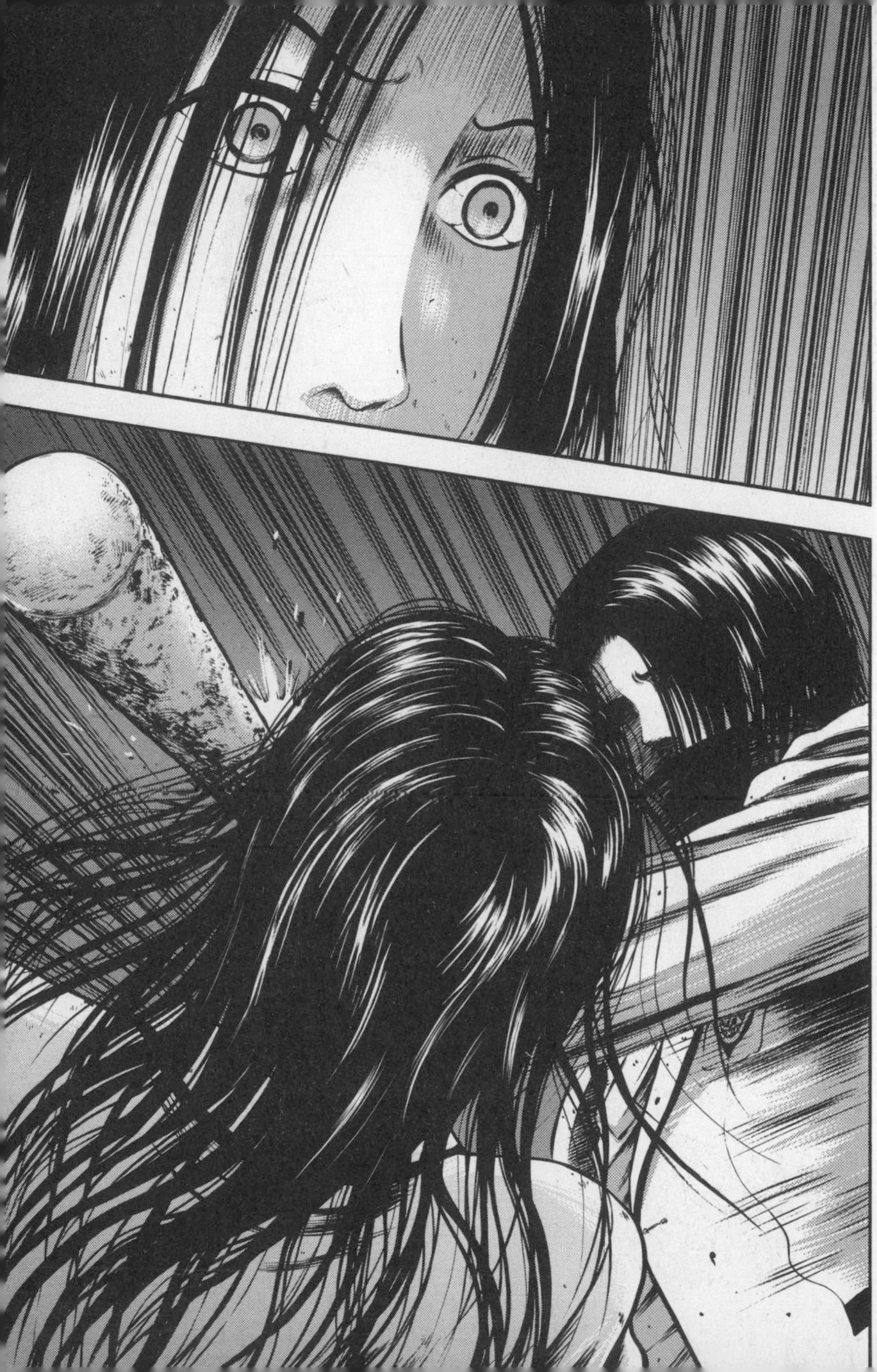

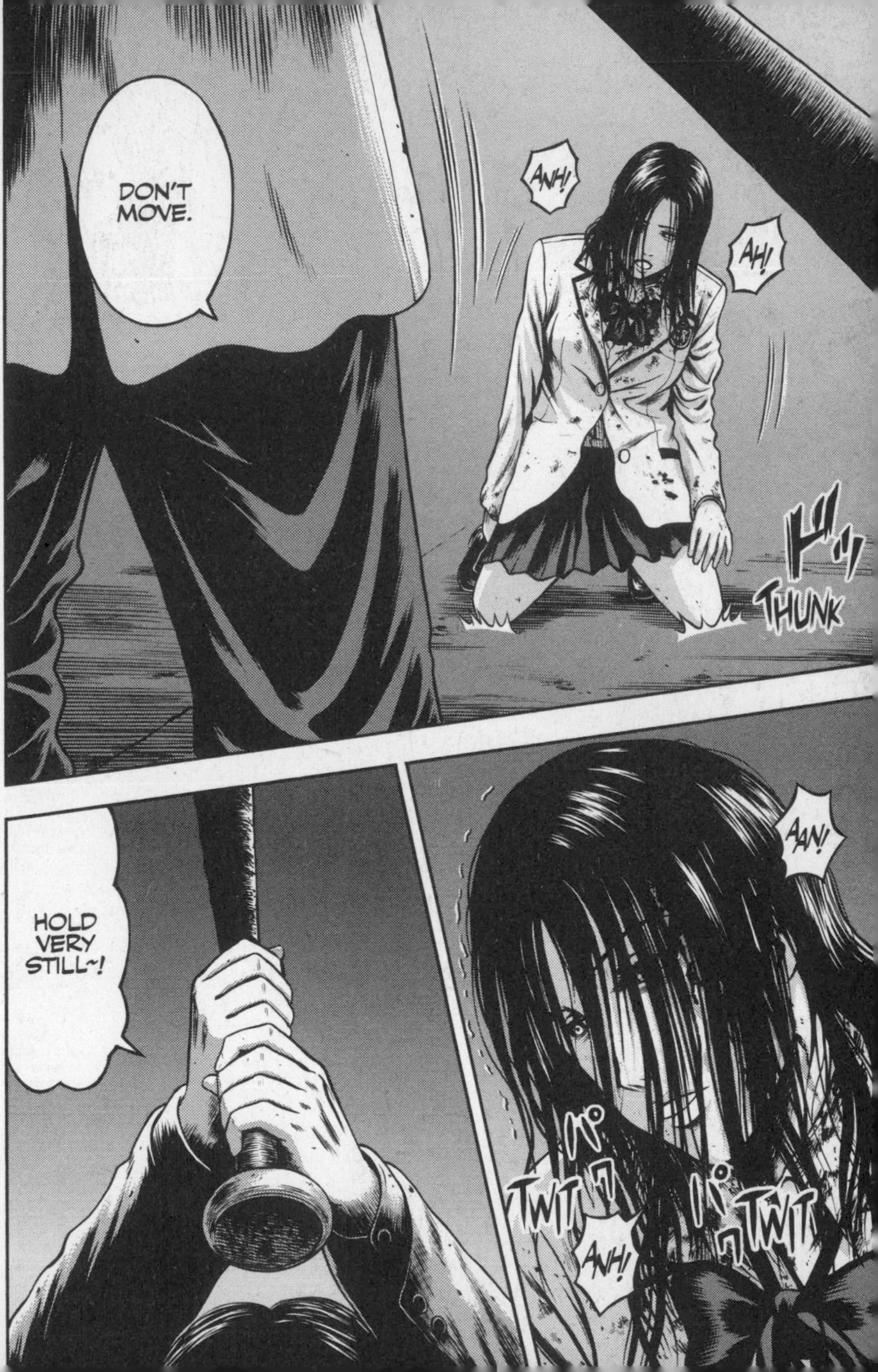
ANH!
AH!
ドッ
THUNK
DON'T MOVE.
AAN!
パッ
TWIT
パッ
TWIT
ANH!
HOLD VERY STILL~!

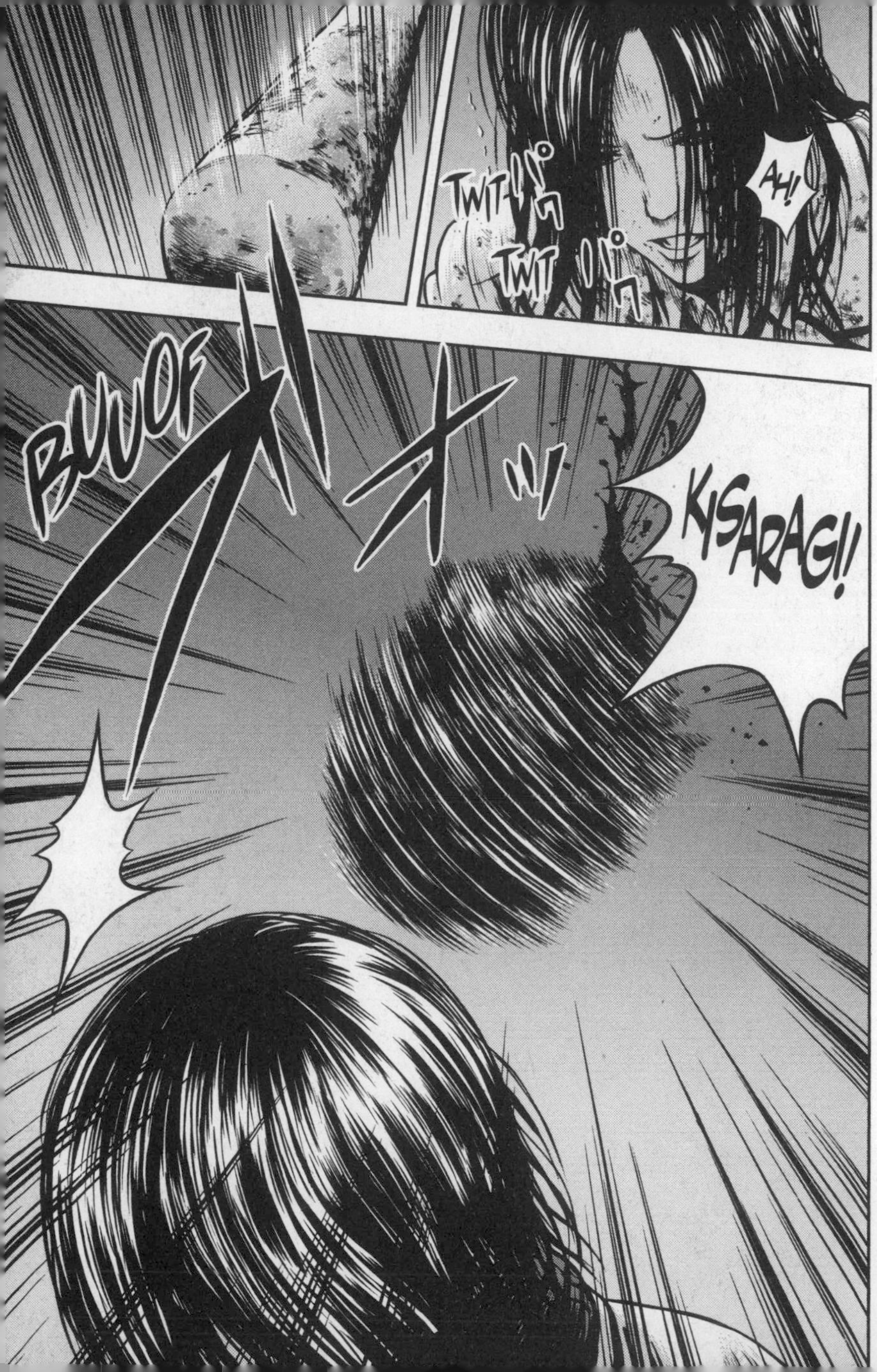
AH!
TWIT
TWIT
BUOF
KISARAGI!!

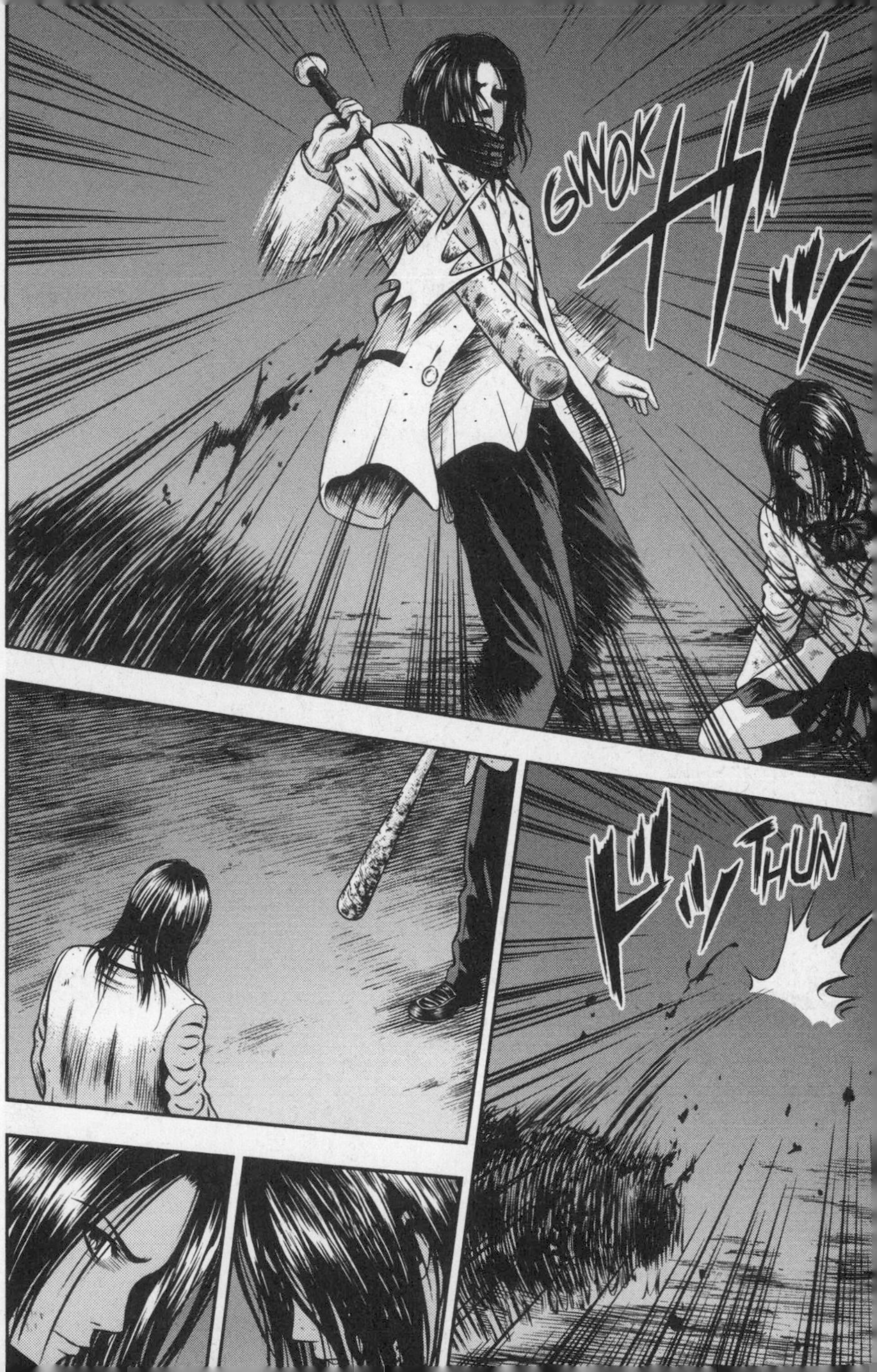
GWOK
THUN

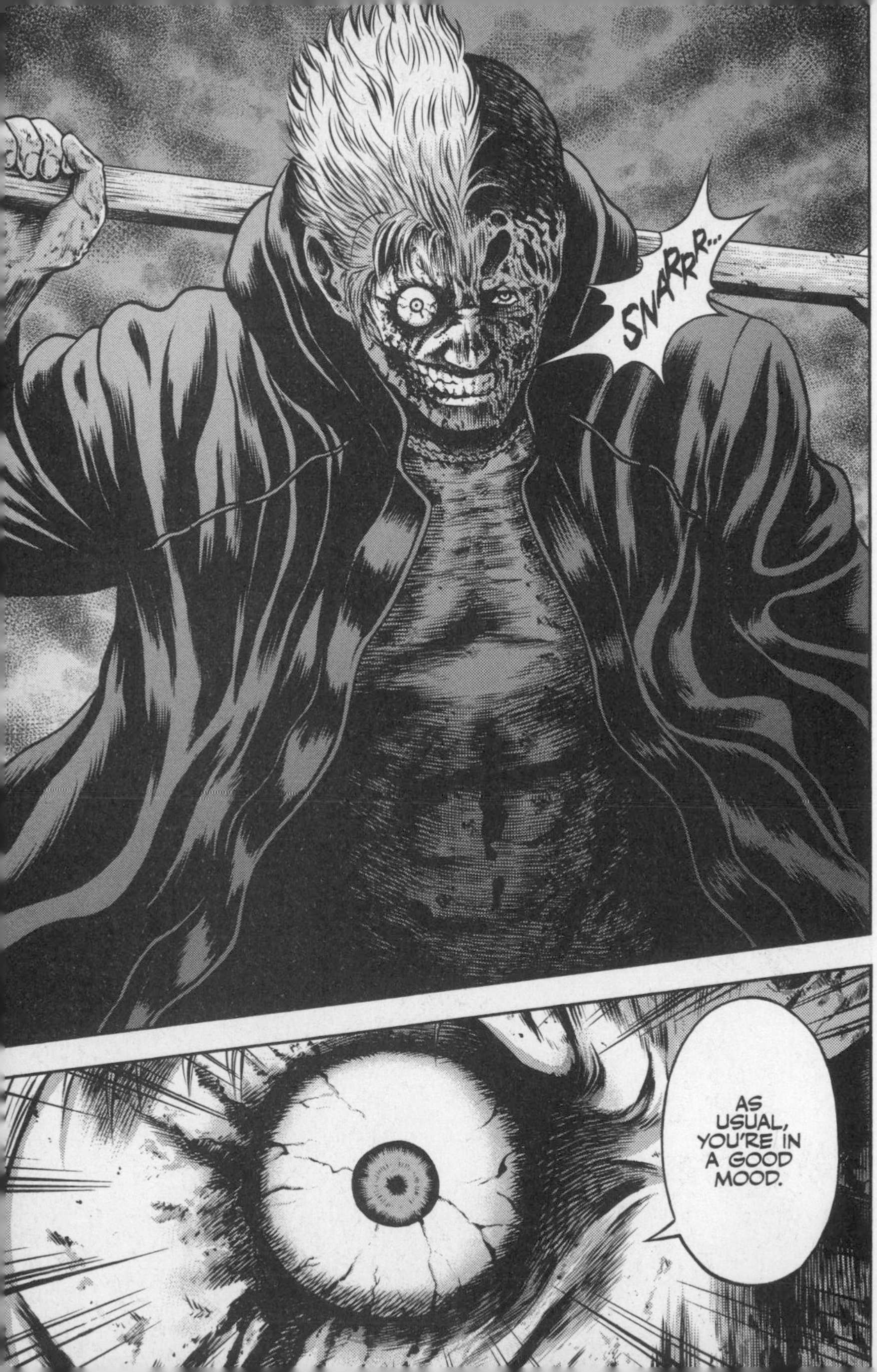
SNARRR...
AS USUAL, YOU'RE IN A GOOD MOOD.

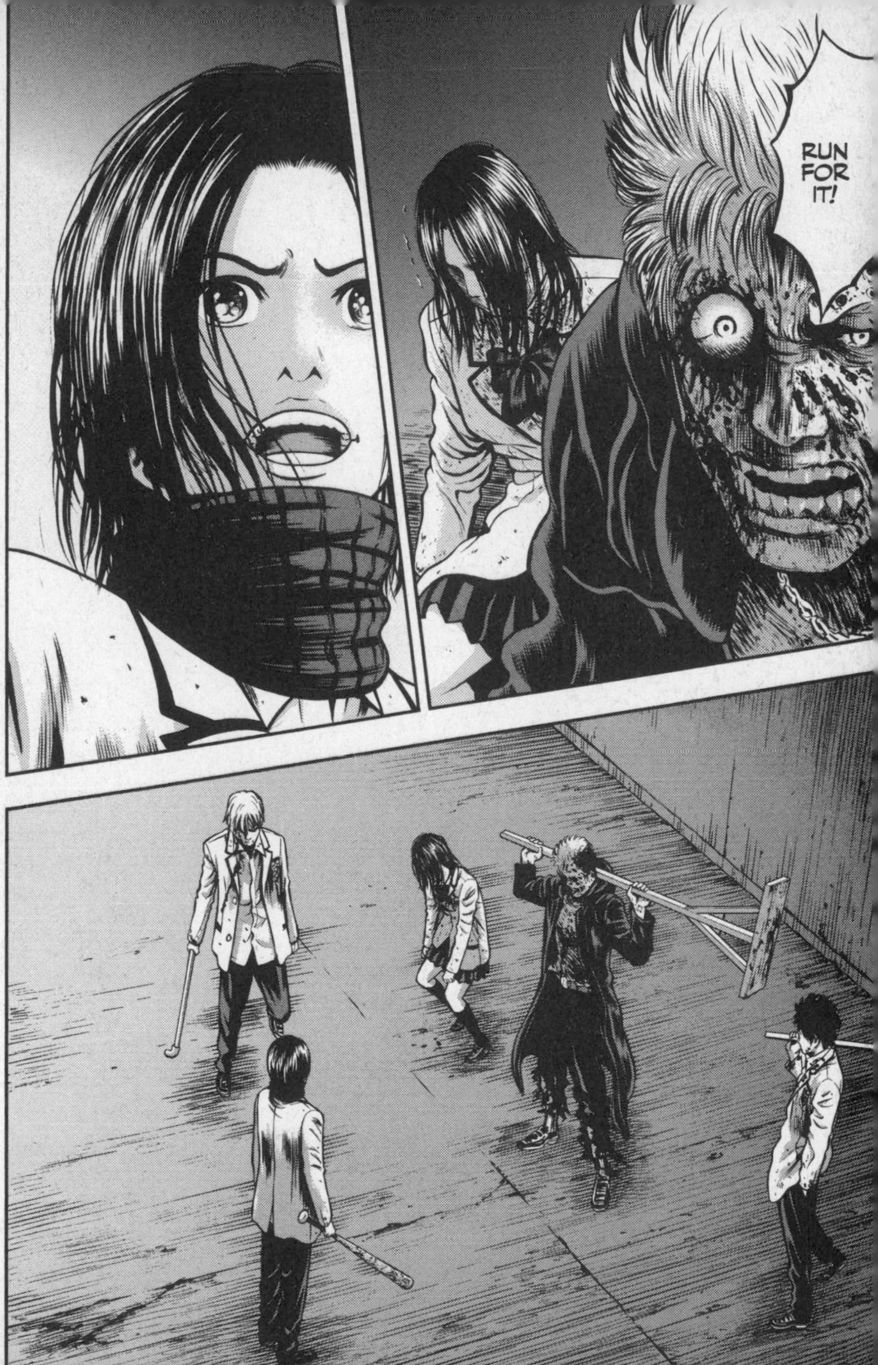
RUN FOR IT!

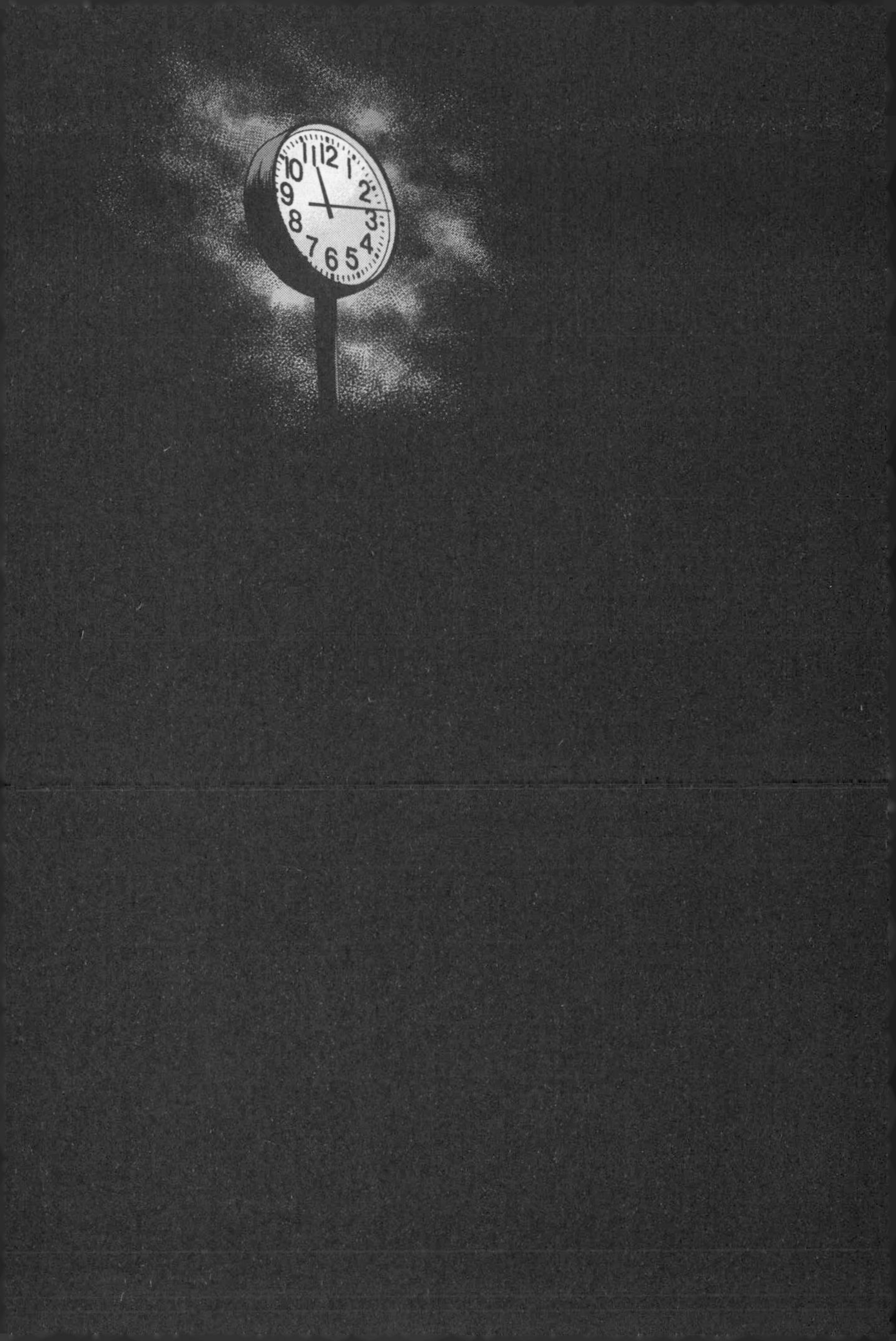

HOUR OF THE ZOMBIE

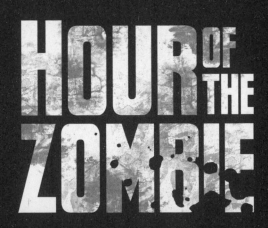

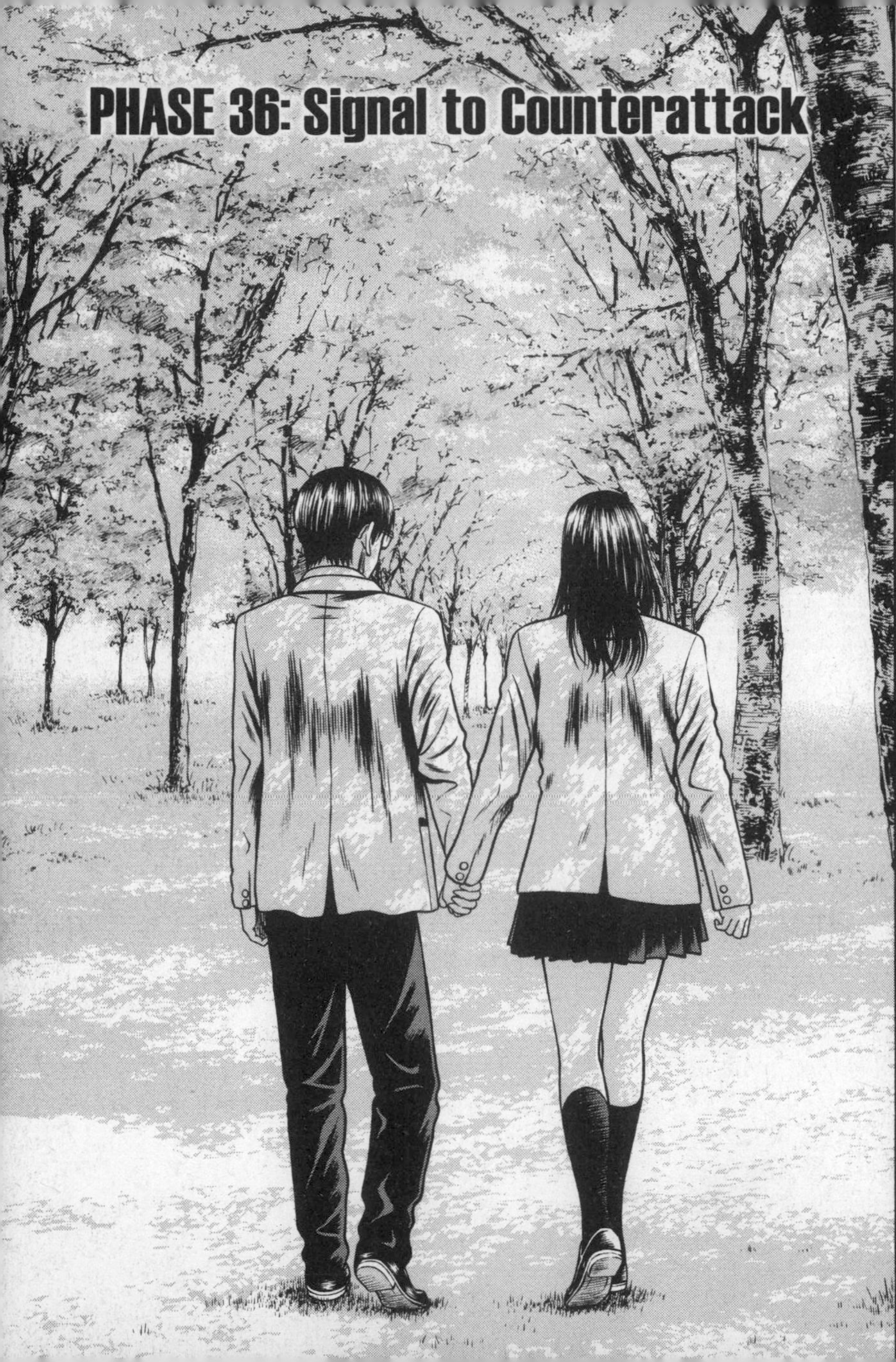
PHASE 36: Signal to Counterattack

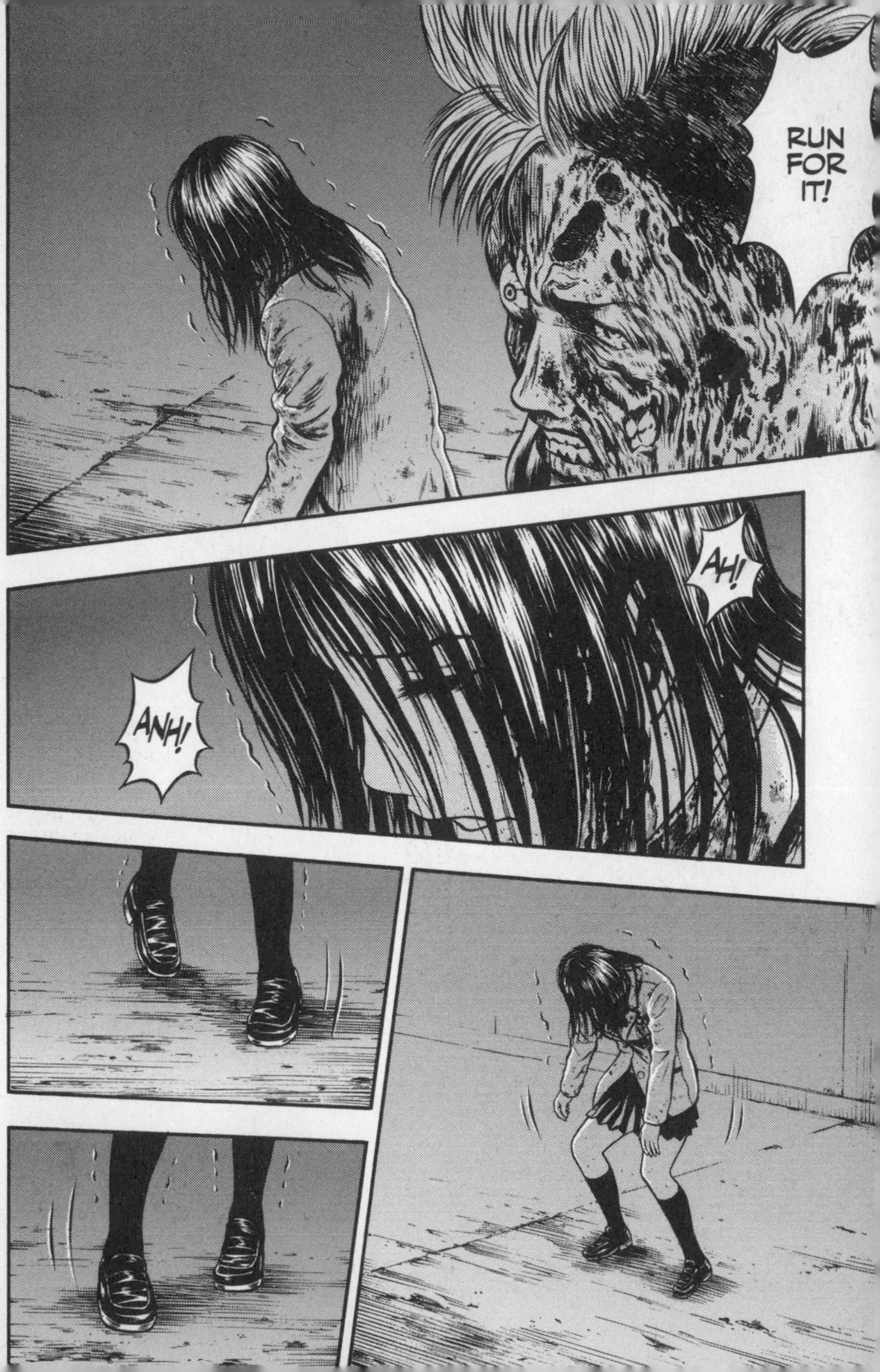
RUN FOR IT!
AH!
ANH!

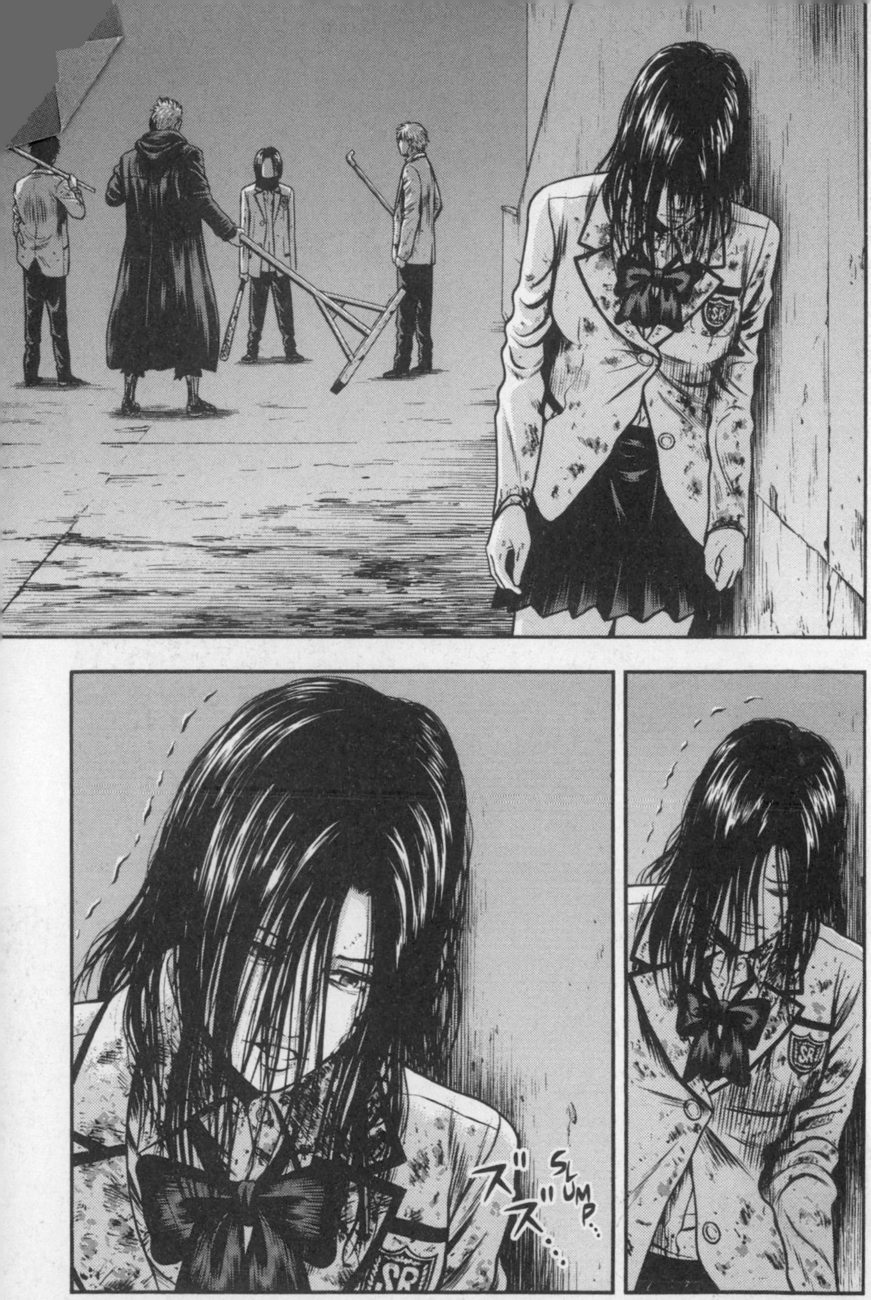
ズ゛ズ゛ズ…
SLUMP...

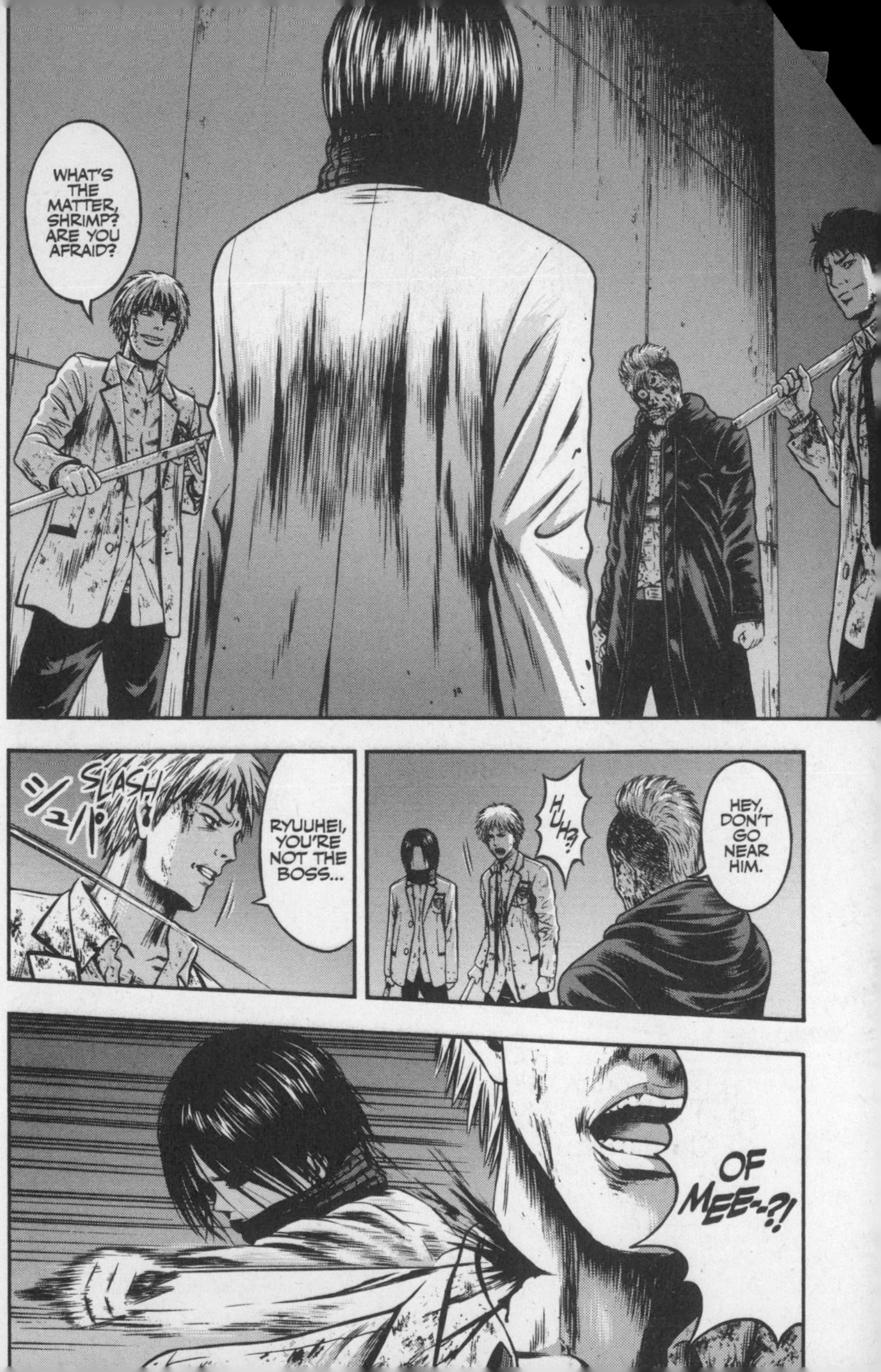
WHAT'S THE MATTER, SHRIMP? ARE YOU AFRAID?
HEY, DON'T GO NEAR HIM.
HUH?!
RYUUHEI, YOU'RE NOT THE BOSS...
SLASH
シュパ
OF MEE--?!

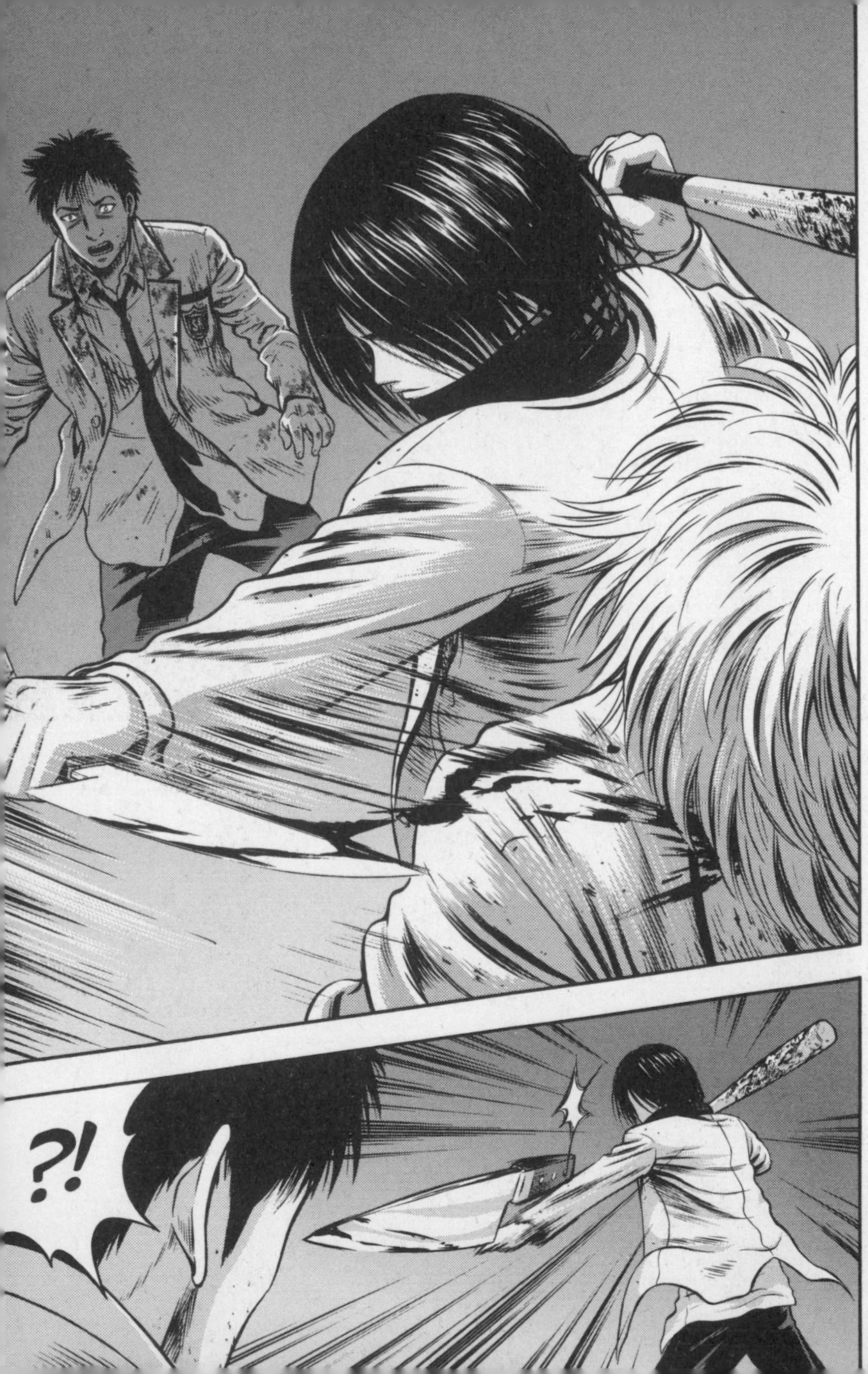
?!

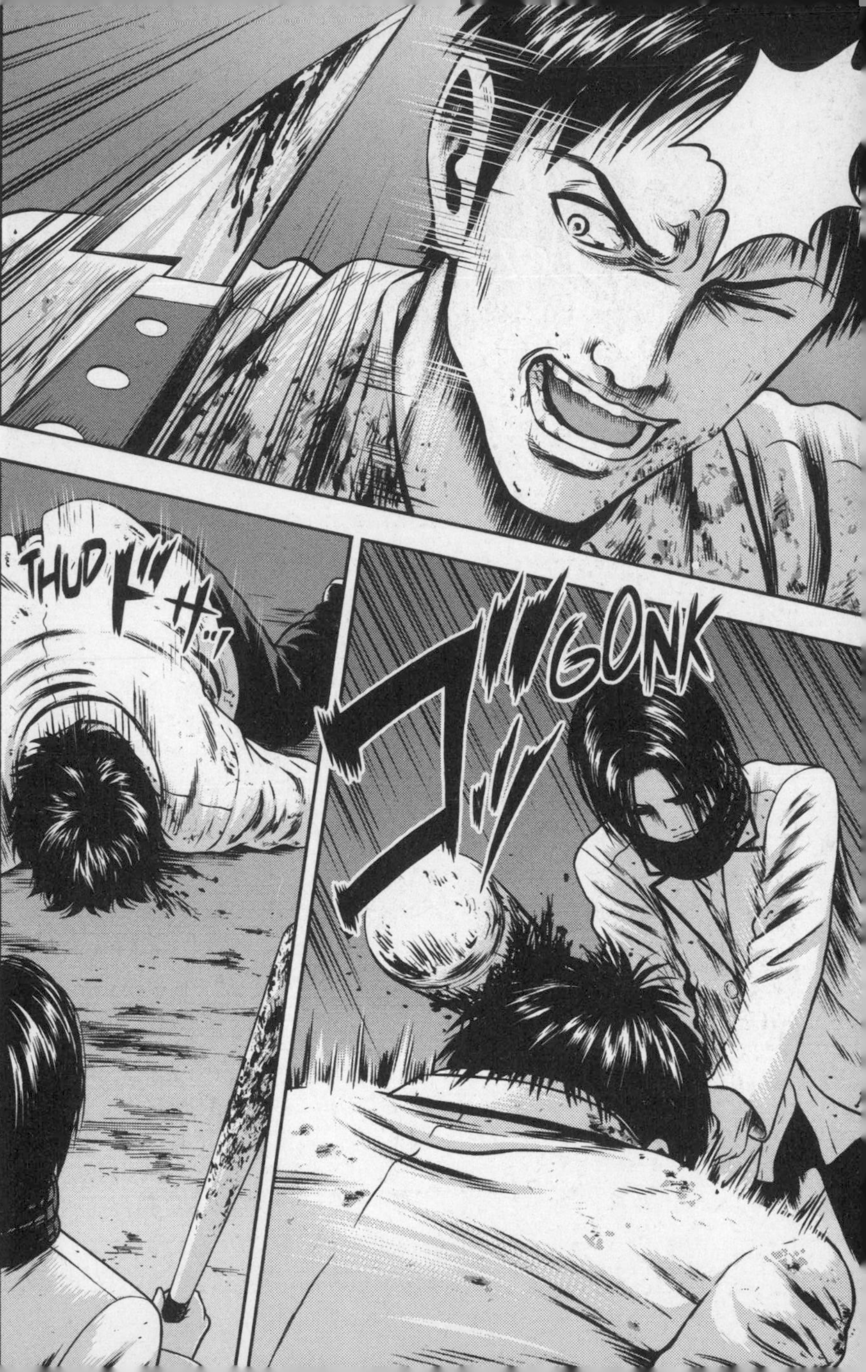
GONK
THUD

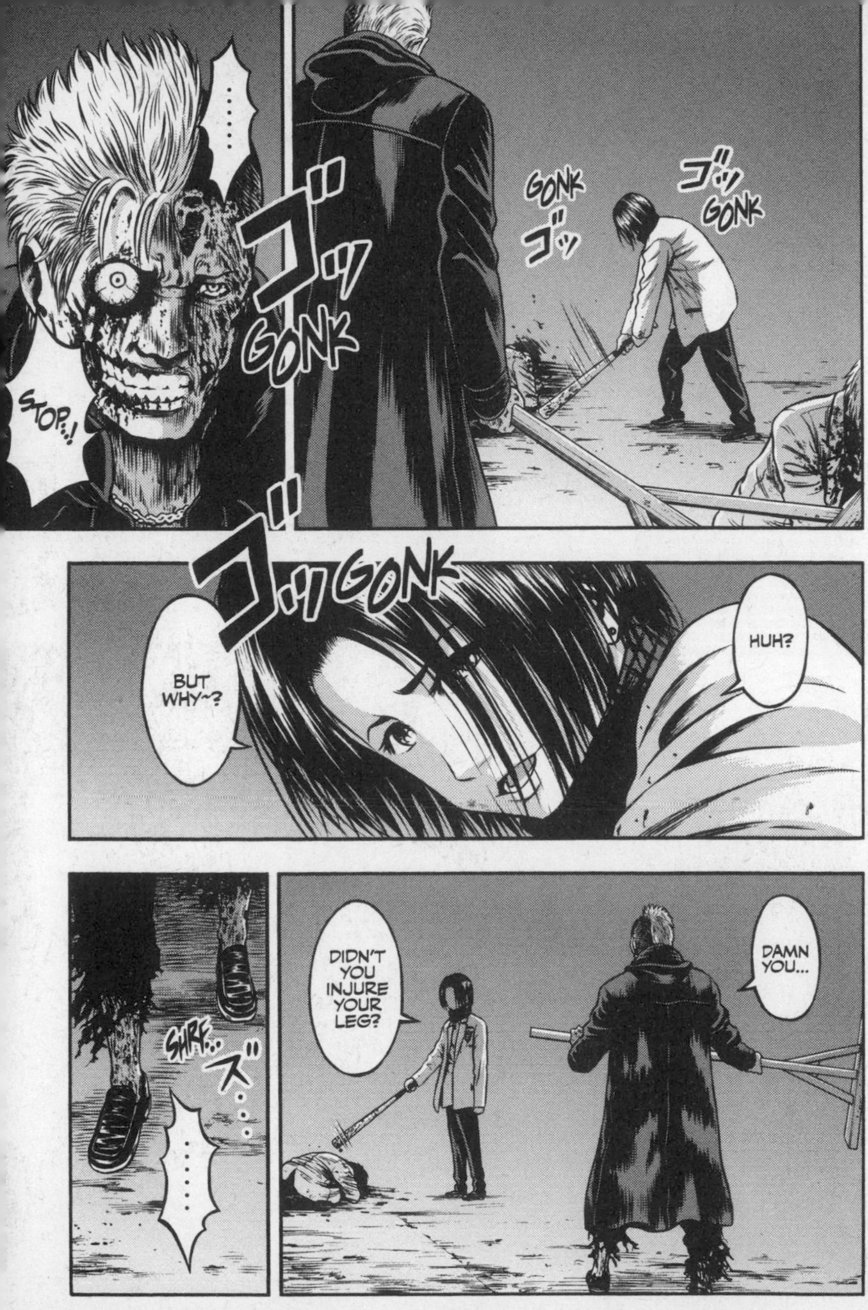
ゴッ GONK
GONK ゴッ
......!
ゴッ GONK
STOP..!
HUH?
ゴッ GONK
BUT WHY~?
DAMN YOU...
DIDN'T YOU INJURE YOUR LEG?
SHRF... ズ...
......

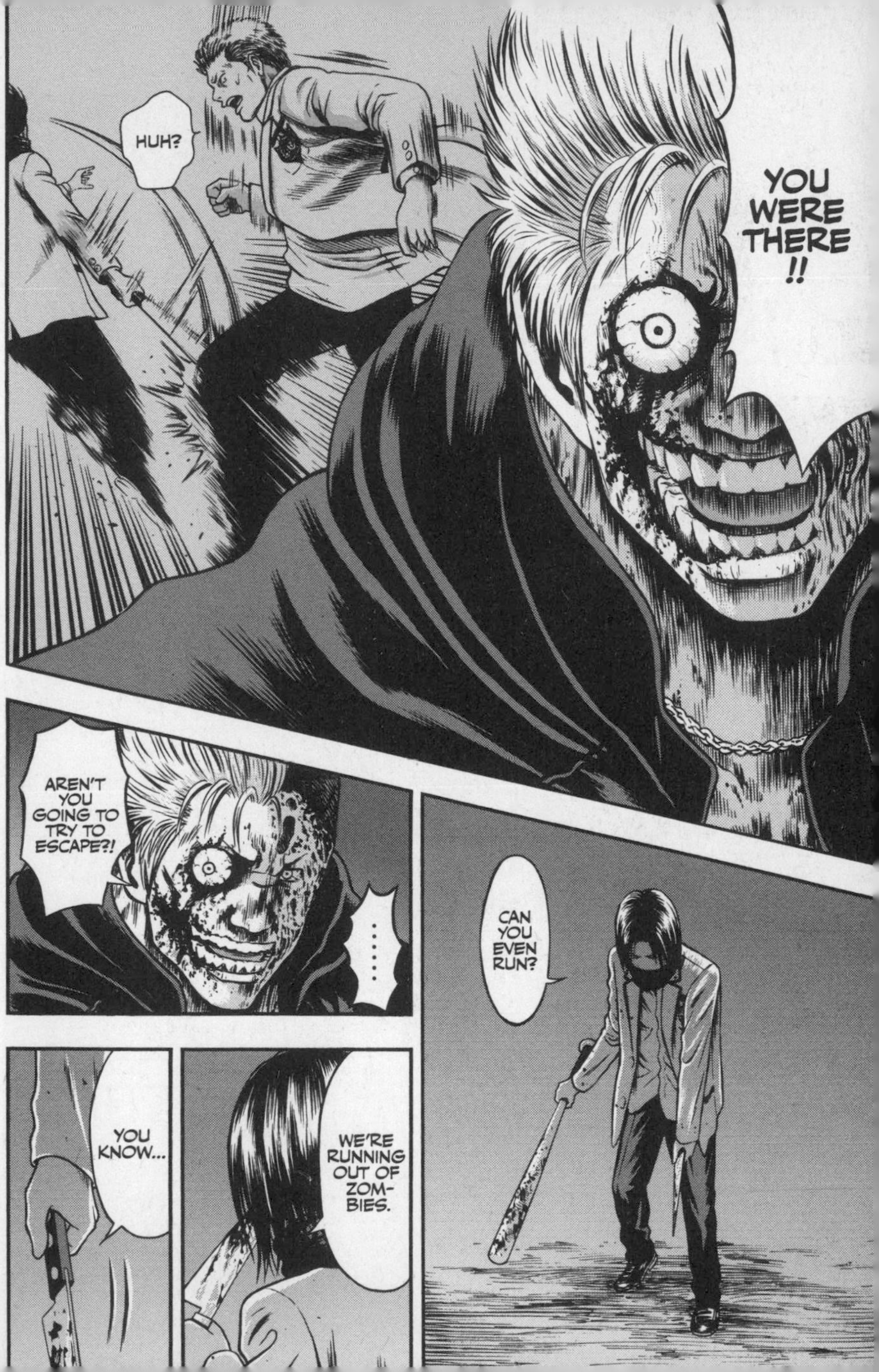
YOU WERE THERE !!
HUH?
CAN YOU EVEN RUN?
AREN'T YOU GOING TO TRY TO ESCAPE?!
......
WE'RE RUNNING OUT OF ZOM-BIES.
YOU KNOW...

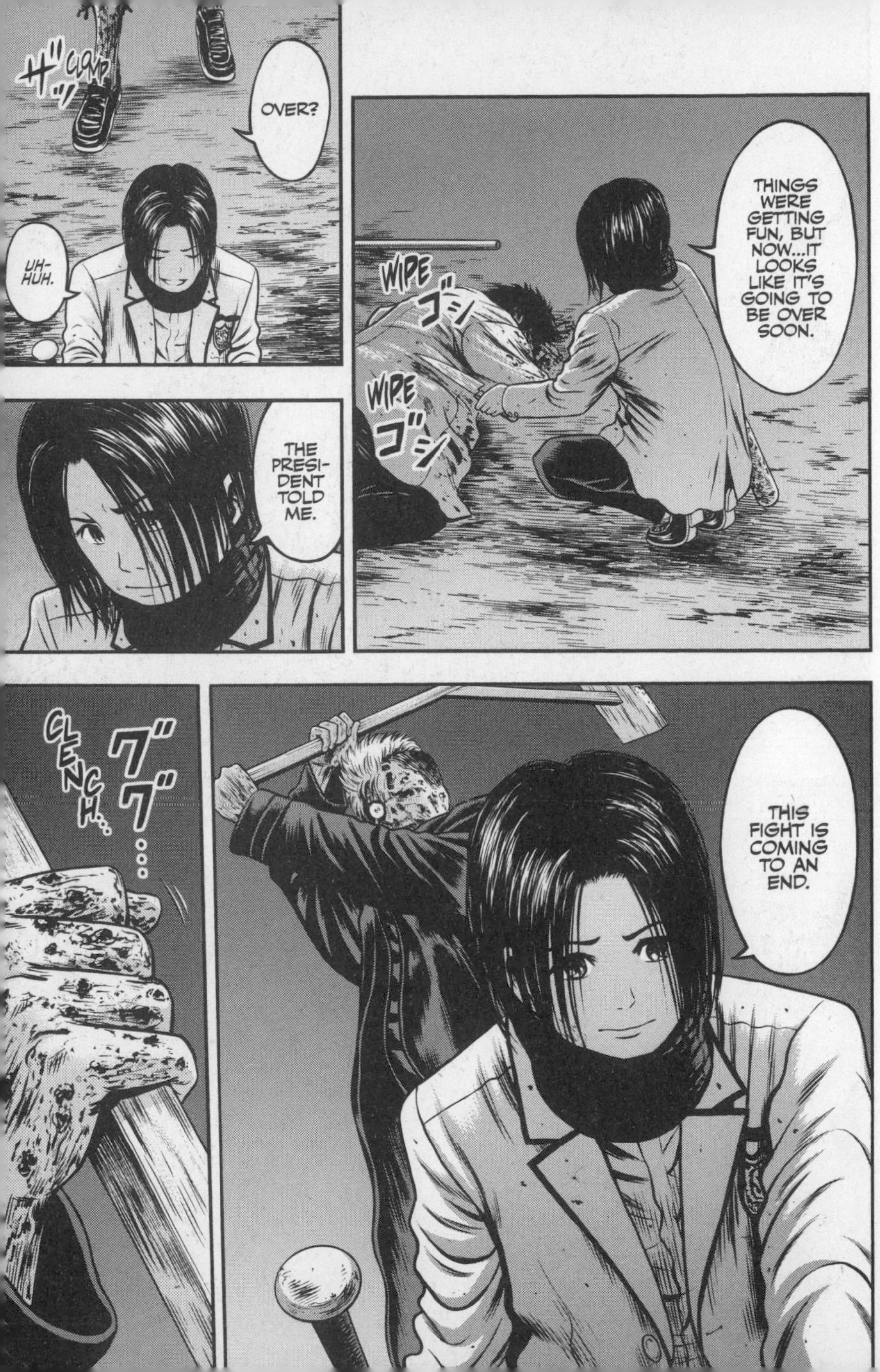
THINGS WERE GETTING FUN, BUT NOW...IT LOOKS LIKE IT'S GOING TO BE OVER SOON.
WIPE
ゴシ
WIPE
ゴシ
ザッ
CLOMP
OVER?
UH-HUH.
THE PRESI-DENT TOLD ME.
THIS FIGHT IS COMING TO AN END.
ググ…
CLENCH...

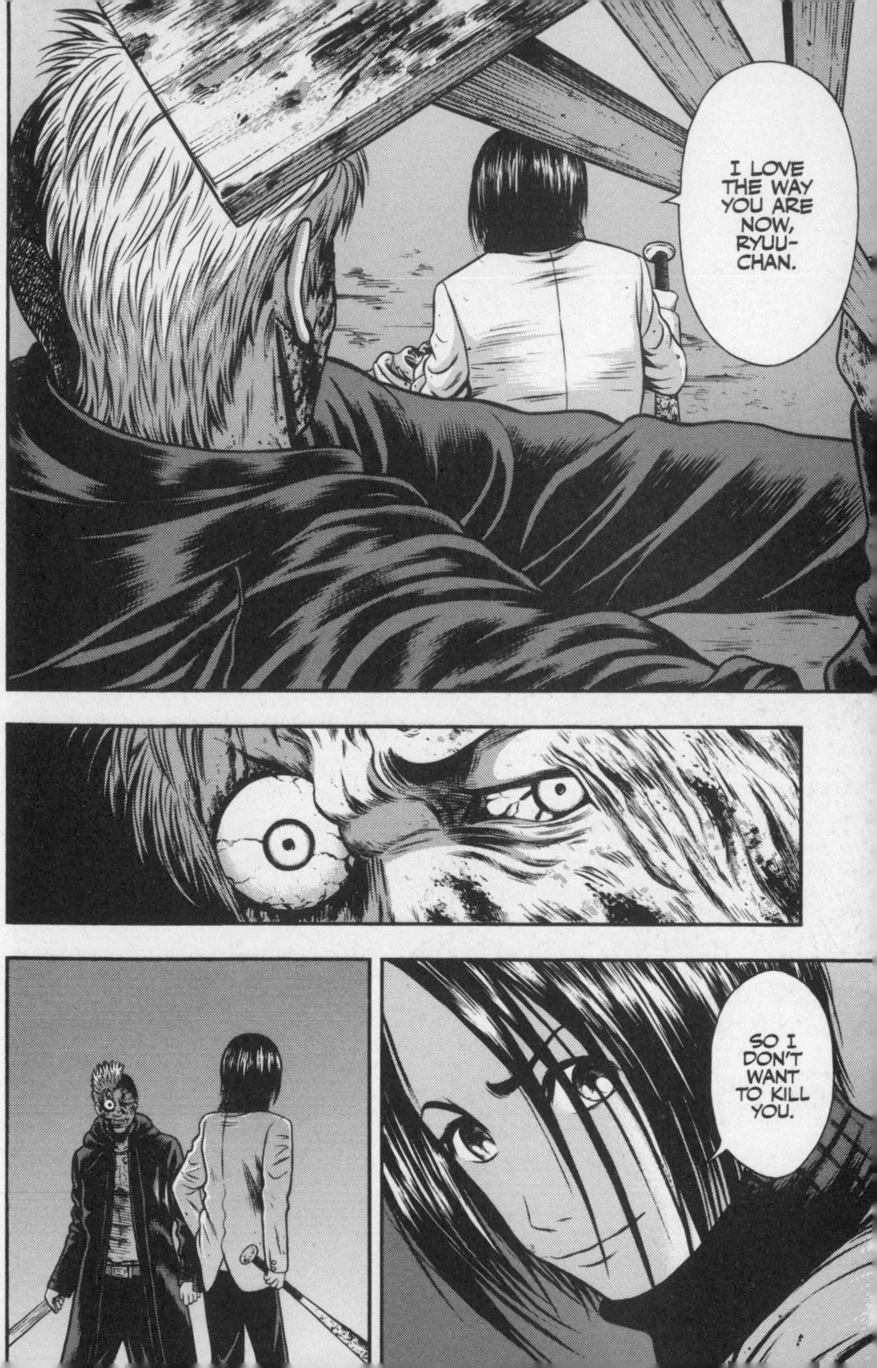
I LOVE THE WAY YOU ARE NOW, RYUU-CHAN.
SO I DON'T WANT TO KILL YOU.

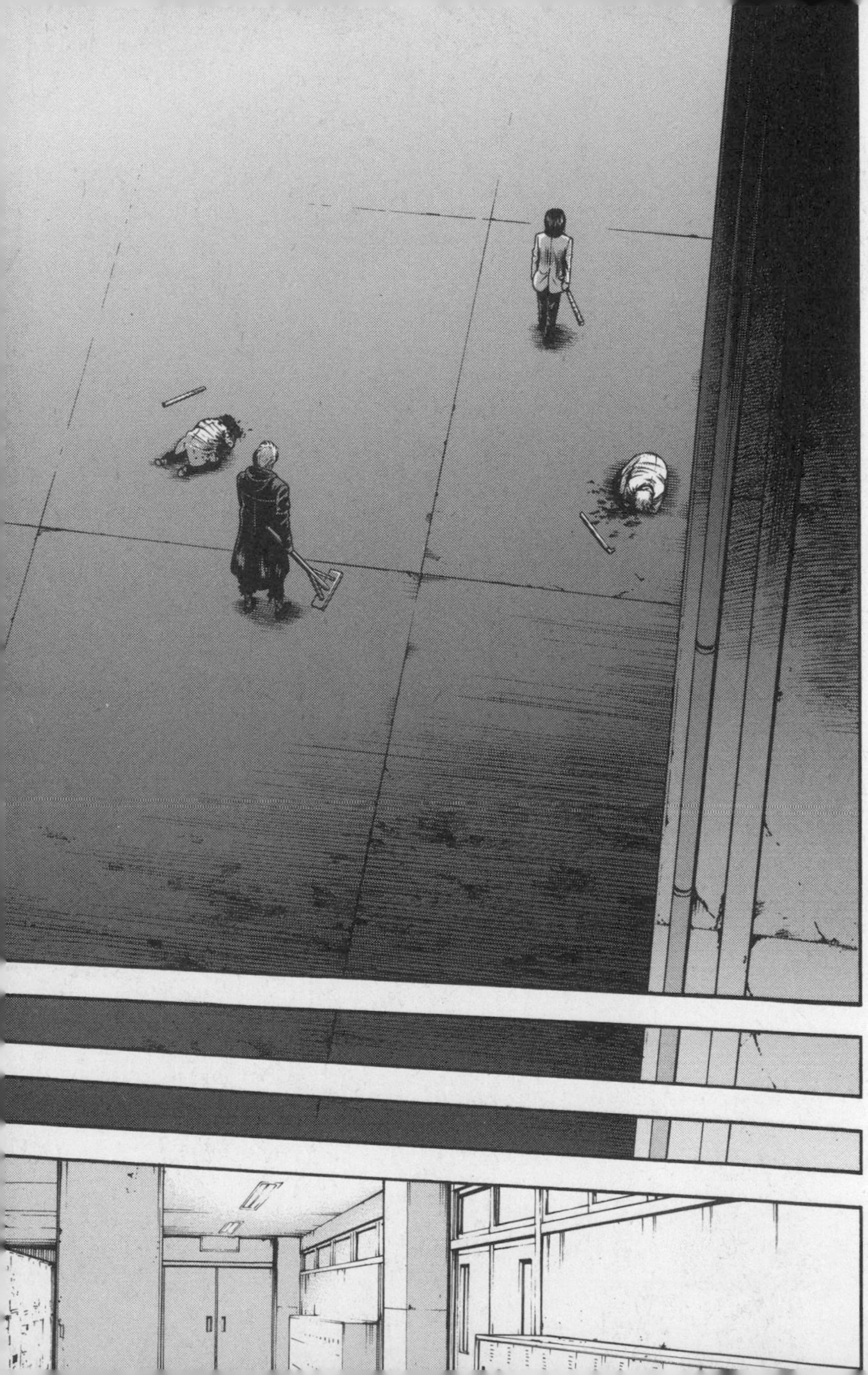

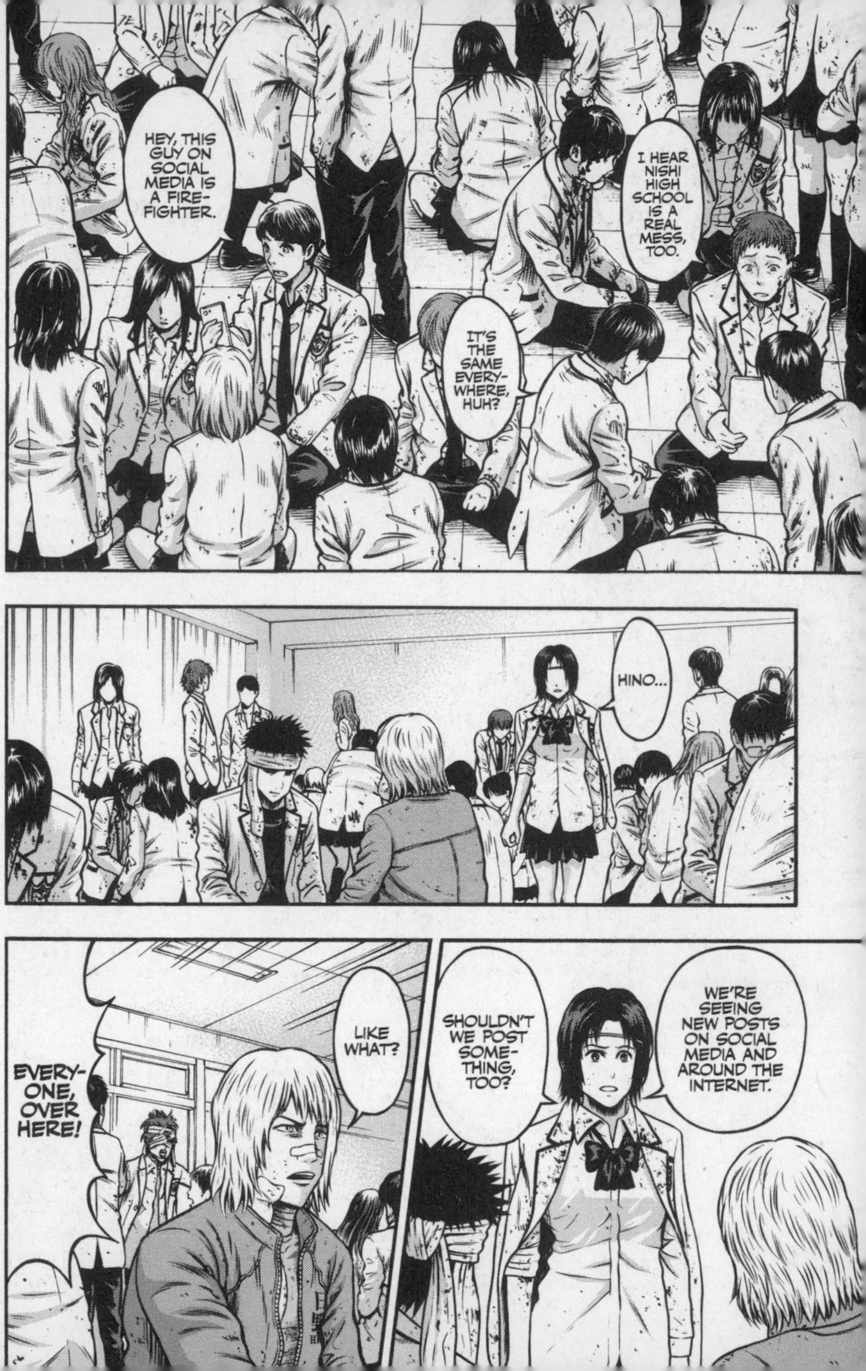
I HEAR NISHI HIGH SCHOOL IS A REAL MESS, TOO.
IT'S THE SAME EVERY-WHERE, HUH?
HEY, THIS GUY ON SOCIAL MEDIA IS A FIRE-FIGHTER.
HINO...
WE'RE SEEING NEW POSTS ON SOCIAL MEDIA AND AROUND THE INTERNET.
SHOULDN'T WE POST SOME-THING, TOO?
LIKE WHAT?
EVERY-ONE, OVER HERE!

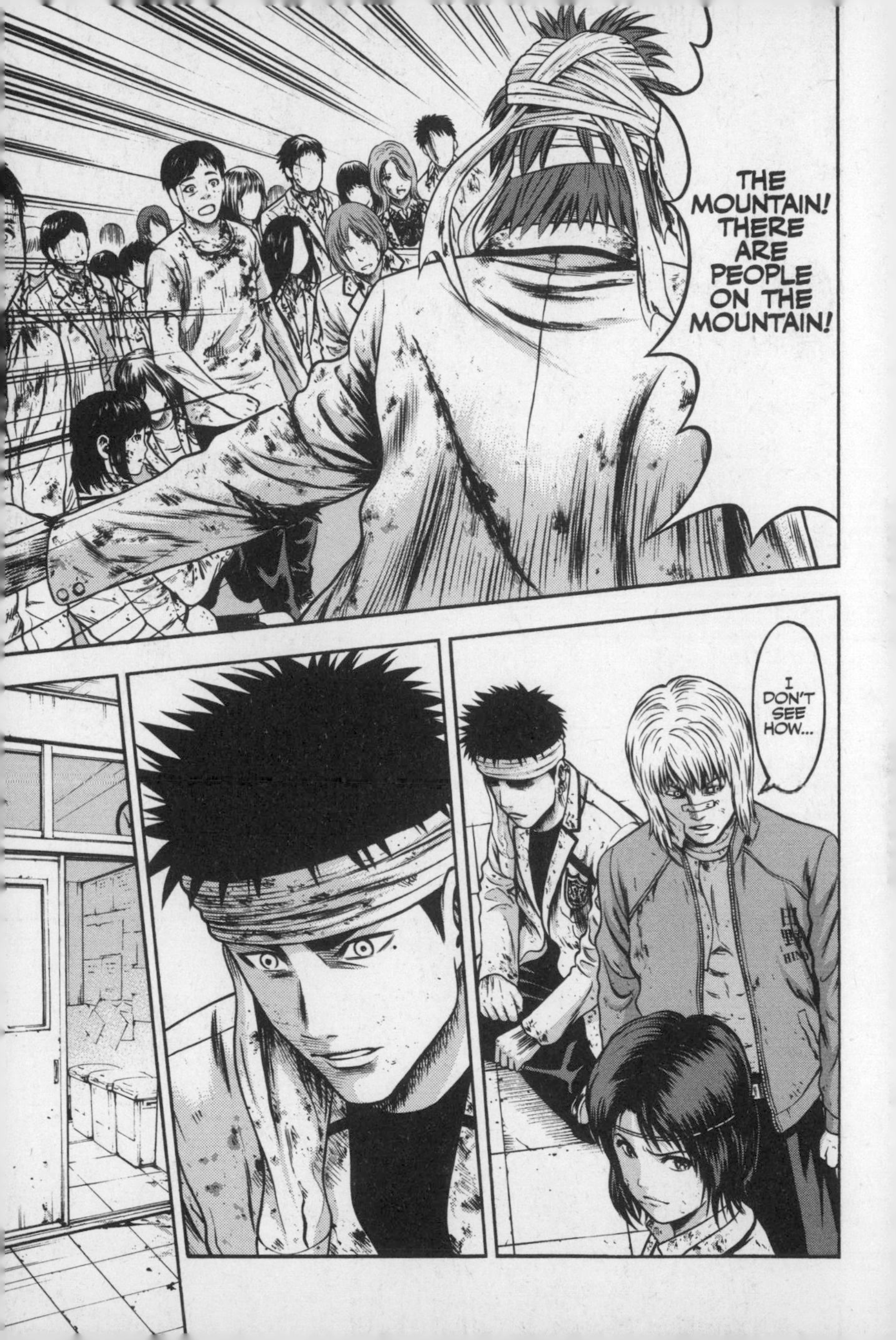
THE MOUNTAIN! THERE ARE PEOPLE ON THE MOUNTAIN!
I DON'T SEE HOW...

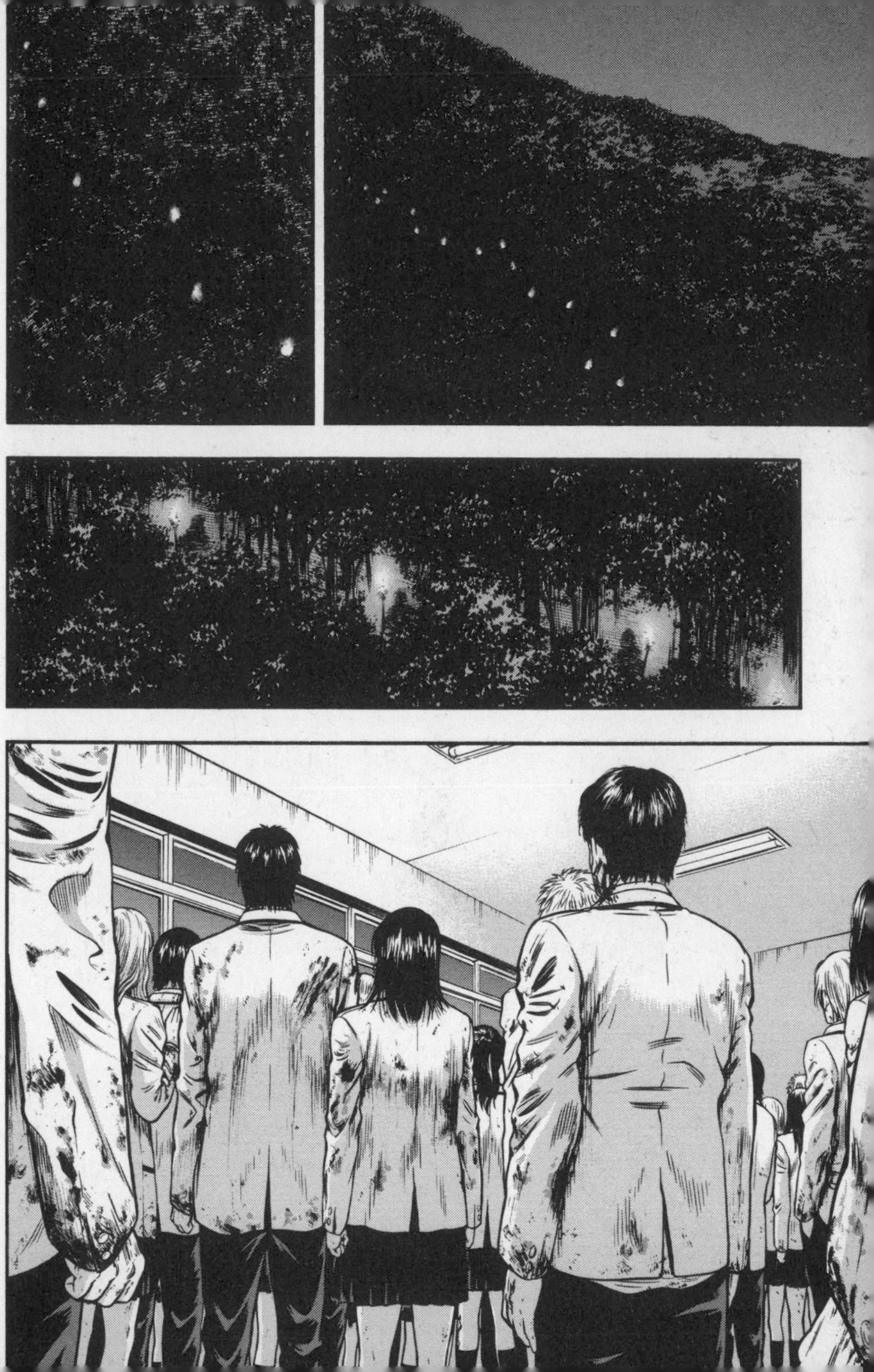

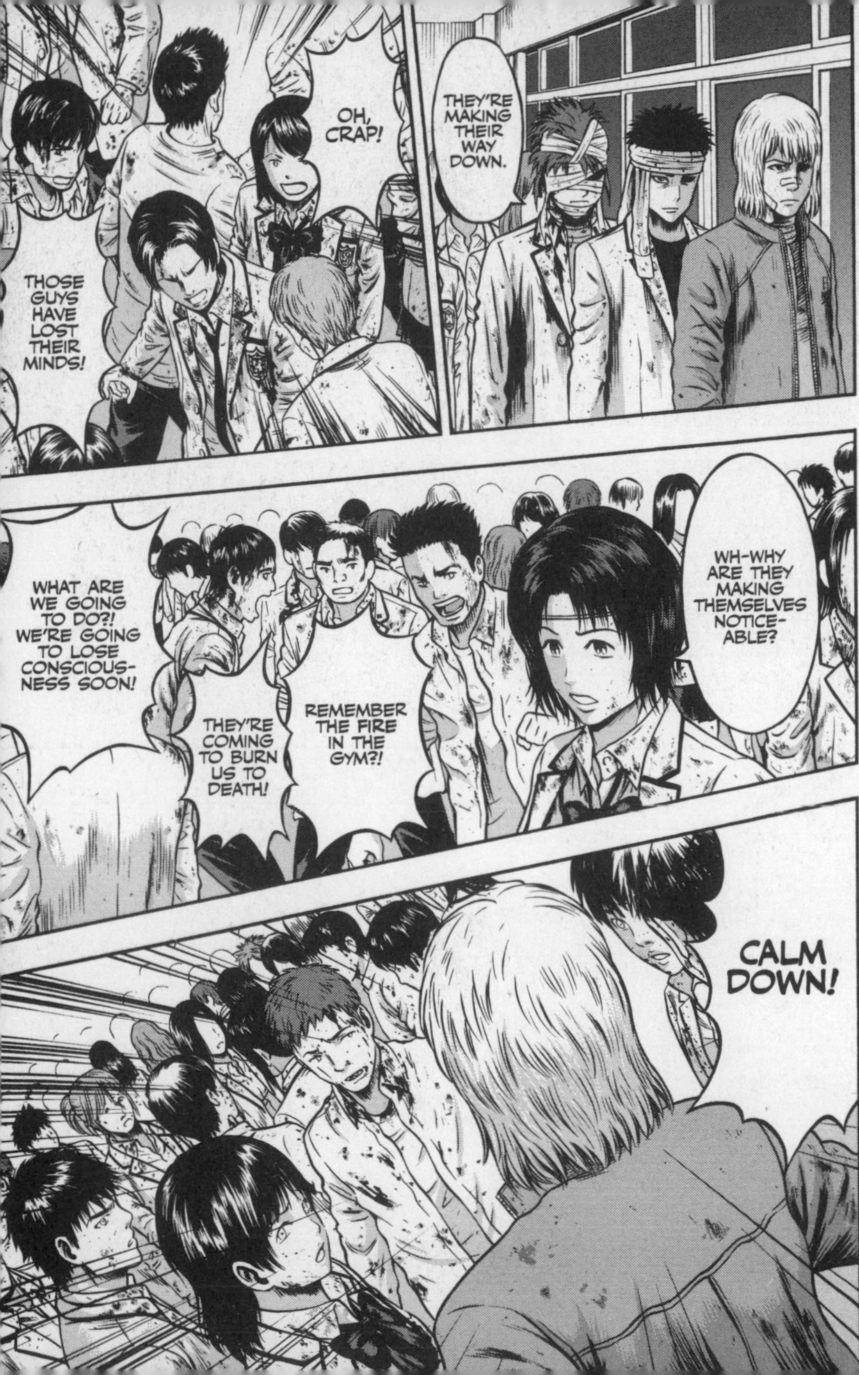
THEY'RE MAKING THEIR WAY DOWN.
OH, CRAP!
THOSE GUYS HAVE LOST THEIR MINDS!
WH-WHY ARE THEY MAKING THEMSELVES NOTICE-ABLE?
REMEMBER THE FIRE IN THE GYM?!
THEY'RE COMING TO BURN US TO DEATH!
WHAT ARE WE GOING TO DO?! WE'RE GOING TO LOSE CONSCIOUS-NESS SOON!
CALM DOWN!

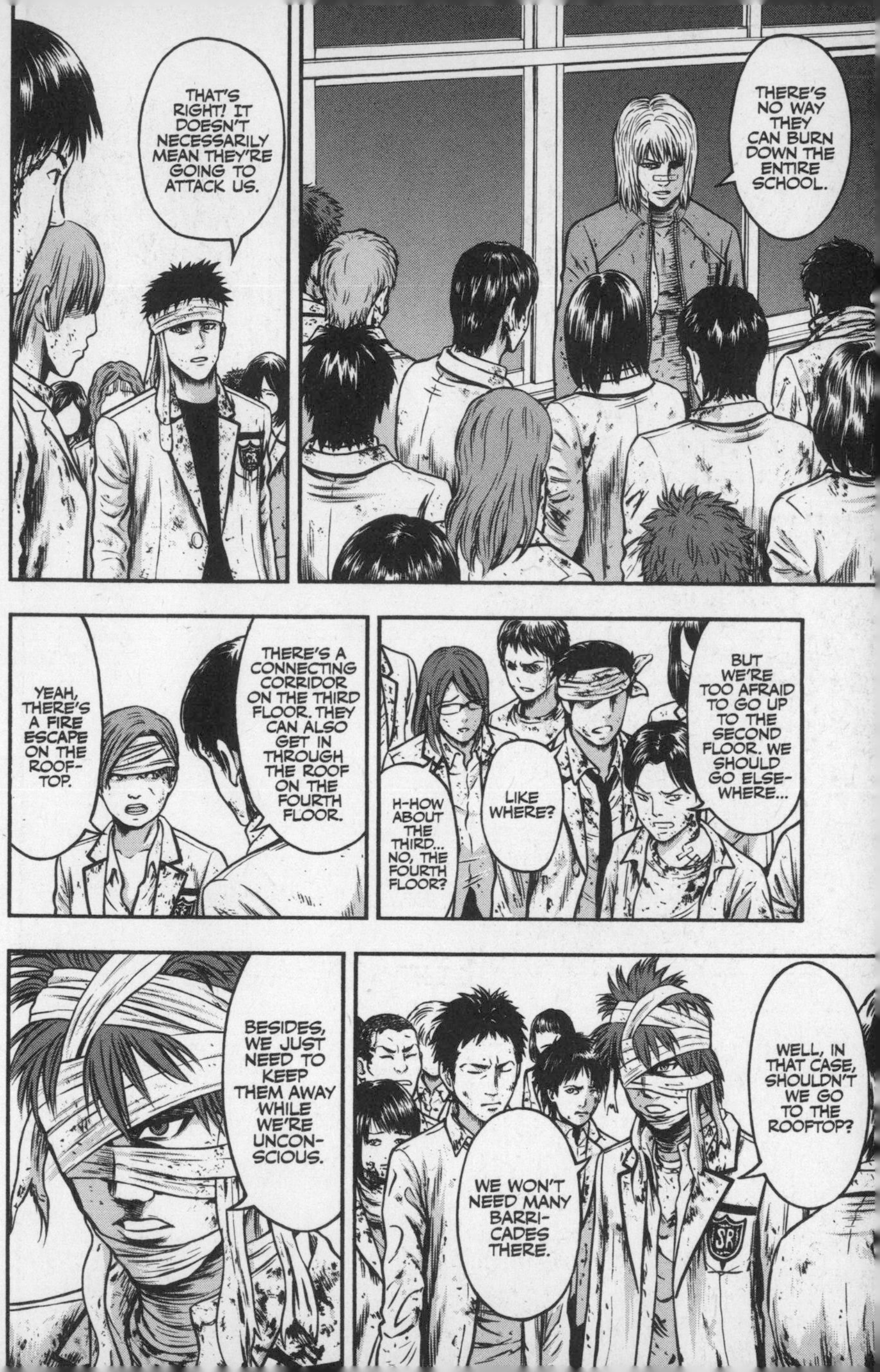
THERE'S NO WAY THEY CAN BURN DOWN THE ENTIRE SCHOOL.
THAT'S RIGHT! IT DOESN'T NECESSARILY MEAN THEY'RE GOING TO ATTACK US.
BUT WE'RE TOO AFRAID TO GO UP TO THE SECOND FLOOR. WE SHOULD GO ELSE-WHERE...
LIKE WHERE?
H-HOW ABOUT THE THIRD... NO, THE FOURTH FLOOR?
THERE'S A CONNECTING CORRIDOR ON THE THIRD FLOOR. THEY CAN ALSO GET IN THROUGH THE ROOF ON THE FOURTH FLOOR.
YEAH, THERE'S A FIRE ESCAPE ON THE ROOF-TOP.
WELL, IN THAT CASE, SHOULDN'T WE GO TO THE ROOFTOP?
WE WON'T NEED MANY BARRI-CADES THERE.
BESIDES, WE JUST NEED TO KEEP THEM AWAY WHILE WE'RE UNCON-SCIOUS.

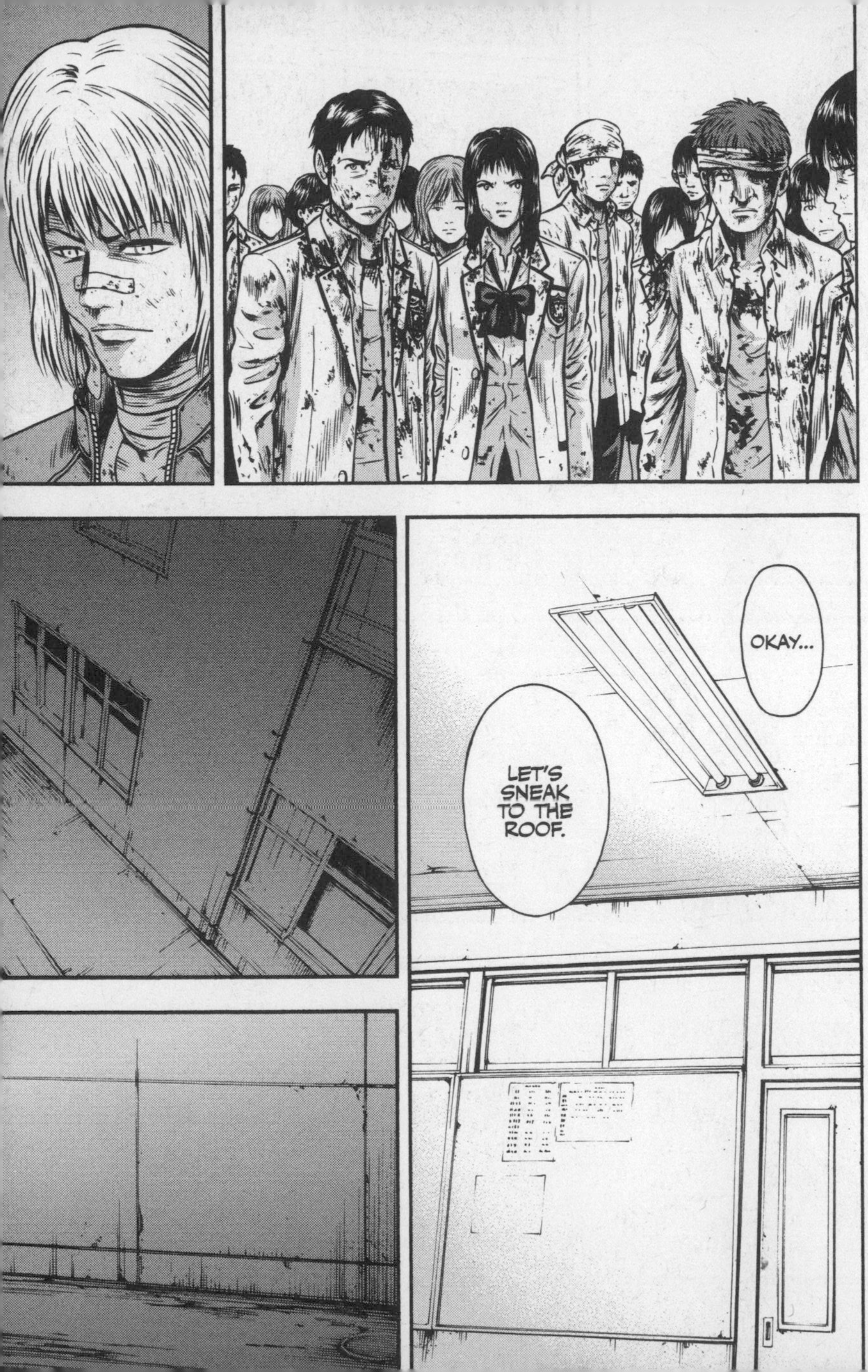
OKAY...
LET'S SNEAK TO THE ROOF.

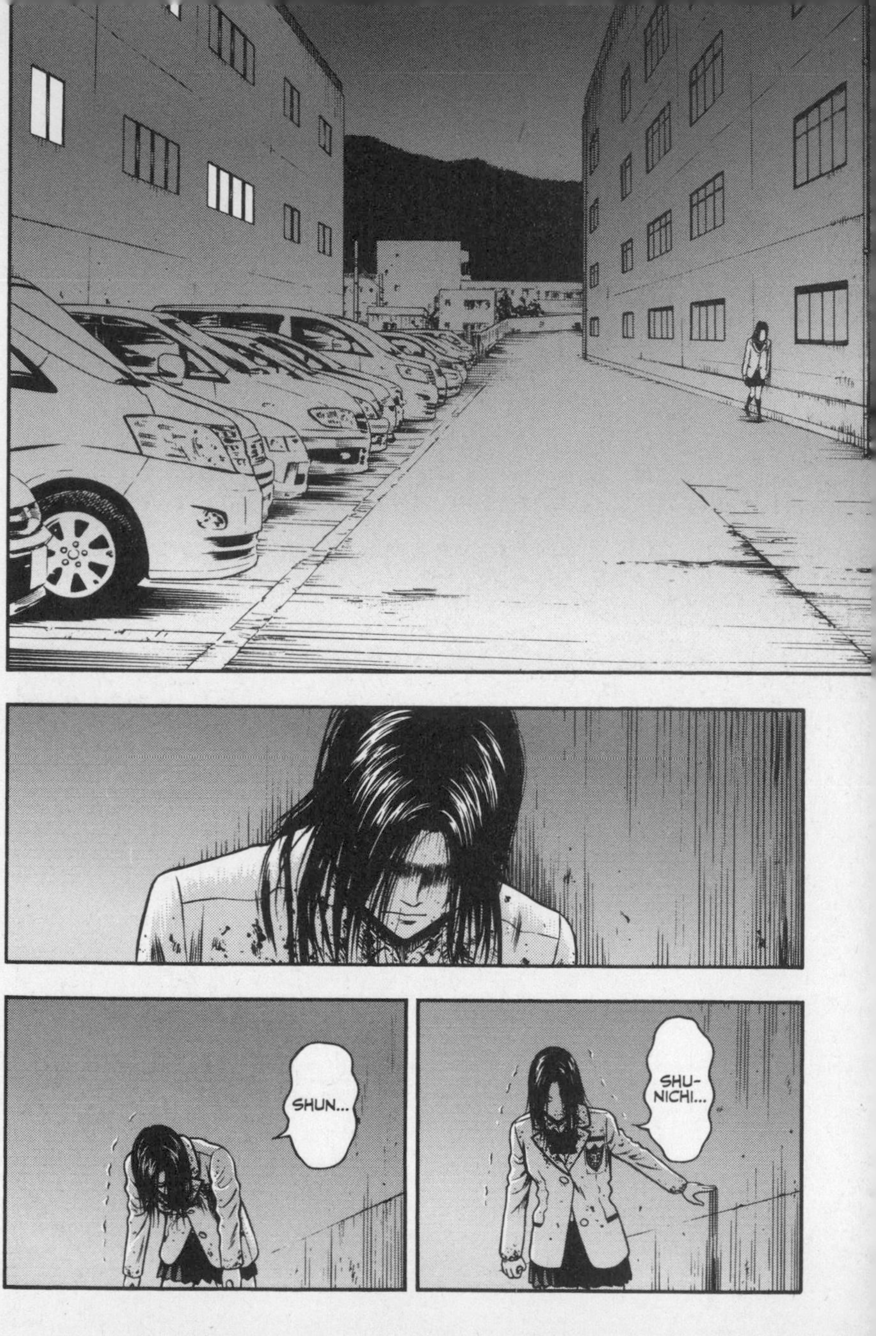
SHU-NICHI...
SHUN...

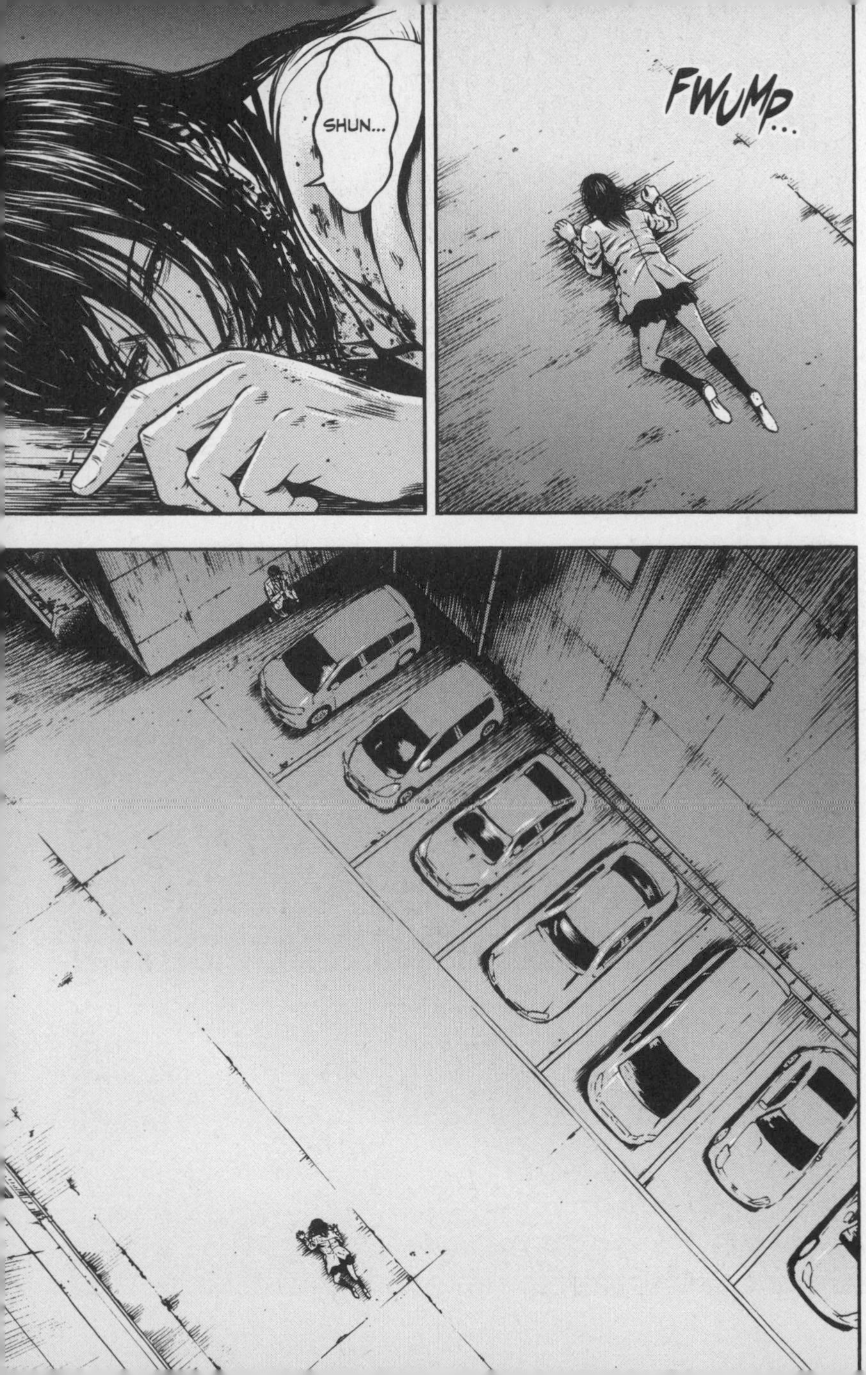
FWUMP...
SHUN...

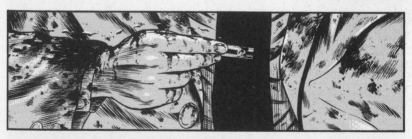

ド ド
ッ ッ
BLRB. BLRB

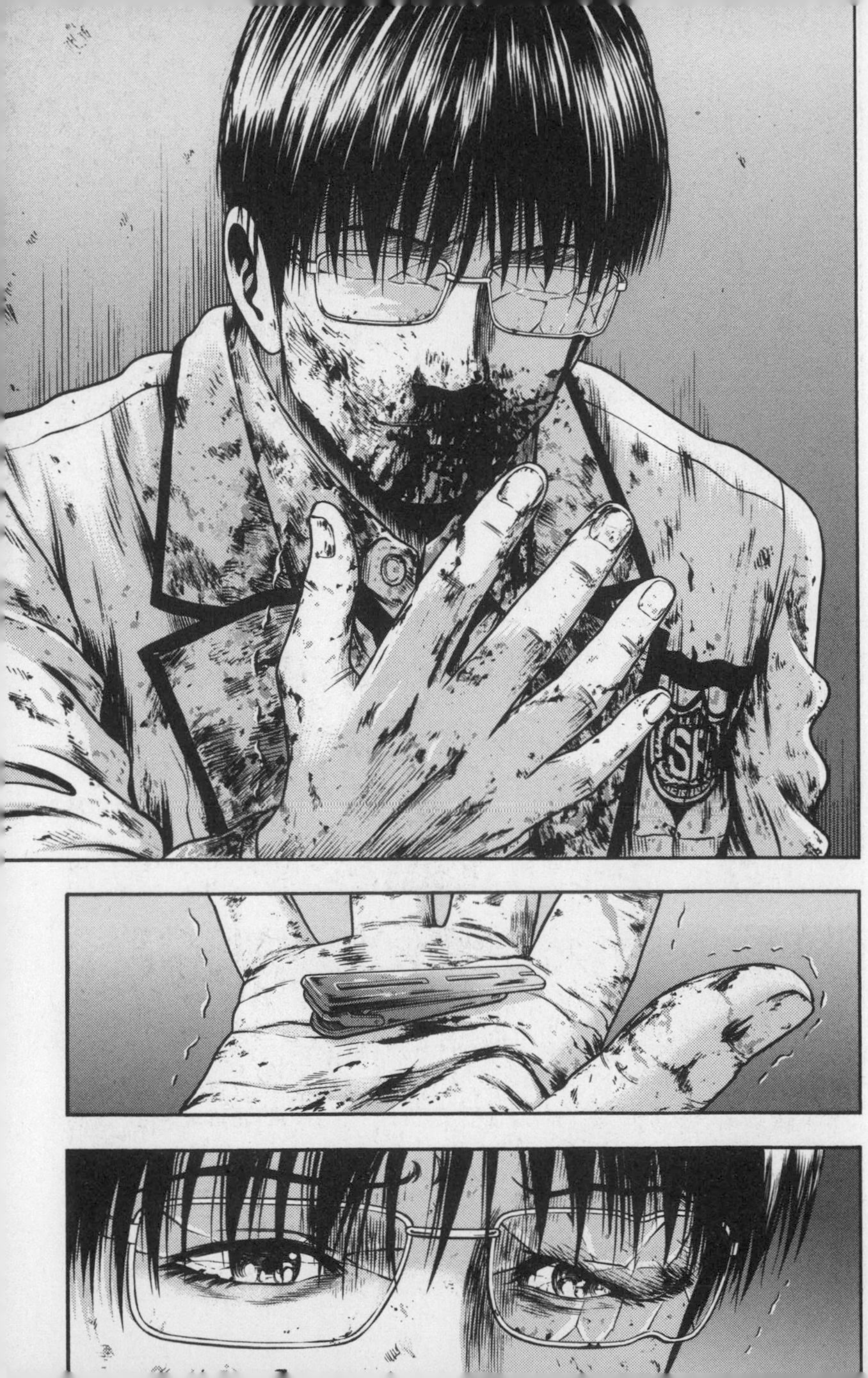

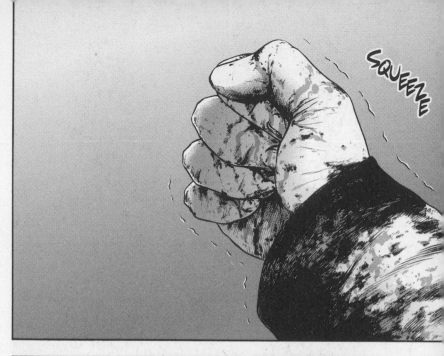

SQUEEZE

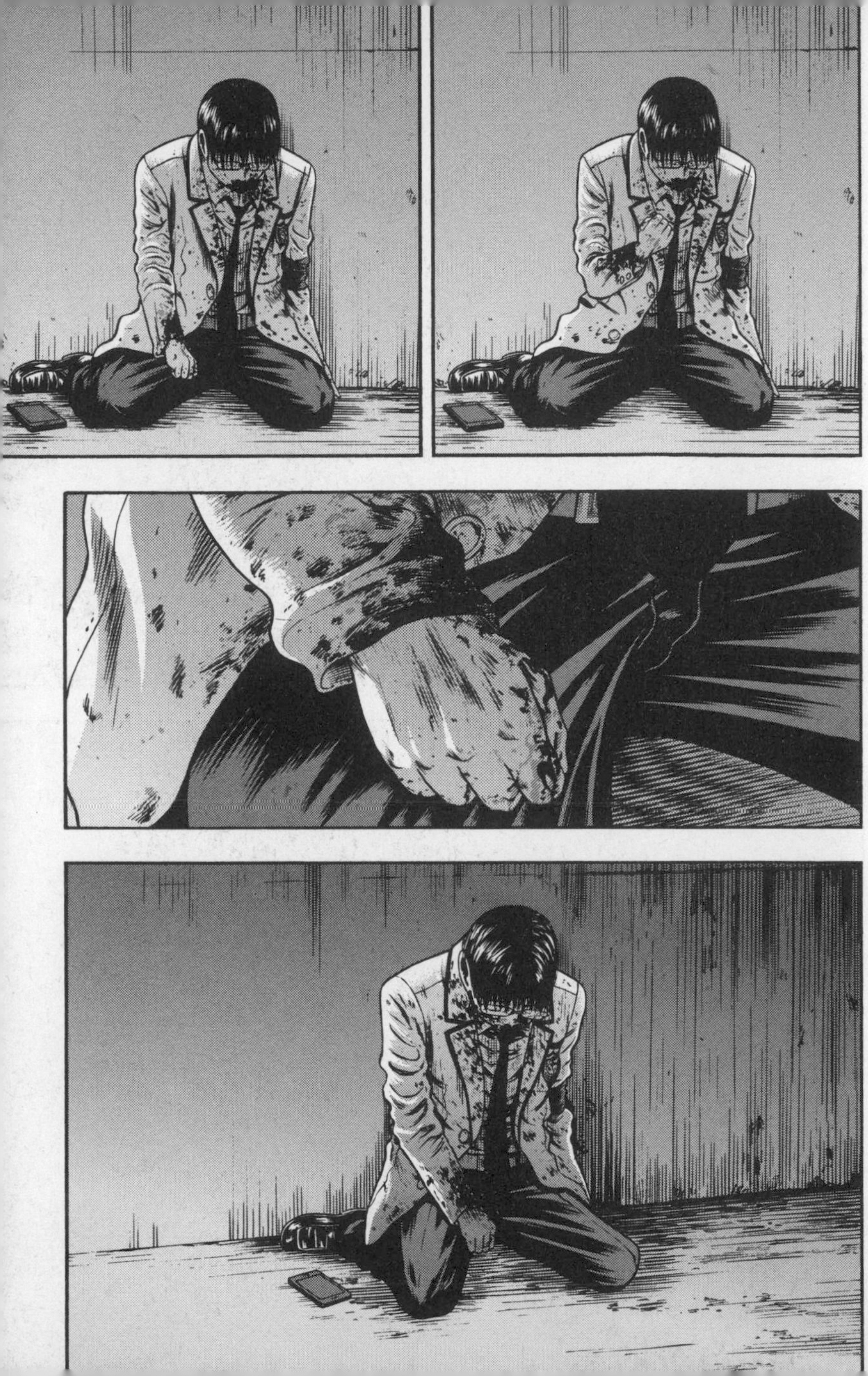

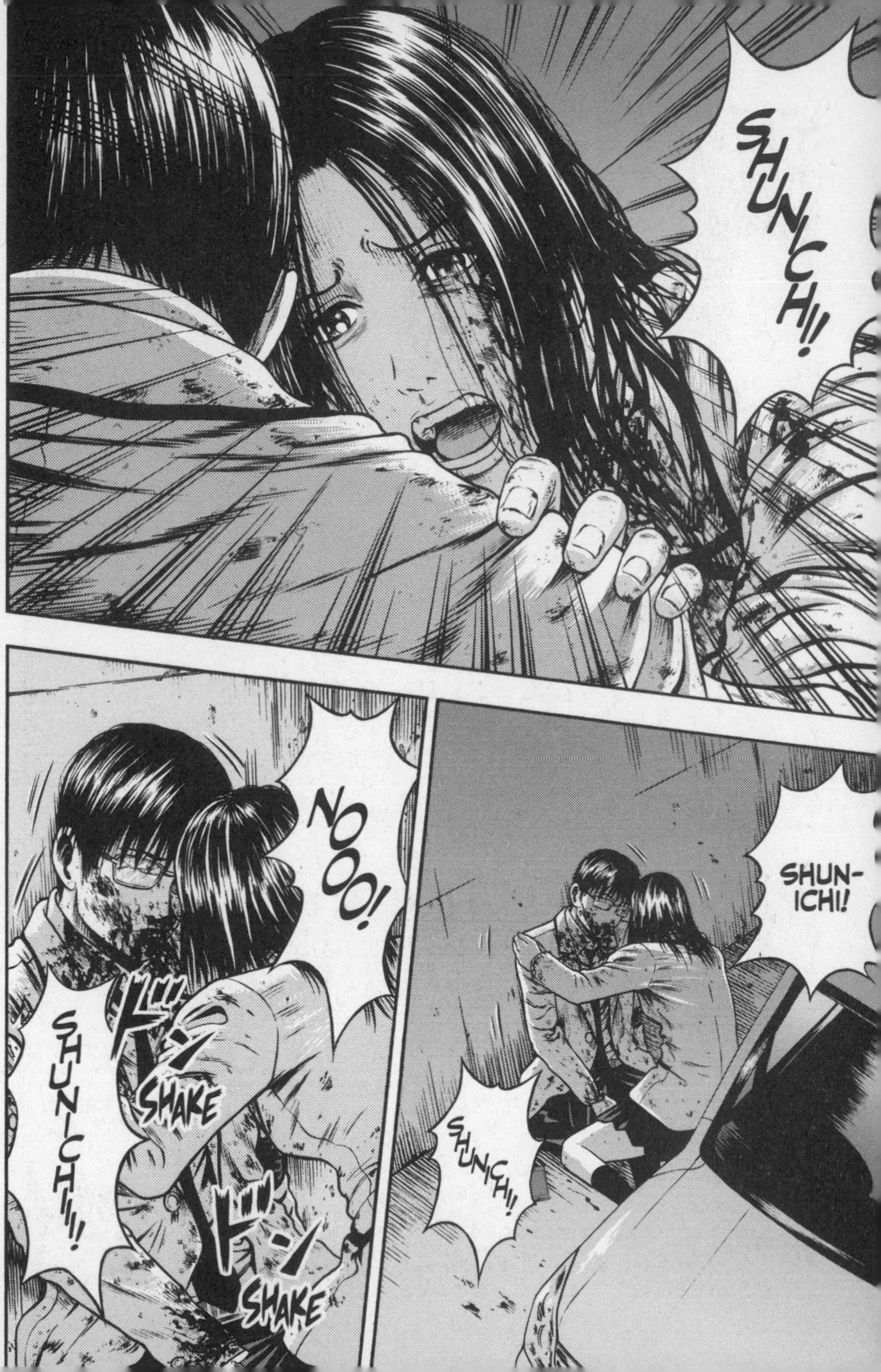
SHUNICHI!!
SHUN-ICHI!
SHUNICHI!!
NOOOO!
SHUNICHI!!!!!
SHAKE
SHAKE

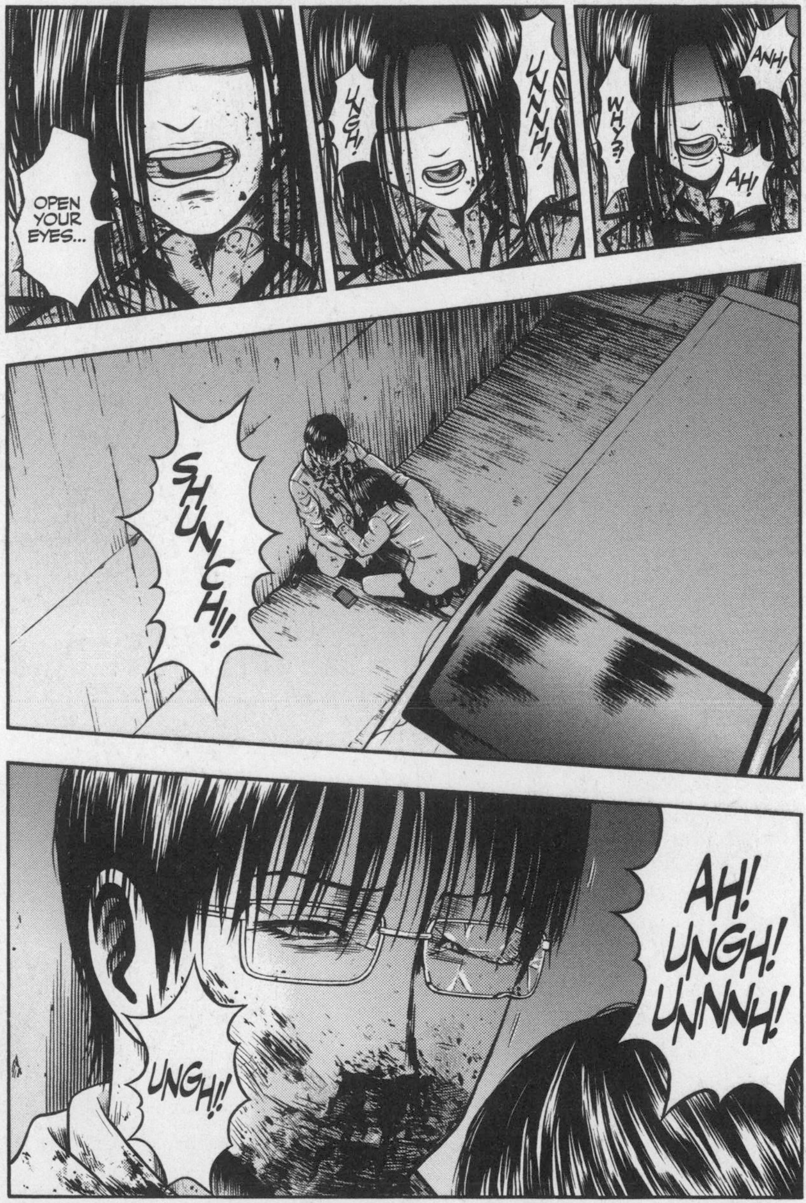
ANH!
WHY?!
AH!
UNNNH!
UNGH!
OPEN YOUR EYES...
SHUNCH!!
AH! UNGH! UNNNH!
UNGH!!

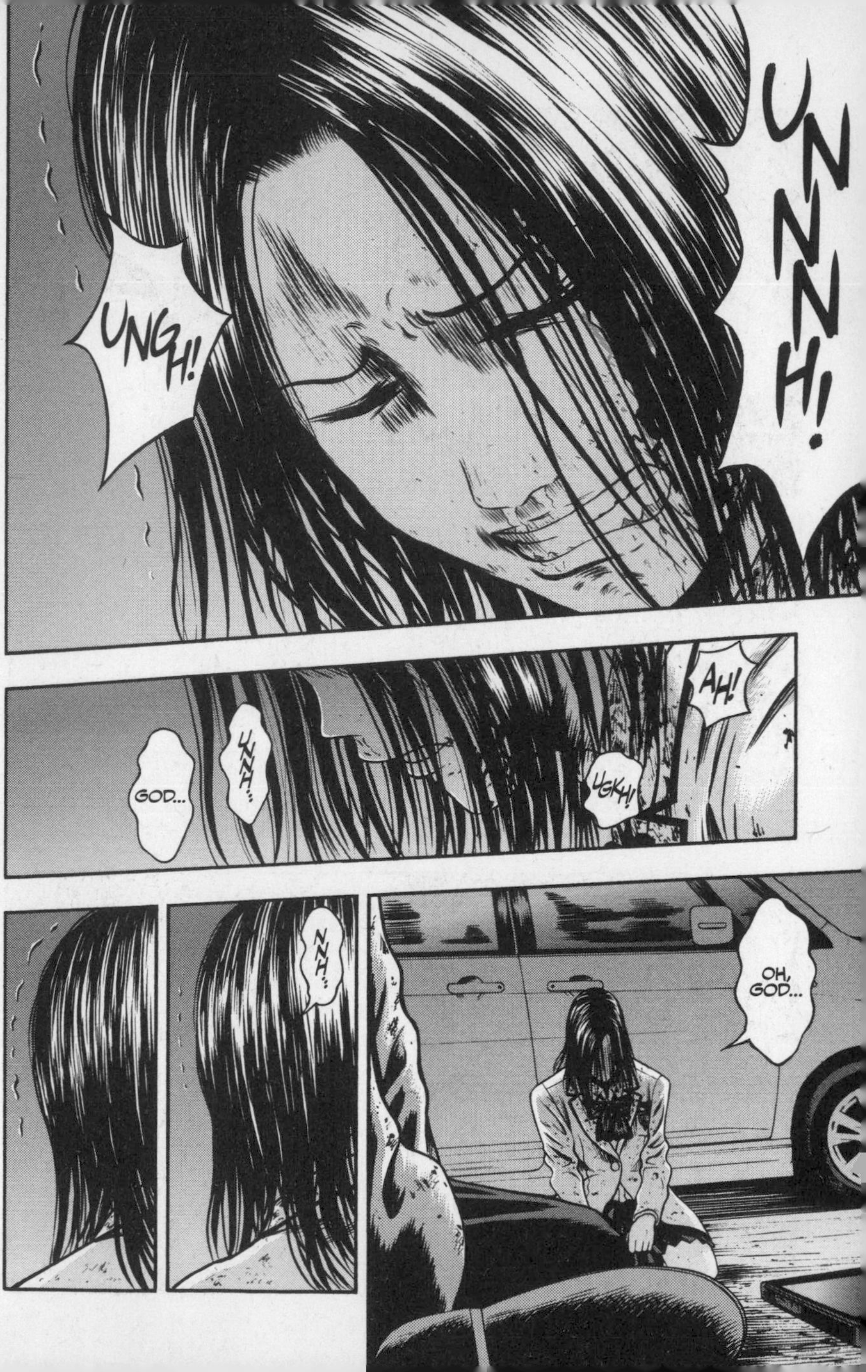
UNNNH!
UNGH!
AH!
UGKH!
UNNH...
GOD...
OH, GOD...
NNH...

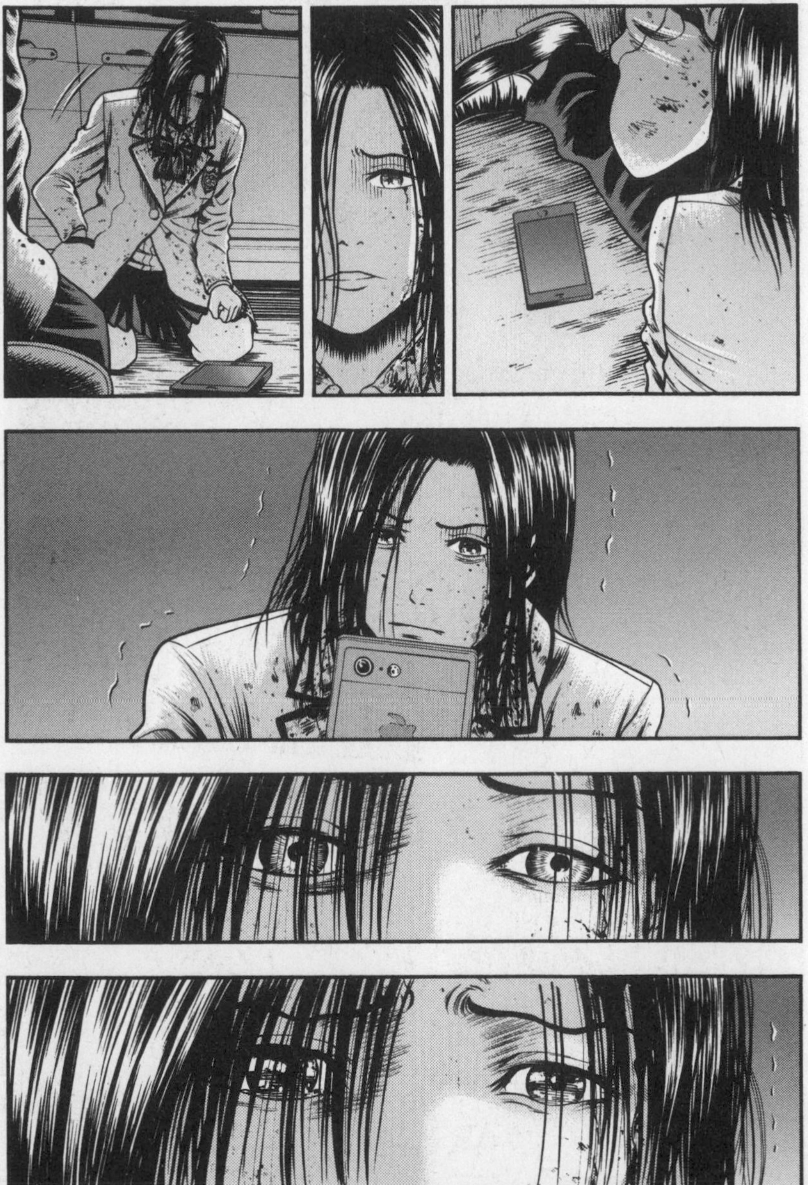

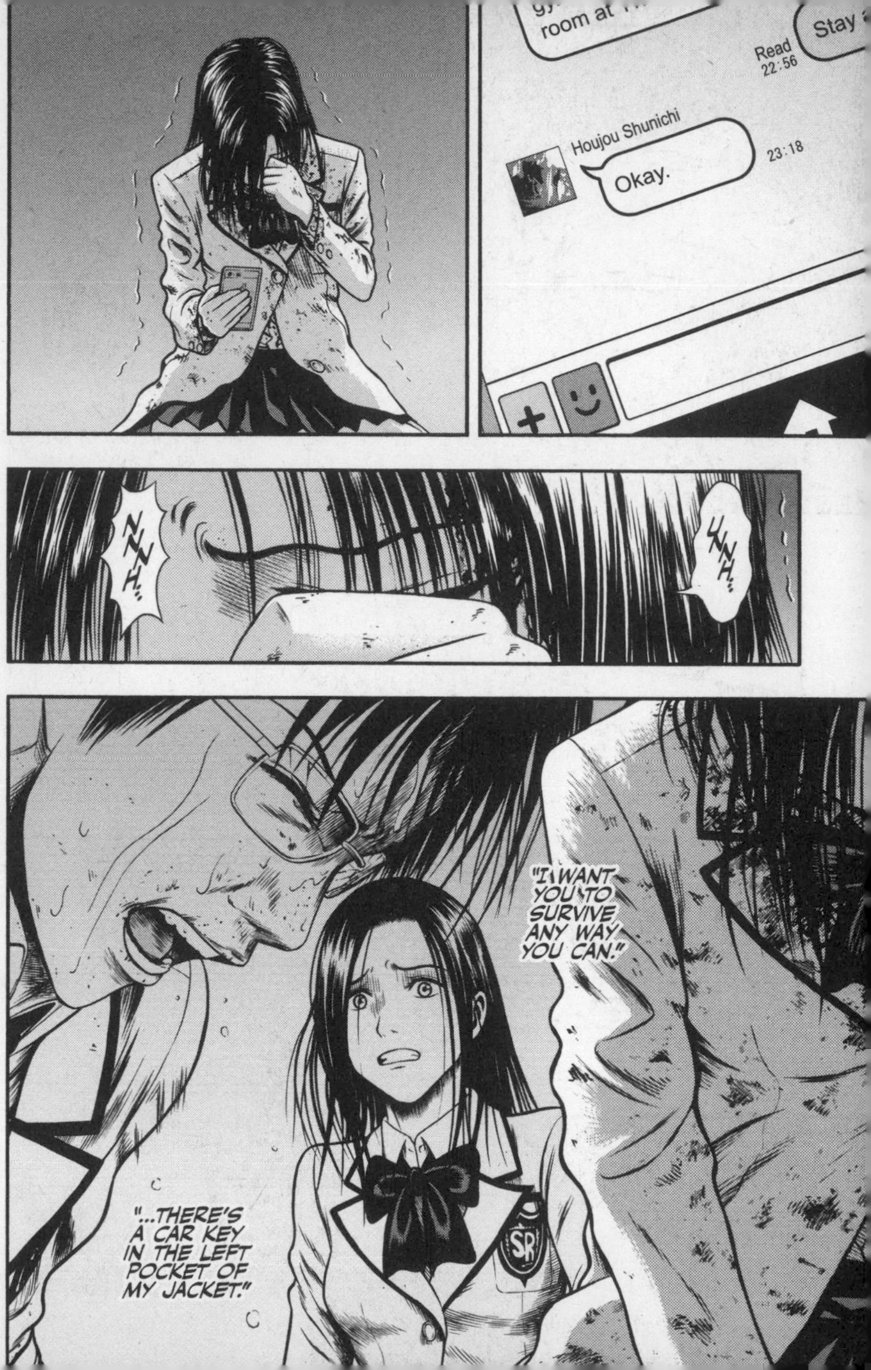
room at
Stay
Read 22:56
Houjou Shunichi
Okay.
23:18
UNH...
NNNH...
"I WANT YOU TO SURVIVE ANY WAY YOU CAN."
"...THERE'S A CAR KEY IN THE LEFT POCKET OF MY JACKET."

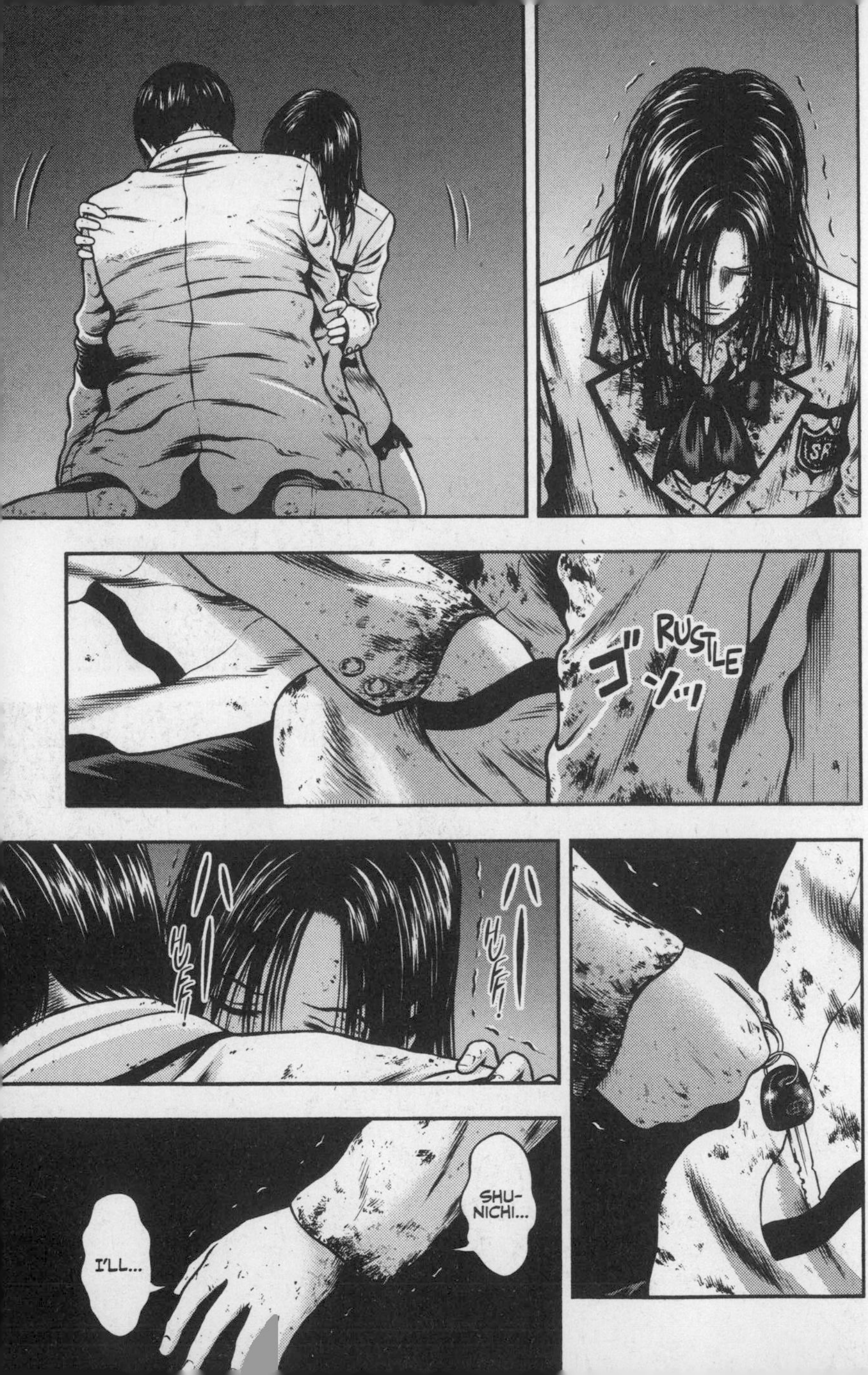

ゴソッ
RUSTLE
HUFF!
HUFF!
SHU-NICHI...
I'LL...

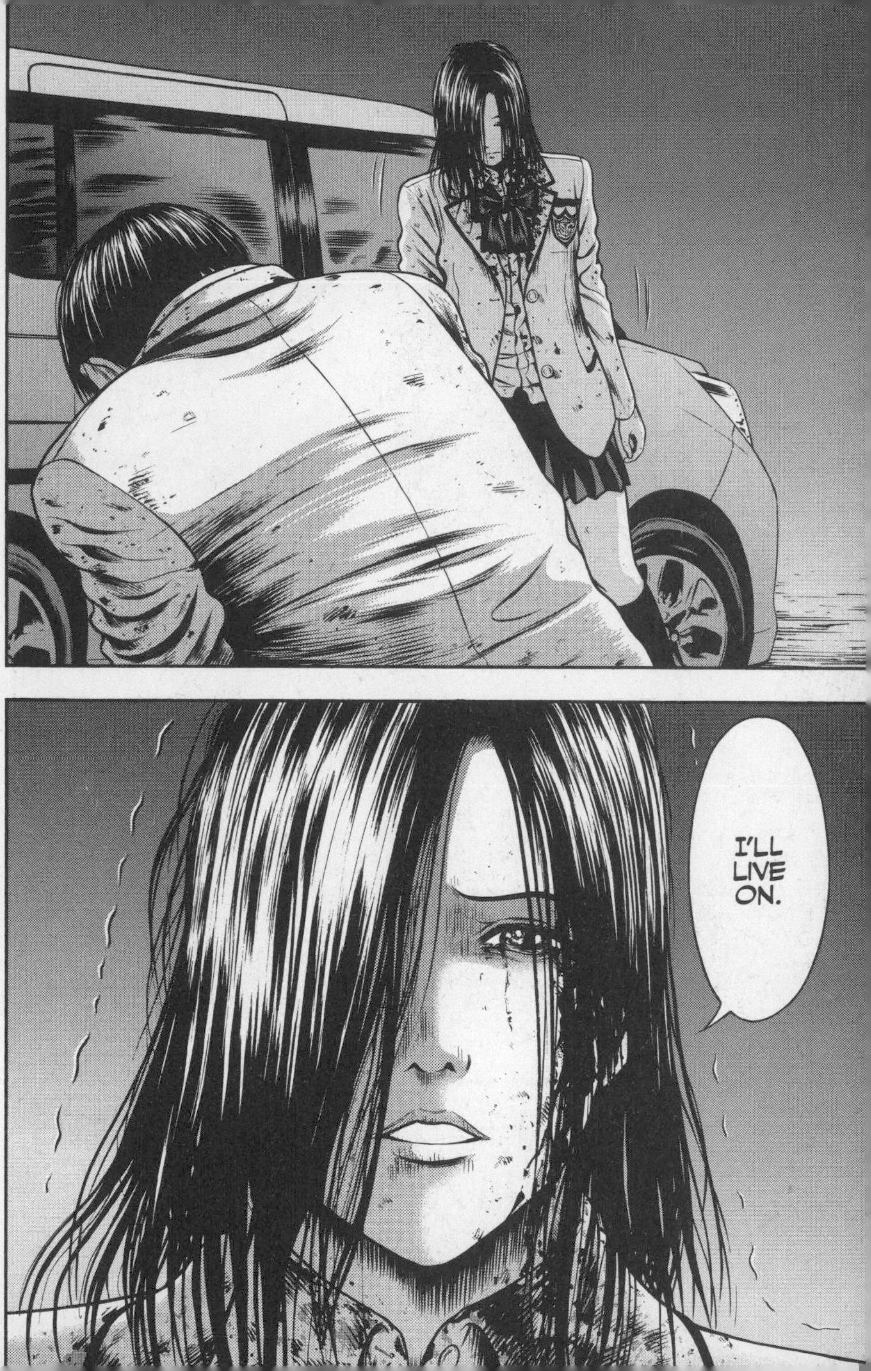
I'LL LIVE ON.

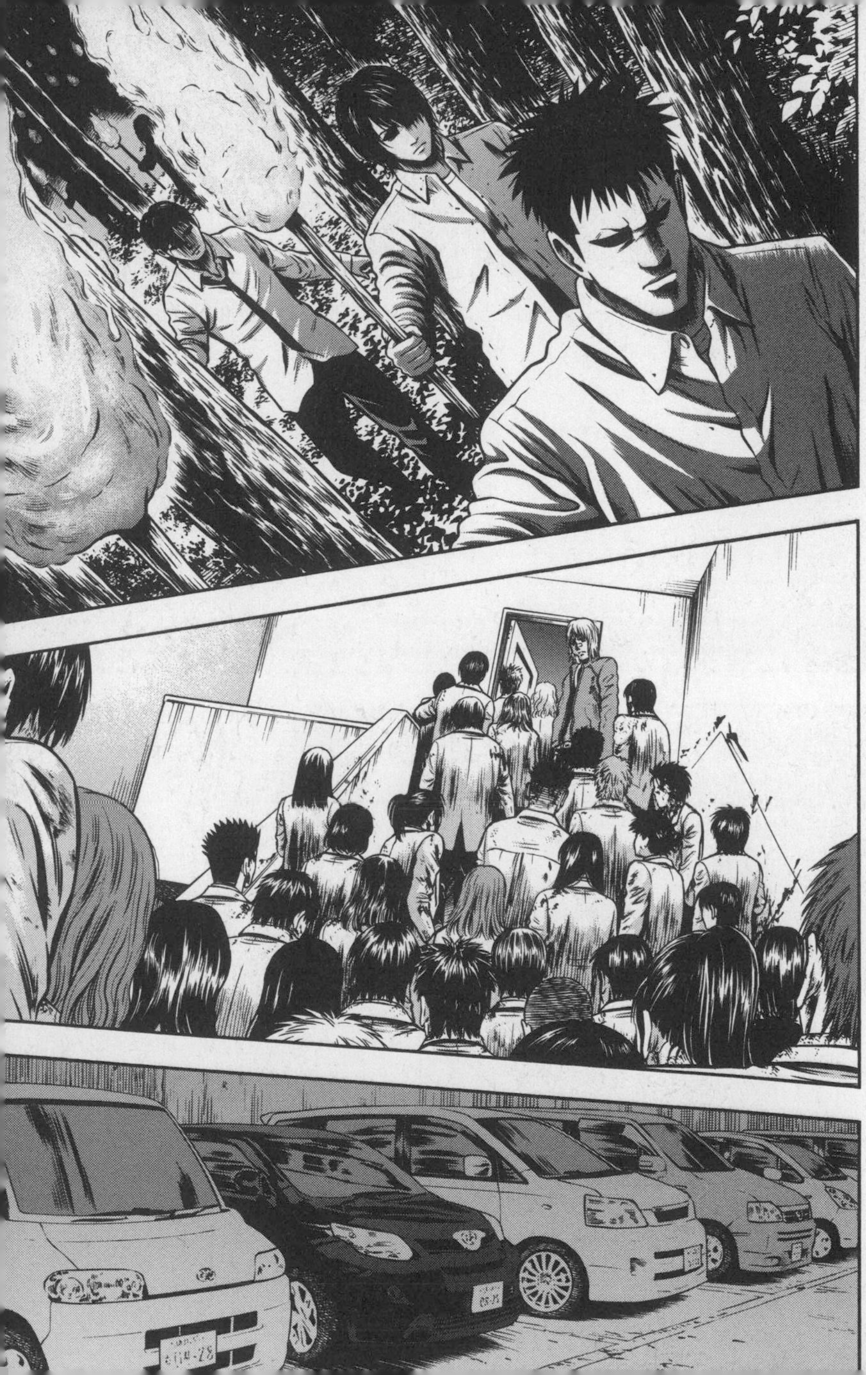

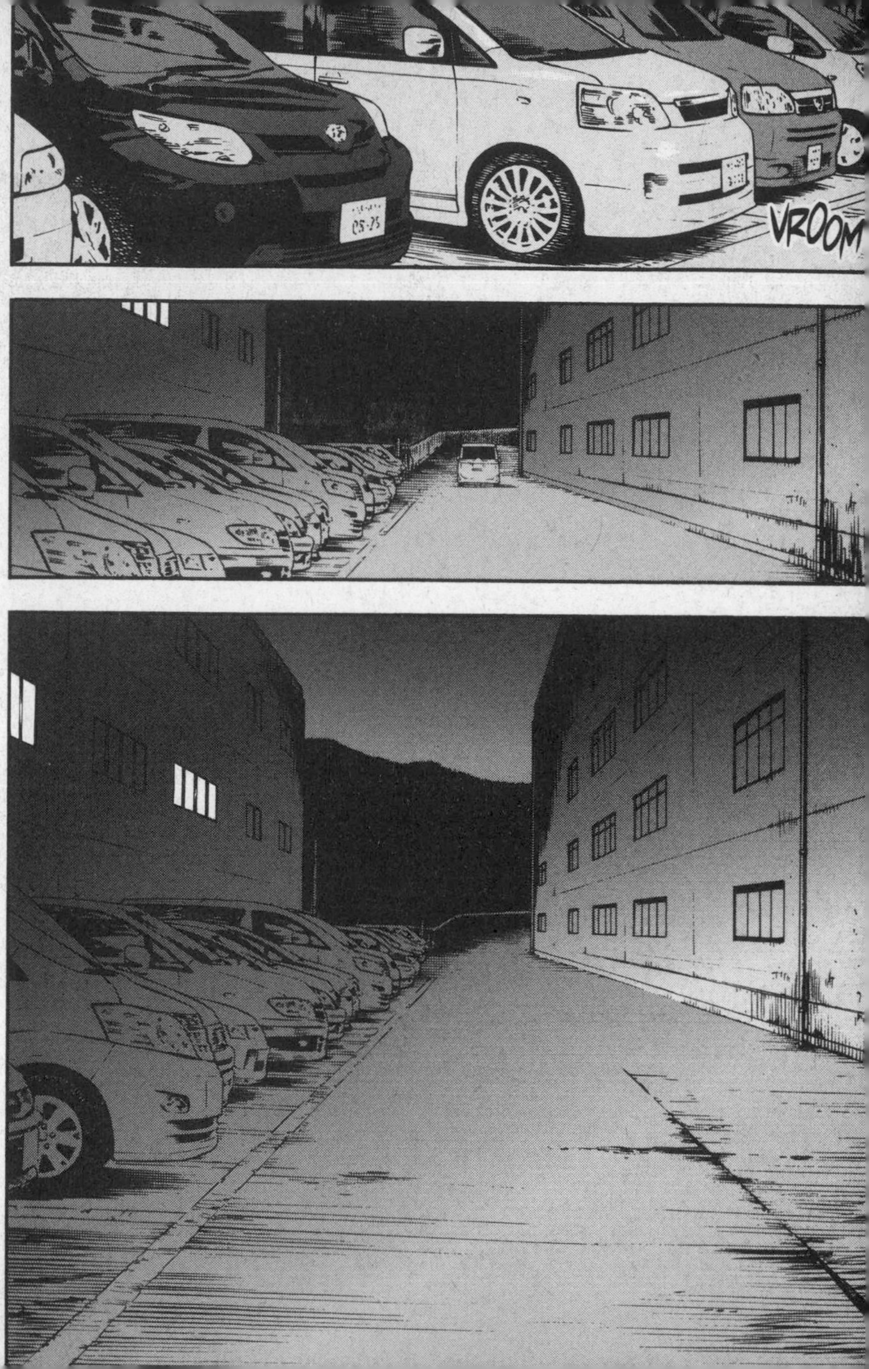
VROOM

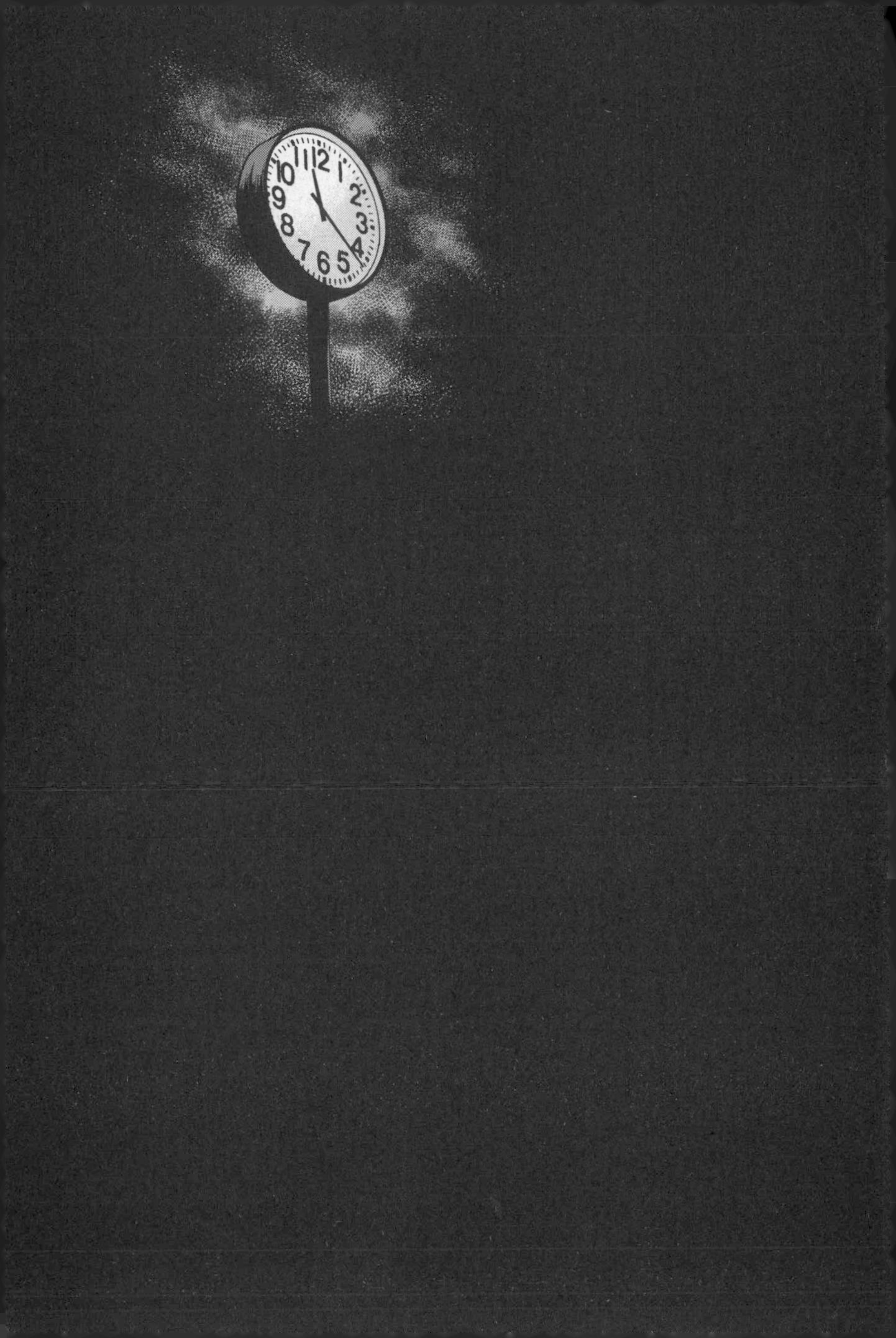

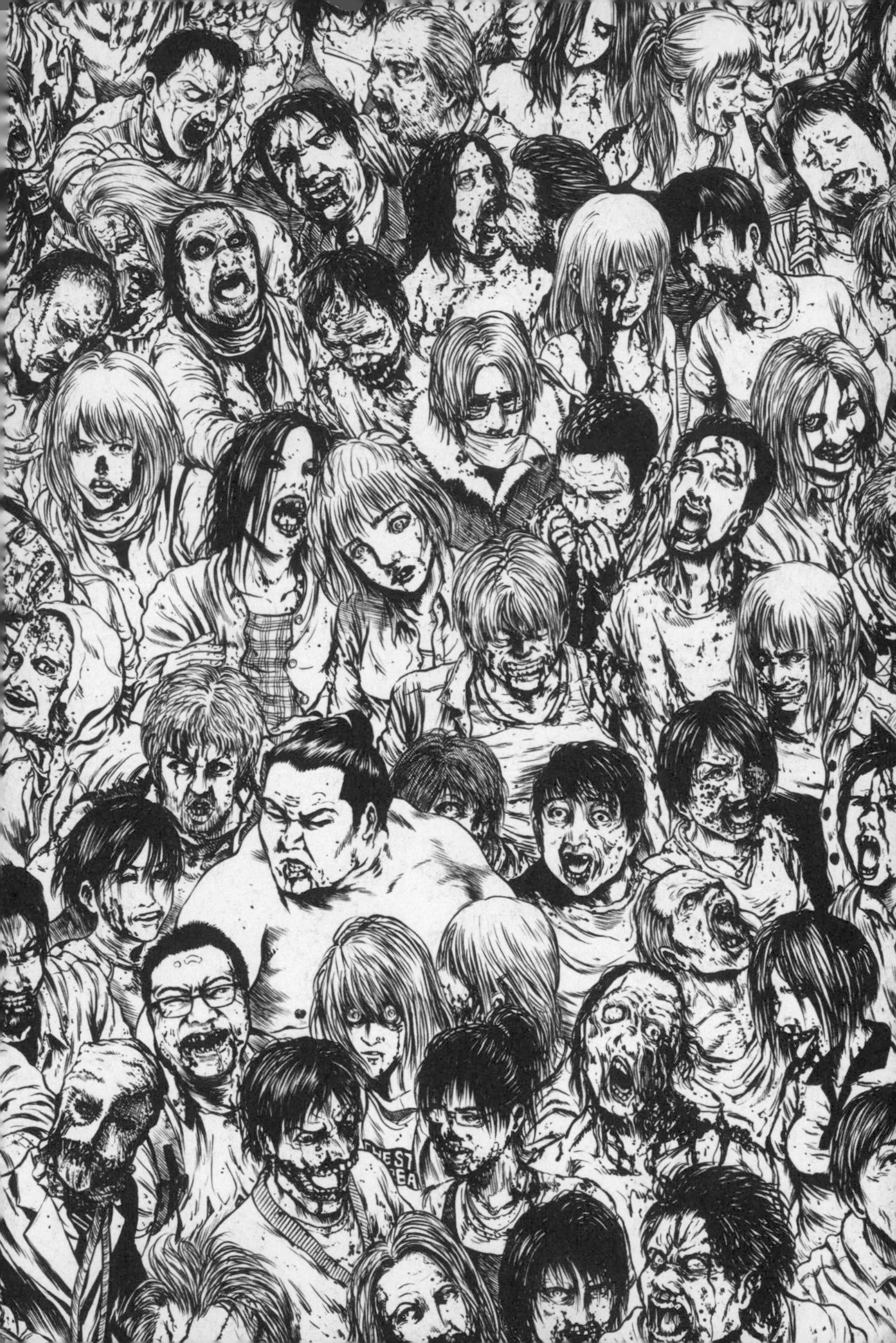

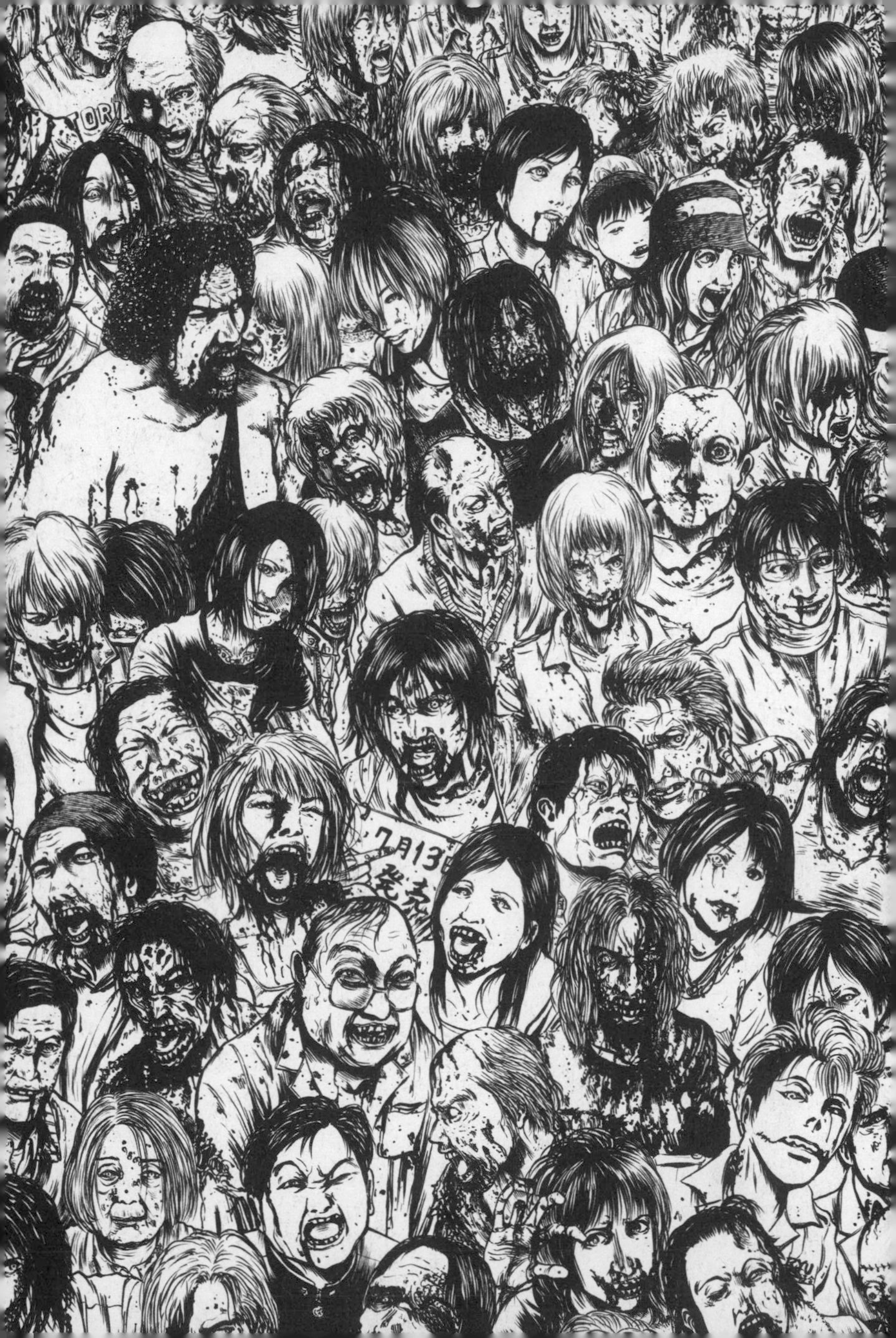
TORI
7月13
発売

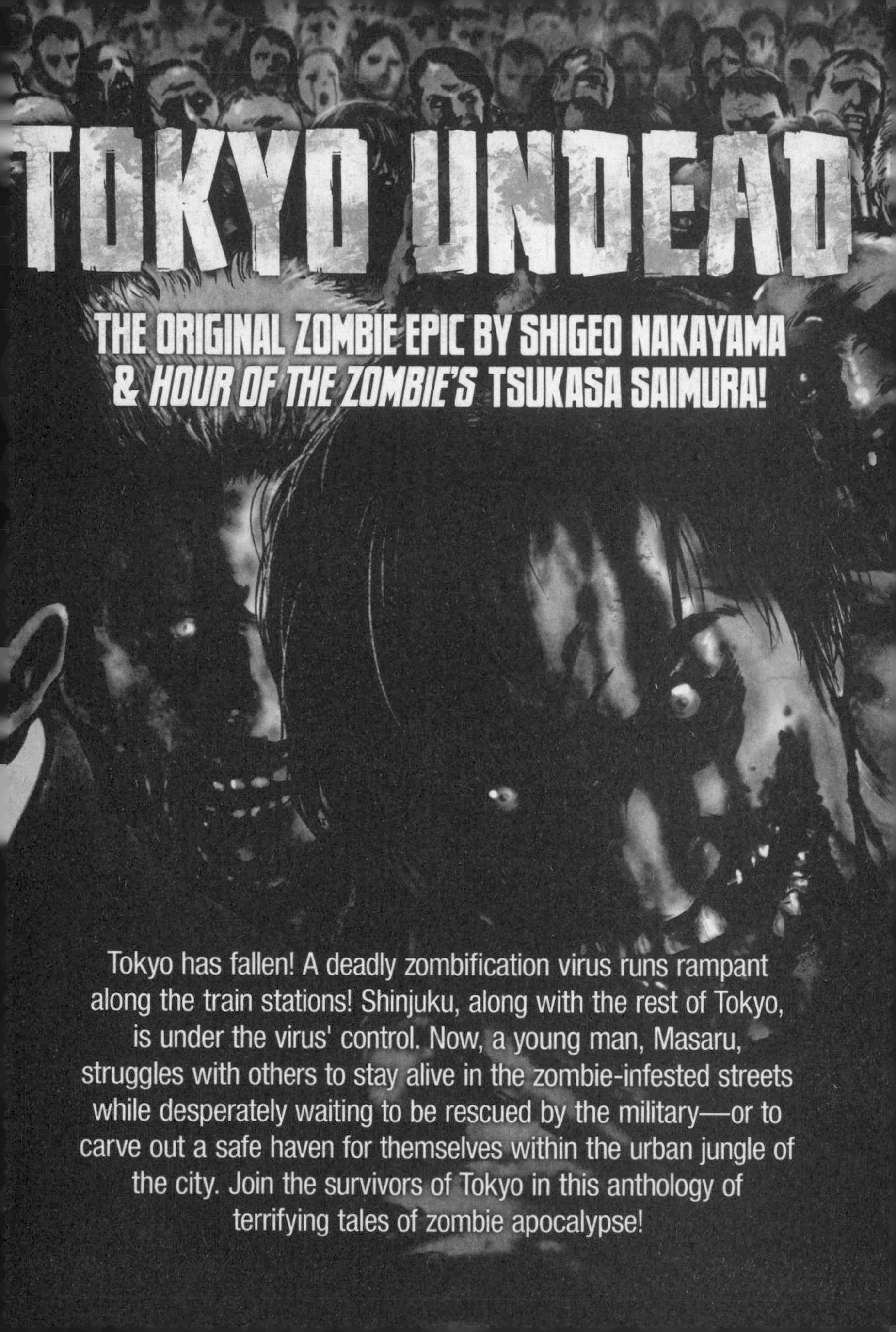

TOKYO UNDEAD

THE ORIGINAL ZOMBIE EPIC BY SHIGEO NAKAYAMA & *HOUR OF THE ZOMBIE'S* TSUKASA SAIMURA!

Tokyo has fallen! A deadly zombification virus runs rampant along the train stations! Shinjuku, along with the rest of Tokyo, is under the virus' control. Now, a young man, Masaru, struggles with others to stay alive in the zombie-infested streets while desperately waiting to be rescued by the military—or to carve out a safe haven for themselves within the urban jungle of the city. Join the survivors of Tokyo in this anthology of terrifying tales of zombie apocalypse!

SEVEN SEAS ENTERTAINMENT PRESENTS

HOUR OF THE ZOMBIE

story and art by **Tsukasa Saimura**   **VOLUME 7**

TRANSLATION
Elina Ishikawa

ADAPTATION
Janet Houck

LETTERING AND COVER
Nicky Lim

LOGO DESIGN
Karis Page

PROOFREADER
Cae Hawksmoor

EDITOR
J.P. Sullivan

PRODUCTION ASSISTANT
CK Russell

PRODUCTION MANAGER
Lissa Pattillo

EDITOR-IN-CHIEF
Adam Arnold

PUBLISHER
Jason DeAngelis

IGAI -THE PLAY DEAD/ALIVE- VOLUME 7
© TSUKASA SAIMURA 2017
Originally published in Japan in 2017 by TOKUMA SHOTEN PUBLISHING
CO., LTD., Tokyo. English translation rights arranged with TOKUMA SHOTEN
PUBLISHING CO., LTD., Tokyo, through TOHAN CORPORATION, Tokyo.

Seven Seas books may be purchased in bulk for promotional, educational, or
business use. Please contact your local bookseller or the Macmillan Corporate
and Premium Sales Department at 1-800-221-7945, extension 5442, or by
e-mail at MacmillanSpecialMarkets@macmillan.com.

Seven Seas and the Seven Seas logo are trademarks of
Seven Seas Entertainment, LLC. All rights reserved.

ISBN: 978-1-626926-89-9

Printed in Canada

First Printing: September 2018

10 9 8 7 6 5 4 3 2 1

FOLLOW US ONLINE: *www.sevenseasentertainment.com*

READING DIRECTIONS

This book reads from *right to left*, Japanese style.
If this is your first time reading manga, you start
reading from the top right panel on each page and
take it from there. If you get lost, just follow the
numbered diagram here. It may seem backwards at
first, but you'll get the hang of it! Have fun!!

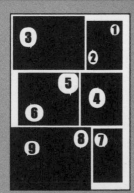